THE KNOWLEDGE OF GOD IN CALVIN'S THEOLOGY

THE KNOWLEDGE OF GOD IN CALVIN'S THEOLOGY

BY EDWARD A. DOWEY, JR.

WILLIAM B. EERDMANS PUBLISHING COMPANY
GRAND RAPIDS, MICHIGAN

255 JEFFERSON AVE., S.E., GRAND RAPIDS, MI 49503

PRINTED IN THE UNITED STATES OF AMERICA

LIBRARY OF CONGRESS CATALOGING-IN-PUBLICATION DATA

Dowey, Edward A.
The knowledge of God in Calvin's theology /
by Edward A. Dowey. — Expanded ed.
p. cm.
Includes bibliographical references and index.
ISBN 0-8028-0107-2 (pbk.)
1. God — Knowableness — History of doctrines — 16th century.
2. Calvin, Jean, 1509-1564 — Contributions in theology of knowableness of God. I. Title.
BT98.D63 1994
231′.042′092—dc20 94-29693
CIP

Portions of the material added to this expanded edition were previously published. The publisher gratefully acknowledges permission to reprint the following:

Chapter VI was first published as "The Structure of Calvin's Theological Thought As Influenced by the Two-Fold Knowledge of God," in *Calvinus ecclesiae Genevensis Custos,* ed. W. H. Neuser (Frankfurt: Peter Lang, 1984), pp. 135-148.

Appendix 5 was first published as "John Calvin: A Sixteenth Century Portrait," review in *Journal of the American Academy of Religion*, 57 (1988), 845-48.

To
MARGARET TURNER DOWEY
and
THE REVEREND ATKINSON DOWEY
my best teachers

CONTENTS

PREFACE TO THE EXPANDED EDITION

ALTHOUGH MANY YEARS have gone by, and much has been written on the subjects covered in this volume, the work as a whole does not seem to have been entirely superseded. It apparently brought to the fore certain subject matter in Calvin's writings that is still more comprehensively treated here than elsewhere. Also assessments of the structure of Calvin's *Institutes* and of his thought in general, as developed here, are both widely accepted and also widely debated today. Some writers have revised, refined, and extended these views. Almost incidentally to the specialized title of the book, knowledge of God, it has been found useful as a general introduction to Calvin's thought, particularly among theological students. Um so besser!

Now, before continuing in this preface of 1993, it might be well for the reader to turn at once to the preface of 1952, *infra,* to see the original intended scope of the work and the status of the problem in Calvin studies up to that time. Further the preface to the second printing in 1965, *infra,* contains comments on the literature of the intervening thirteen years, plus some mild retractions and some defense in response to criticisms. We now proceed in a similar vein with a few generalizations, but without attempting a review of the literature within this preface. However, the newly added Chapter VI is carried on in dialogue with other treatments of our subject, and the new Appendix VI offers a critical evaluation of the celebrated book of Professor William J. Bouwsma, *John Calvin, A Sixteenth Century Portrait* (Oxford University Press, 1988). Otherwise, the text remains as it first appeared, warts (such as male gendered speech) and all.

Strictly speaking, although our subject matter is the theology of a thinker of five centuries ago, the method of this study is (in the writer's present estimate) not adequately historical. This means insufficiently genetic. What we have here is more analytical and theological in the sense that the prime concern throughout is the possible yield for contemporary theological thinking. These modes are not mutually exclusive, but they are different, and represent changes mentioned in the opening section of Chapter VI, *infra.* It is probably in the area of fresh historical and philological work more than any other that immense progress has been made, for instance, in the opening up of fifteenth century studies, both theological and humanistic. Further, there is the increased hermeneutical sophistication which now permeates good historical writing and reading. Nonetheless, it seems that this volume has avoided serious stumbling in what have been taken as its chief contributions: exposition of what knowledge of God means and how it functions in Calvin's thought, and the structure of his thought as a whole.

Some newer studies have investigated in detail the putative background of Calvin in knowledge theory, with mixed results. So far, I do not find Calvin interested in technical epistemology, a word I would no longer use in discussing his views, just so long as theological assertions are supported adequately. This is comparable to Calvin's eclectic use of philosophy and psychology in discussing the nature of the soul.

It would promote clarity and accuracy in Calvin scholarship generally if Calvin's own terminology of the "two-fold" knowledge were used exclusively as Calvin used it for the knowledge of God the Creator and Redeemer. This technical term should not be carelessly applied to the "knowledge of God and ourselves," as often happens. For the latter, the term correlative knowledge (or the like) would avoid confusion.

Accommodation as a major characterization of the knowledge of God was first developed in the Calvin literature in this book in 1952 (*infra* Chapter I, part 1, and Appendix I). That was long before Quirinus Breen, and soon many others, alerted students of Calvin to the important role of classical and humanistic rhetoric in Calvin's way of thought and expression. These pages, in my view, are happily defensible as they stand, particularly on the theological meaning and role of accommodation, despite my innocence of rhetoric at that time. More account of rhetoric is now taken, both in the new Chapter VI, and in Appendix VI on Bouwsma.

The best studies of the last few years on the structure of Calvin's thought appear to me to be those of Mary Potter Engel, who presents Calvin's "perspectival" theology, and Brian G. Armstrong, who expounds its "hypothetical" structure. These are two quite independent, yet harmonious analyses, both of which offer refinements and improvements of the suggestions in our chapters V and VI, rather awkwardly described as Calvin's "double presupposition."

Although the parameters of the problem in which the classic debate between Karl Barth and Emil Brunner took place (*infra,* Appendix III) may no longer be in position, one might say that fundamentally the same problem is before us again when theological voices deal with the fateful issues of ecology, gender, and social liberation in terms of divine justice and grace. Calvin's method is one in which the knowledge of the Creator is presupposed when speaking of redemption, and grace is presupposed when speaking of the creation — the whole within a Trinitarian setting, yet with important continuities and discontinuities remaining. A mastery of Calvin's brilliant and delicate thought by the contemporary theologian cannot but be "useful" (Calvin's word), both positively and in avoiding pitfalls. If this be so, then the reappearance of this volume may still make some contribution to living theology as well as to debates among historians of thought. One hopes so.

Edward A. Dowey

Princeton, New Jersey
October 24, 1993

PREFACE TO THE SECOND PRINTING

RESEARCH AND WRITING for the first printing of this volume were completed fifteen years ago. At that time, few books had been written on the knowledge of God according to Calvin, but 1952 saw publication of several volumes on the subject (listed on pp. 257–258) by T. H. L. Parker, W. E. Stuermann, and myself. (My review of Parker and Stuermann appears in *Theology Today,* XII, 1 [April, 1955], 115–117.) Two more by R. A. Wallace and Werner Krusche (Krusche's, though dated 1957, was completed in 1953) were evidently being written at the same time. Unhappily this meant that the writers could not benefit by one another's work. The results are rather diffuse and uneven. A later volume, H. J. Forstman's *Word and Spirit,* does not succeed in advancing the discussion or in bringing the earlier contributions into focus.

The book by Krusche, *Das Wirken des heiligen Geistes nach Calvin,* one of the ablest monographs in the entire Calvin literature, and an article by John T. McNeill, "The Significance of the Word of God for Calvin," have brought me to some *retractiones.* This retouching will be done in the next few pages along with comments on the recent literature. Otherwise, I am happy to have this volume appear as it did before, with some minor corrections. Were I to begin all over, the most extensive changes would be in the first and last chapters. Many things would be differently expressed, but the basic orientation would remain.

The most numerous and substantive discussions in the recent literature have concerned Calvin's view of Scripture. The old Warfield-Seeberg opinion that Calvin fathered the seventeenth-century orthodox doctrine of inspiration has been revived without much change by K. S. Kantzer. McNeill develops and improves views held earlier by Doumergue and Clavier in which Calvin is seen to hold that the doctrine or subject matter is inspired, but not the words. With remarkable sensitivity to nuance in Calvin, Krusche manages to do justice to the authentic insight in each position. "Inspiration," he writes, "is not related only to the matter (*Sache*), so that it is left to us to distinguish between the inspired contents and the uninspired form; it extends also to the form, but to the form only insofar as it is the form of this particular matter. The Holy Spirit rules also the choice of words, —and this rule is so severe that it is *as if* he had dictated the words, placed them in the mouths of the biblical witnesses,—but only in order that these words faithfully (*fideliter*) deliver the matter." (Krusche, p. 183, italics added; cf. p. 173 *et passim*.)

To explain the "as if" (Calvin's *quasi* or *quodammodo*), Krusche offers a distinction between *grammatikalische Wortwörtlichkeit* and *wortgetreue Wiedergabe*. The former is a pleonasm equivalent to word-for-word literalism, including errorless syntax. The latter is probably best expressed as a repetition faithful to words, not as such, but because of the meaning they bear. The former is an attribute of a text, the latter describes a process of communication. According to Krusche, Calvin's view of the writing down of Scripture is that of the *wortgetreue Wiedergabe* of divine revelation which lies in "another dimension" from the seventeenth-century view of a sacred errorless text.

The formulation of Krusche may come closer to verbal inspiration than McNeill might wish. Yet there is a refinement that recognizes a difference between text and communication. It allows for those places, forced upon my attention by McNeill, where Calvin discovers factual but not substantive error in the original text. This further account of the "as if," a term borrowed from Warfield (*infra* pp. 101 f.), represents a genuine gain. Since Krusche had studied Warfield carefully, it may be that he borrowed the expression inadvertently. At any rate, he avoids more clearly than I did Warfield's incorrect assimilation of Calvin to the position of Reformed scholasticism. My own expressed intent (let the reader judge) would have been much better served by avoiding here and there the unqualified use of "dictate" or "verbal inerrancy."

Nonetheless, it must be urged upon Krusche and McNeill that despite their close attention to the text of Calvin's Jeremiah lectures, neither has noticed that Calvin in commenting on Jeremiah 38:28 attributed to the Holy Spirit a secretarial dictation process in which not a "syllable" is to be omitted (*infra,* p. 93). This statement is not normative for Calvin but it should be given enough weight to qualify the opinion that the seventeenth century offered an "absolute *novum.*" (Krusche, p. 184, takes this phrase from H. Cremer.) There were roots in Calvin and before Calvin for what evolved in that century.

It is not enough, however, to set Calvin apart from orthodoxy by emphasizing the figurative or "as if" character of so-called dictation. Much more important, and certainly the main point in the treatment (*infra,* pp. 148–220), is to show that both inspiration and the "witness" of the Spirit are subsidiary in Calvin to his teaching about faith in the *Institutes,* Book III. Christ, not a book, is the *scopus fidei.* Joseph Haroutunian develops this succinctly in his fine introduction to *Calvin: Commentaries.*

A responsible comment here requires the mention of two widely quoted books of comprehensive title. The first, R. E. Davies, *The Problem of Authority in the Continental Reformers,* depends for its Calvin materials largely on secondary works. On the subject at hand it attributes "verbal and mechanical" inspiration to Calvin, defending Warfield against Doumergue, on the basis of battles fought in the first quarter of the century. Davies' book, however, was published in 1946 and showed no knowledge of Peter Brunner, Peter Barth, or Niesel, who certainly had reoriented the discussion and might well have opened for the author a fresh understanding of Calvin. The second book, J. K. S. Reid, *The Authority of Scripture: a Study of Reformation and Post-Reformation Understanding of the Bible,* falls short, also by undue dependence upon others, of the solid work we need on this topic. Well intentioned in rescuing Calvin from orthodoxy, Reid's chapter on Calvin is careless in terminology and capricious in citing both Calvin and secondary writers. In the confusion he mistakes friend and foe. Reid's classification of viewpoints in a Supplementary Note lists wrongly Seeberg and Otto Ritschl among those who deny that Calvin held the view of verbal inspiration. My book is placed among those holding for "infallibility" (*sic*), then reclassified on the same page as holding "an intermediary position." The entire latter half of this book, which contains the most extensive study yet published in defense of the view Reid himself shares, namely that Calvin's views of both Scripture and faith are christocentric, apparently remained unread. Instead, as students often report in consternation, Professor Reid, while discussing modern fundamentalism (p. 162), attributes to me personally the view that the Bible derives from documents "errorless in their original form." This amusing result is achieved by excising the words "according to Calvin," from the sentence at the top of page 101, *infra*. There, in fact, I was reluctantly ascribing to Calvin a view clearly not shared between Benjamin Warfield and myself!

The most inclusive thesis in the present volume continues to reflect, in the mind of the writer, a sound analysis of Calvin. That is to say that the "two-fold knowledge of God" as Redeemer and Creator, the latter dependent upon the former, the two in dialectical relationship, and the whole rooted in faith, is basic to Calvin's mode of thought in all its branches. It has been suggested by Krusche and developed in the yet unpublished Harvard dissertation of E. David Willis that a fuller Trinitarian setting is achieved for the knowledge of God when closer attention is given to Calvin's treatment of the *filioque* together with the so-called *extra-Calvinisticum*. This results in a profounder unity of the knowledge of God without resolving the dialectic as here described. I refrain from taking a position on this until I see the matter more clearly. But it appears to be a fruitful line of thought, and it carries out a suggestion (*infra,* p. 222) which had in fact been part of the original program for the present work. The choice of law as the theme for the demonstration worked out in the last chapter is supported remarkably by Krusche (pp. 184 ff.).

By contrast, the polemic of T. H. L. Parker in an Appendix to the American reprint of his book misses the mark. The claim that problems of the *duplex cognitio Domini* arise from my "rearranging" of the *Institutes* is made so irresponsibly as to cast doubts on Parker's desire to be taken seriously. His second claim, concerning the treatment of "inexcusability," may have something in it. But I fail to see the difference between his summary on page 125 and my own expressed view. A glance at Mr. Parker's bibliography and text reveals a second-hand acquaintance with the continental debates from which his own case (and mine) derives. He might profit from the brief account, *infra,* Appendix III.

E.A.D., Jr.

Princeton, New Jersey
October, 1964

PREFACE

All who write about Calvin deal directly or indirectly with the problem of the knowledge of God, but there is no single book that touches all the issues involved. Two articles on the subject, one by Warfield, "Calvin's Doctrine of the Knowledge of God," in his *Calvin and Calvinism,* and one by Lobstein, "La Connaissance religieuse d'après Calvin," in *Revue de théologie et de philosophie* (Lausanne), are of basic importance, but neither is comprehensive. The most serious omission in both instances is the lack of a study of Calvin's doctrine of faith. At the root of this is a failure to take seriously Calvin's fundamental distinction between the knowledge of God the Creator and the knowledge of God the Redeemer, and thus to assume (as Calvin himself did not) that the problem of knowledge is dealt with and done with when the doctrines of the revelation in creation and in Scripture have been formulated, in the first book of the *Institutes.* In fact, the doctrine of faith in Book III is just as much an epistemological introduction to the *Institutes* as is Book I, chapters i–ix. Calvin's doctrine of Scripture stands in a very difficult-to-describe relation to that of faith, but at least as good a case can be made for subsuming it under the doctrine of faith, as for the reverse, which is the usual procedure. Lobstein goes beyond Warfield in this respect, but he uses an oversimplified distinction which identifies Calvin's doctrine of Scripture as "scholastic" and his doctrine of faith as "evangelical," with a very short study of the latter, and without any account of the interrelation of the two. Two works by Peter Brunner, *Vom Glauben bei Calvin,* and "Allgemeine und besondere Offenbarung in Calvins Institutio," in *Evangelische Theologie,* cover some issues slighted by Warfield and Lobstein, but with emphasis on the objective revelation rather than on the knowledge of it. If to the aforementioned we add the appropriate works of Gloede, *Theologia naturalis bei Calvin,* Peter Barth, *Das Problem der natürlichen Theologie bei Calvin,* and the "problems," of Bauke, *Die Probleme der Theologie Calvins,* we shall have a collection of literature that covers in separate studies all the problems raised in the present work save one: the problem of the basic significance of the *duplex cognitio Domini*. But these writings over a period of thirty years that included one of the major theological upheavals since the Reformation, proceed from such differing bases that no consistent picture is given in them of the group of problems which they, in a general way, cover. The following pages are an effort to treat these problems together and from a single point of view. The point of view is, I hope, everywhere identifiable and so expressed as to help, not hinder, the main purpose of the book, which is a critical exposition of Calvin's theological epistemology.

It would have been possible to study much of the material that follows under the four headings of the first chapter. But this, in the process of writing, seemed always to tend toward a falsification of Calvin's thought by giving it a form not his own. Therefore, the four categories of the opening chapter are treated only in so far as is necessary to define them. They are given fuller meaning as they recur throughout the later sections.

Permission to quote at length from the collected works of Warfield has been granted by the Presbyterian and Reformed Publication Company which owns the copyright of these works, formerly in the hands of the Oxford University Press.

In the completion of this work, I owe particular thanks to the friendship and advice of Professor Emil Brunner, of the University of Zürich, and also to the Central Library of Zürich, which permitted me the indispensable use of the works of Calvin in my pleasant Swiss pension room for more than a year.

E.A.D., Jr.

New York City
October, 1951

Note on Translations and Citations

Whenever possible the English translations of Calvin's works listed in the bibliography have been used in the text and footnotes. Quotations, however, have been altered freely and without notation, and in addition Latin and French words have been added in parentheses or notes where they served to clarify or emphasize.

Since most readers will have Calvin's works only in translation, the first part of each citation is in a form applicable to any translation. The *Institutes* is referred to by Book, chapter, and paragraph as follows, I.ii.2. In addition, for those who use the sources a second part has been added to each reference in parentheses, such as, (OS III. 35. 11–14), which means *Opera Selecta,* Volume III, page 35, lines 11–14. Commentaries and sermons are cited by the appropriate verses from the Bible, for example, Com.Ez.9:3. The latter continues, (CO XL.196d), which means *Calvini Opera,* Volume XL, page 196, and the last quarter of the page when divided into equal parts, a,b,c,d.

The various Latin editions of the *Institutes* are referred to in notes by an abbreviation of the year in which they appeared, the edition of 1536 becoming "ed.'36." French editions are cited, for example, as "Fr. ed. '60."

If English translations of German and French works are nonexistent or were not available, I have made my own.

E.A.D., Jr.

THE KNOWLEDGE OF GOD IN CALVIN'S THEOLOGY

·I·

GENERAL CHARACTERISTICS OF THE KNOWLEDGE OF GOD

CALVIN'S THEOLOGY exalts the category of knowledge. It is overwhelmingly a "theology of the word," and it gave birth to a theological tradition that even today is best described by this phrase. Calvin's thought has its whole existence within the realm of God as revealer and man as knower. Because of this, one of the most common rebukes leveled against Calvin is that he overintellectualized the Christian faith. Some of the sting of this rebuke—some, if not all—will be removed when we discover what Calvin meant by knowledge, particularly knowledge of God. The word knowledge, we may say in anticipation and in apparent contradiction, is not purely noetic in Calvin's theology, and therefore its ubiquity is not *ipso facto* evidence of an intellectualized faith.

As is frequently the case with ideas that are so fundamental, so immediate to the consciousness of a philosopher or theologian as is knowledge to Calvin, no exact definition of it can be found in his writings, nor can one be constructed. Rather, we must try to grasp what is meant by the knowledge of God through the part it plays in his whole way of thinking. The four categories that are the four divisions of this introductory chapter are meant to orient us in this pursuit.

THE ACCOMMODATED CHARACTER OF ALL KNOWLEDGE OF GOD

The term accommodation refers to the process by which God reduces or adjusts to human capacities what he wills to reveal of the infinite mysteries of his being, which by their very nature are beyond the powers of the mind of man to grasp. For "God cannot be comprehended by us except as far as he accommodates (*attemperat*) himself to our standard."[1] The term includes within its scope all the noetic aspects of the Creator-creature relation. It points to a gap between God and man that is bridged only by God "in some way descending"[2] to meet the limitations of human nature, never by man himself overcoming them. These limitations are of two varieties, essential and accidental.[3] Calvin always recognizes that man was at creation and essentially remains a finite creature and that in addition he is accidentally a sinful creature. Thus, accommodation is of two varieties: (*a*) the universal and necessary accommodation of the infinite mysteries of God *to finite comprehension,* which embraces all revelation, and (*b*) the special, gracious accommodation *to human sinfulness* which is connected with the work of redemption. By this separation we are anticipating a distinction to be made and defined more closely in later chapters. For the present we are more interested in it as a qualitative distinction than as a description of the sources of revelation.

THE ACCOMMODATION OF GOD'S REVELATION TO FINITE COMPREHENSION.—The essence of God is unknown and inaccessible to us, according to Calvin, and all speculations about it are blasphemy. Here lies a chief error of schoolmen and philosophers alike, who discuss the being of God apart from the revelation of his will. "Those, therefore, who in considering this question propose to inquire what the essence of God is (*quid sit Deus*) only trifle with frigid speculations—it being much more important for us to

[1] Com. Ez. 9:3, 4 (CO XL.196d). "For since he is in himself incomprehensible, he assumes, when he wishes to manifest himself to men, those marks by which he may be known." Com. Gen. 3:8 (CO XXIII.65d). "God in his greatness can by no means be fully comprehended by our minds . . . there are certain limits within which men ought to confine themselves, in as much as God accommodates (*attemperat*) to our measure what he testifies of himself." Com. Rm. 1:19 (CO XLIX.23c). "He accommodates (*attemperat*) himself to our capacity in addressing us." Com. I Cor. 2:7 (CO XLIX.337d).

[2] "It was necessary that he should assume a visible form, that he might be seen by Moses not as he was in his essence but as the infirmity of the human mind could comprehend. For thus we believe that God, as often as he appeared of old to the holy patriarchs, decended in some way (*descendisse quodammodo*) from his loftiness, that he might reveal himself as far as was useful and as far as their comprehension would admit." Com. Ex. 3:2 (CO XXIV.35c).

[3] These two terms in their Aristotelian sense are routine distinctions for Calvin.

know what kind of being (*qualis sit*) God is, and what things are agreeable to his nature."[4] See Appendix 1 on anthropomorphism.

The three "epithets" for God's essence, "immensity," "spirituality," and "simplicity," [5] are not positive descriptions which form a base for philosophizing and theologizing, but boundaries or limits which deny the access of philosophers and theologians to the essence of God. These words mean, respectively, that God's essence is *not* finite, *not* material, and *not* divisible—in short, not comprehensible.

What is taught in the Scriptures concerning the immensity and spirituality of the essence of God should serve not only to overthrow the foolish notions of the vulgar but also to refute the subtleties of profane philosophy. . . . But although God, to keep us within the bounds of sobriety, speaks but rarely of his essence, yet, by those two epithets, which I have mentioned, he supersedes all gross imaginations, and represses the presumption of the human mind. For surely, his immensity ought to deter us that we may not attempt to measure him with our senses; and his spiritual nature prohibits us from entertaining any earthly or carnal speculations concerning him.[6]

Even the simplicity of God's essence, when viewed alone as a positive attribute, gives a false picture, "a bare and empty name of God, which floats in our brains, and not the true God," [7] be-

[4] I.ii.2 (OS III.35.11–14). "God appeared under a visible form to his servant: could Ezekiel on that account do as scholastic theologians do—philosophize with subtility concerning God's essence and know no end or moderation in their dispute! By no means, but he restrained himself within fixed bounds." Com. Ez. 1:25–26 (CO XL.57c).

[5] "Quod de immensa et spirituali Dei essentia traditur in Scripturis . . . parce de sua essentia disserit, duobus tamen illis quae dixi epithetis." I.xiii.1 (OS III.108.23, 29). "Simplicem Dei essentiam . . ." I.xiii.2 (OS III.109.24). God's "immensity" and "spirituality" receive no detailed discussion by Calvin, while his "simplicity" is a constant foil to the tri-unity throughout I.xiii.

Calvin speaks most often of *virtutes Dei,* sometimes of *attributa* and *epitheta;* cf. Warfield, "Calvin's Doctrine of God," in *Calvin and Calvinism,* p. 164. Warfield collects them all together, divided into properties of God "in himself" and "toward us," and summarizes their development in the *Institutes, ibid.,* pp. 164–173.

[6] I.xiii.1 (OS III.108.23–109.1). "For since the nature of God is spiritual, it is not allowable to imagine respecting him anything earthly or gross; nor does his immensity permit of his being confined to place," Com. Ex. 3:4 (CO XXIV.37d).

[7] I.xiii.2 (OS III.109.22).

cause within the "unity of essence" there is "a distinction of persons between the Father and the Son, not only with respect to men, but it is so in God Himself." [8] But this is a wholly mysterious relation, not to be investigated. The classic doctrine of the Trinity is not meant to describe the objective *jenseits* life of God, but is a protective terminology guarding the Biblical teaching from this and other heresies.[9] Precisely in connection with the doctrine of the Trinity, Calvin writes "For how can the infinite essence of God be defined by the capacity of the human mind, which could never yet certainly determine the nature of the body of the sun, which the eye beholds daily? Indeed, how can it, by its own efforts, penetrate into an examination of the substance (*substantiam*) of God, when it is totally ignorant of its own? Wherefore let us willingly leave to God the knowledge of himself." [10]

It is the work, power, activity, or will of God rather than his being or essence that we know, and then only in so far as it is directed toward us.

For God, otherwise invisible (as we have already said) clothes himself, so to speak, in the image of the world (*mundi imaginem quodammodo induit*), in which he presents himself to our observation. . . . Therefore as soon as the name of God sounds in our ears or a thought of him suggests itself, let us clothe him with this most beautiful attire; finally, let the world be our school, if we desire rightly to know God.[11]

Whence we conclude this to be the right way and the best method of seeking God: not with presumptuous curiosity to attempt an examination of his essence, which is rather to be adored than too minutely investigated; but to contemplate him in his works, in which he approaches and familiarizes, and in some measure communicates himself to us.[12]

[8] Com. Heb. 1:2 (CO LV.11a).

[9] The "invented" names of the trinitarian formularies tell us nothing beyond Scripture. "I could wish them, indeed, to be buried, provided that all were agreed upon this belief, that the Father, Son, and Spirit, are the one God and that nevertheless the Son is not the Father, nor the Spirit the Son, but that they are distinguished from each other by some peculiar property." I.xiii.5 (OS III.113.28–114.2, and *passim*).

[10] I.xiii.21 (OS III.136.13–18).

[11] Com. Gen. "Argument" (CO XXIII.8d).

[12] I.v.9 (OS III.53.18–23).

His essence is indeed incomprehensible, so that his divinity is not to be perceived by the human senses, but on each of his works he has inscribed his glory in characters so clear, unequivocal, and striking that the most illiterate and stupid cannot exculpate themselves by the plea of ignorance.[13]

Although he is himself invisible, in a manner he becomes visible to us in his works.[14]

Man must keep his thoughts within the limits imposed by the temporal and spatial creation. Speculations about infinite time and infinite space are forbidden, as are those concerning possible activities of God that do not directly concern man.[15] The best answer to the question of what God did with his power before he created the world is that "he had been making hell for overcurious men."[16] Even within the time-space creation, man knows God's will only in a very limited way. Calvin's doctrine of providence, or the continuing relation of Creator and creation, is permeated in an almost uncanny manner with the immediate presence of a mysterious will. Every wind, every drop of rain, is a special volition of God's will.[17] Man is consciously surrounded by its work. Yet it remains a mysterious will emanating from the "secret purpose of the Father," his "secret" or "mysterious judgments," or his "secret counsel." "God claims a power unknown to us in governing the world," and while it is not an unjust will, "the reasons governing it are concealed from us."[18]

The works of God have double significance both as limits to human knowledge and as limited self-revelations of God. Calvin is no nature mystic elevated to ecstasy by the "power of being." Subpersonal metaphysical categories have almost no place in his theology. He does recognize a kind of hierarchy in creation consisting of existence, motion, life, and finally thought.[19] The latter, which is the differentia of human life, is the summit of creation and the correlate of its revelatory character. It is here, with revela-

[13] I.v.1 (OS III.45.4–8).
[14] Com. Heb. 11:3 (CO LV.146a).
[15] I.xiv.1 (OS III.153.5–37); Com. Gen. "Argument" (CO XXIII.10a).
[16] *Ibid.*
[17] I.xvi.7, *passim.*
[18] I.xvii.1–2 (OS III.202.33, 41; 203.16; 204.4; 205.12–19).
[19] Com. Acts 17:28 (CO XLVIII.416/17).

tion and the knowledge of it, that Calvin's theology begins. It is no accident that the *Institutes,* from the first edition to the last, opens with the category of knowledge, "the *knowledge* of God and ourselves," not speculations about being or existence. Calvin is here a kind of Kant, an epistemologist not a metaphysician, with reference to both God and the world. For Calvin the *raison d'être* of creation—the goal of accommodation—is God's revelation to man and the resultant possibility of glorifying God by worship and obedience.[20] Lobstein points out that this teleology follows "quite naturally" from Calvin's practical religious interest.[21] It comes also from his logos doctrine. "Now as God, in creating the world, revealed himself by that Word, so he formerly had him concealed with himself, so that there is a two-fold relation: the former to God, and the latter to men." [22] "The Word was, as it were, hidden before he revealed himself in the external structure of the world." [23] "No sooner was the world created than the Word of God came forth into external operation; having been formerly *incomprehensible in his essence,* he then became *publicly known by the effect of his power."* [24] The incomprehensible essence of the Third Person of the Trinity (Calvin is not yet speaking of Christ and the Incarnation), through the exertion of his power in creating the world, becomes "publicly known," that is, reveals himself to men. Further, under the words "In him was life, and the life was the light of men," Calvin adds that the Eternal Word preserves those things which had been created, displaying his "power" in the "steady and regular order of nature," giving "life" to both inanimate and animate creatures, but more especially in "that part of life in which men excel other animals . . . *the light of understanding* . . . [and] as it is not in vain that God imparts his light to their minds, it follows that *the purpose for which they were created was, that they might acknowledge him who is the Author of so excellent a blessing.* And since

[20] Com. Isa. 34:17 (CO XXXVI.589b); Com. Gen. 1:26 (CO XXIII.27d); Com. Ps. 8:6 (CO XXXI.92b). Cf. Geneva Catechism, 1545, 1st question (CO VI.10b).

[21] "La Connaissance réligieuse," pp. 67 f.

[22] Com. Jn. 1:1–4 (CO XLVII.2a).

[23] *Ibid.* (p. 3b).

[24] *Ibid.* (p. 4a), italics added.

this light, of which the Word was the source has been conveyed from him to us, it ought to serve as a mirror, in which we may clearly behold the divine power of the Word."[25]

Not only is the creation as such a revelation of God, but the very method by which it took place was peculiarly adapted, or accommodated, to our instruction. God might, by a sudden act of will have brought all things into being at once, but rather than thus confounding our reason, he "took the space of six days for the purpose of accommodating (*temperaret*) his works to the capacity of men." Removing the occasion for men to slight his glory, "he distributed the creation of the world into successive portions, that he might fix our attention and compel us, as if he had laid his hand upon us, to pause and to reflect."[26] Further, God both created light (Gen. 1:3), and brought herbs and grasses to the earth (Gen. 1:11), before creating the sun (Gen. 1:13–16), simply to show man that he, not the sun, is the source of light and growth, "that we may learn from the order of the creation itself, that God acts through the creatures, not as if he needed external help, but because it was his pleasure."[27]

THE ACCOMMODATION TO HUMAN SINFULNESS.—When we turn to the special or historical revelation—not God's works in general, but his works of redemption—we find the reduction or accommodation of God to man's capacities extended. The Redeeming Word, like the Creative Word, is spoken by the Eternal Wisdom of God through the created order, but in a special language accommodated to the aggravated condition of *sinful* creaturliness.

For there are two distinct powers which belong to the Son of God: the first, which is manifest in the architecture of the world and the order of nature; and the second, by which he renews and restores fallen nature. As he is the eternal Word of God, by him the world was made, by his power all things continue to possess the life which they once received; man was endued with an unique gift of understanding, and though by revolt he lost the light of understanding, yet he still sees and understands, so that what he naturally possesses from the grace of the Son of God is not entirely destroyed. But since by his

[25] *Ibid.* (p. 4c), italics added.
[26] Com. Gen. 1:5 (CO XXIII.18a).
[27] Com. Gen. 1:11 (CO XXIII.20b).

stupidity and perverseness he darkens the light which still dwells in him, it remains that a new office be undertaken by the Son of God, the office of Mediator, to renew by the spirit of regeneration man, who had been ruined.[28]

This is one of the fundamental statements in Calvin's theology. Just as the universal revelation of God arises from God's Creative Word, so this special accommodation to human sinfulness occurs exclusively through the self-abasement that God undertook when the Eternal Son assumed the office of Mediator.[29] There is no redemptive knowledge of God, whether patriarchal, prophetic, or apostolic, apart from the mediatorial office of Christ.[30] All the various forms through which the special revelation has come at various times are simply to be understood as further accommodations of God to the peculiar needs of each age. We shall enter later into a fuller discussion of the developing forms of revelation—the "oracle" or message transmitted, and the accompanying dreams, visions, and physical miracles.[31] For the present it will suffice to show the caution with which Calvin treats some of those aspects of special revelation where the temptation is strong to say that God is known immediately. For him the principle of accommodation always intervenes.

Calvin, contrary to the scholastic tradition [32] and with an excellent appreciation of Old Testament ways of thinking, eschews all philosophizing in connection with the revelation of the name of God and links it with his power. He does not deny that in the name Jahweh the "eternity and primary essence of God is expressed." [33] But, "how would it have profited Moses to gaze upon

[28] Com. Jn. 1:5 (CO XLVII.7a). "For he assumed the character of Mediator in order to approach to us by descending from the bosom and incomprehensible glory of his Father." II.xv.5 (OS III.479.22–23); cf., II.xvi.1 (OS III.482.9). See also Appendix I.

[29] ". . . because God himself would remain absolutely hidden (*procul absconditus*) if we were not illuminated by the brightness of Christ." III.ii.l (OS IV.8.12).

[30] *Infra*, pp. 157 ff. [31] *Infra*, pp. 93 ff.

[32] Cf. Gilson, *The Spirit of Medieval Philosophy*, pp. 93 ff., 446 f., 461. This writer often uses the term "the metaphysics of Exodus." Also in *God and Philosophy*, chaps. i–ii.

[33] Com. Ez. 1:25–26 (CO XL.53d); cf. Com. Acts 17:28 (CO XLVIII.416d–417c).

the secret essence of God as if it were shut up in heaven, unless, being assured of his omnipotence, he had obtained from thence the buckler of his confidence?"[34] This name of God is "to be understood of the knowledge of him in so far as he makes himself known to us, for I do not approve of the subtle speculations of those who think the name of God means nothing else but God himself. It ought rather to be referred to the works and properties (*virtutes*) by which he is known, than to his essence."[35] Elsewhere, commenting on the words "I, I am Jahweh, and there is no Savior besides me," Calvin characteristically notes that the second clause is added

> that we may not suppose that his eternal essence only is here exhibited, but also his power and goodness, which he constantly exercises toward us and by which he abundantly reveals himself. . . . The world falls into the mistake of giving a naked and empty name to God, meanwhile transferring his authority to another.[36]

God does not boast of power which lies concealed within himself, but of that which he manifests toward his children. . . .[37]

When the prophet speaks of the strength and power of God, he does not mean power which is unemployed (*otiosam potentiam*), but that which is effectual and actual, *which is actually exerted on us,* and which conducts to the end what he had begun.[38]

The name "strong" is attributed to God, as often in other passages, because it is not enough to acknowledge God's eternal essence unless we also ascribe strength to him. But for this we shall leave him nothing but a bare and empty name, as the wicked do, who with the mouth confess God and then transfer his power to this and that.[39]

[34] Com. Ex. 3:14 (CO XXIV.44a). The comment on Ex. 3:14 throughout stresses the "power and government" of God. His "incomprehensible essence" is to be admired, but is not to serve as a first term in our philosophy, as Plato's *τὸ ὄν*.

[35] Com. Ps. 8:1 (CO XXXI.88c).

[36] Com. Isa. 43:11 (CO XXXVII.89d).

[37] Com. Gen. 17:1 (CO XXIII.234c).

[38] Com. Isa. 26:4 (CO XXXVI.429a), italics added.

[39] Com. Isa. 44:8 (CO XXXVII.111c). Note *supra,* in the references to Com. Isa. 43:11 and 44:8, as well as Ex. 3:14 that it is by the separation of God's being from his power that idolatry gets a foothold. Both pagan idolatry and Roman saint worship often maintain that God is the One Being, nonetheless, by

Elsewhere the Psalmist "does not speak of the hidden essence of God (*abscondita Dei essentia*), which fills heaven and earth, but of the manifestations of his power, wisdom, goodness, and righteousness, which appear publicly, although they may exceed the measure of our understanding." [40] God's essence remains a mystery even to those who know his name.

God, however, has not only told his name, but in various instances has actually appeared to chosen people or to groups. The presence of God in these theophanies is no exhibition of his essence, it is rather a further illustration that his essence is not only unknowable but also deadly to man [41]—and his "voice" as well [42]—except when graciously veiled under appearances accommodated to human abilities. The emphasis as in the general revelation, remains on the communication of knowledge, and always under the double aspect of revealing-concealing, revealed character and concealed essence.

For when the Lord gives tokens (*signa*) of his presence, he employs at the same time some coverings to restrain the arrogance of the human mind . . . this admonition also pertains to us, that we may not seek to pry into secrets which lie beyond our perception, but rather that every man may keep within the limits of sobriety, according to the measure of his faith.[43]

As therefore our capacity cannot endure the fullness of the infinite glory which belongs to the essence of God, it is necessary whenever he appears to us that he put on a form adapted to our capacity . . . but as I have already said, we ought not to imagine God in his essence to be like any appearance to his own prophet and other holy fathers, but he continually put on various appearances, according to man's

---

thinking to apportion out his power to idols and saints "they impiously tear into pieces the divided divinity."

[40] Com. Ps. 77:15 (CO XXXI.718b); cf. Com. Ps. 86:8 (CO XXXI.794a).

[41] "In sum, therefore, Moses shows us that it was a miracle that the rulers of Israel remained safe and sound, although the terrible majesty of God had appeared to them." Com. Ex. 24:11 (CO XXV.77d); Com. Isa. 6:2 (CO XXXV.128a–b); Com. Ex. 13:21 (CO XXIV.145); Com. Dan. 7:9 (CO XLI.53–55).

[42] "God's voice is deadly to the flesh, unless it is softened by some interposing remedy." Com. Deut. 5:26 (CO XXIV.207b); *ibid.,* 5:24 (p. 206d).

[43] Com. Mt. 17:5 (CO XLV.487c).

comprehension, to whom he wished to give some signs of his presence.[44]

Theophany has the same revelatory function as the sacraments, and it is not uncommon for Calvin, after the example of Paul, to relate the two. The important characteristics that both have in common are (1) a real, but spiritual, presence that is represented by, but not to be identified with, the physical or visionary[45] appearance,[46] (2) a subordination of the sign to its meaning or the message it carries,[47] and (3) the necessity of faith for the reception of the revelation.[48] Here, as everywhere in Calvin's theology, the only successful medium of intercourse between God and fallen man is the word. A sacramental encounter with God's "substance" is out of the question. In connection with Isaiah's temple vision Calvin digresses into a long discussion of the sacraments and characteristically emphasizes that "the chief part of the sacraments

[44] Com. Dan. 7:9 (CO XLI.55b–c).

[45] Calvin displays a curious interest in discovering whether a given appearance is a physical miracle or is purely visionary, although he attaches no theological importance to his conclusion except to deny occasionally a medieval sacramentarian exegesis. In Com. Ez. he is especially insistent on the nonphysical nature of the visionary phenomena. E.g. Com. 1:25, 26 (CO XL.52–57).

[46] By the cloud in the wilderness which went before the children of Israel, God "chose to add also his visible presence to remove all room for doubt. But although the words of Moses seem in some measure to include the Lord in the cloud, we must observe the sacramental mode of speaking (*sacramentalis loquendi ratio*) wherein God transfers his name to visible figures, not to affix to them his essence or to circumscribe his infinity, but only to show that he does not deceitfully expose the signs of his presence to men's eyes, but that the exhibition of the thing signified is at the same time truly conjoined with them. Therefore, although Moses states that God was in the cloud and in the pillar of fire, yet he does not wish to draw him down from heaven or to subject his infinite glory to visible signs, with which the truth may consist without his local presence." Com. Ex. 13:21 (CO XXIV.145b).

[47] At the baptism of Jesus: "Although he [the Holy Spirit] is in himself invisible, yet he is spoken of as beheld when he exhibits any visible sign of his presence. John did not see the essence of the Spirit, which cannot be discerned by the senses of men, nor did he see his power, which is not beheld by human senses, but only by the understanding of faith; but he saw the appearance of a dove, under which God showed the presence of his Spirit. It is therefore spoken by metonymy, in which the name of the spiritual thing is transferred to the visible sign." Com. Mt. 3:16 (CO XLV.127a).

[48] Com. Mt. 17:5 (CO XLV.487d–488a).

[49] Com. Isa. 6:7 (CO XXXVI.134a, and *passim*).

consists in the word."[49] "True knowledge of God is perceived more by the ears than by the eyes."[50]

Calvin does not hesitate to identify certain phenomena among Old Testament theophanies as special appearances of Christ, giving a foretaste of the office he is later to fullfil.[51] But these, together with all the other accompaniments of revelation in the Old and New Testament, are subordinate to the final accommodation to human sinfulness, the Incarnation. Here, as elsewhere, Calvin's principle of accommodation guards the borders. The pattern is the same as previously noted: essence unknown, power exerted for the sake of revelation, with chief emphasis placed upon the revelation itself.

When Christ says, "I am in the Father and the Father in me," Calvin comments,

I do not consider these words to refer to Christ's divine essence, but to the manner of revelation; for Christ, so far as regards his hidden divinity, is not better known to us than the Father. But he is said to be the express image of God because in him God has fully revealed himself, so far as God's infinite goodness, wisdom, and power are clearly manifested in him. Yet the ancients are not wrong when they quote this passage as a proof for defending Christ's divinity; but as Christ does not inquire simply what he is in himself, but what we ought to acknowledge him to be, this description applies to his power rather than to his essence. The Father, therefore, is said to be in Christ, because full divinity dwells in him and displays its power; and Christ, on the other hand, is said to be in the Father because by his divine power he shows that he is one with the Father.[52]

[50] Com. Ex. 33:19 (CO XXV.109a).

[51] E.g., the third angel that appeared to Abraham, but not to Lot, Com. Gen. 19:1 (CO XXIII.267a); the "man" who wrestled with Jacob, Gen. 32:24 ff., is called Christ in Com. Gen. 48:16 (CO XXIII.584d); also in Com. Dan. 7:13, the figure is said to be Christ appearing "like" a man, *sed quasi hominem,* not according to the seed of Abraham, but as *praeludium* and *symbolum* of the "future flesh of Christ," (CO XLI.60, *passim*); and in Dan. 8:16, "he was not clothed with the substance of flesh, but had only a human form and aspect," (CO XLI.110b–c); cf. Com. Ez. 1:25, 26 (CO XL.55a–b, and 52–57, *passim*), where there is a lengthy excursis on the relation of the Trinity to theophany, also 8:2 (p. 178), and 10:19 (p. 223/4).

[52] Com. Jn. 14:10 (CO XLVII.326a); cf. Com. Jn. 1:18; 8:24, 28, 42; 10:30, 38; and 14:1, 7. Even in Jn. 8:58, "Before Abraham was, I am," it is the "power"

Again, it ought to be understood, that in every instance in which Christ declares, in this chapter [Jn. 17] that he is one with the Father, he does not speak simply of his divine essence, but he is called one as regards his *character as Mediator,* and in so far as he is our Head. Many of the fathers, no doubt, interpreted these words as meaning absolutely that Christ is one with the Father, because he is the eternal God. But their dispute with the Arians led them to seize on detached passages, and to twist them into alien meanings. Now, Christ's design was widely different from that of raising our minds to a mere speculation about his hidden divinity. Thus, he reasons from the end, by showing that we ought to be one, otherwise, the unity which he has with the Father would be fruitless and unavailing. To comprehend aright what was intended by saying that Christ and the Father are one, we must take care not to deprive Christ of his *character as Mediator,* but must rather view him as the Head of the Church, and unite him with his members. Thus it agrees best with the context, that in order to prevent that unity of the Son with the Father from being fruitless and unavailing, the power of that unity must be diffused into the whole body of the pious. Hence, too, we infer that we are one with Christ, not because he transfuses his substance into us, but because by the power of his Spirit, he imparts to us his life and all the blessings which he has received from the Father.[53]

While asserting, according to the classical trinitarian formulae, that Christ participates in an identity of essence with the Father, Calvin insists that the "main thing is, in what manner the Father makes himself known to us in Christ." When Christ is called the "image of the invisible God,"

the term image is not related to essence, but has a relation to us. For Christ is called the image of God on this ground, that he makes God in a manner visible to us. . . . [This passage is still valid against the Arians, for only God can represent God, but] we must not insist upon essence alone. The sum is this—that God in himself, that is, in his naked majesty, is invisible, and that not to the eyes of the body only, but also to the minds of men, and that he is revealed to us in Christ alone, that we may behold him as in a mirror.[54]

---

and "efficacy" of Christ exerted as Mediator "in all ages" that points back to his "divine essence." (CO XLVII.215d–216a).

[53] Com. Jn. 17:21 (CO XLVII.387c), italics added.

[54] Com. Col. 1:15 (CO LII.84d–85a).

On II Corinthians 4:4, he writes,

When, however, Christ is called the image of the invisible God, this is not meant merely of his essence, as being the "co-essential of the Father," as they say, but rather has reference to us, because he represents the Father to us. The Father himself is represented as invisible, because he is in himself not apprehended by the human understanding. He exhibits himself, however, to us by his Son, and makes himself in a manner visible.[55]

Three things are to be noted. (1) In the Incarnation Christ's hidden divinity or essence remained unchanged:

Although the infinite essence of the Word is united in one person with the nature of man, yet we have no idea of its incarceration or confinement. For the Son of God miraculously descended from heaven, yet in such a manner that he never left heaven; he chose to be miraculously conceived in the womb of Virgin, to live on the earth, and to be suspended on the cross; and yet he never ceased to fill the universe, in the same manner as from the beginning.[56]

(2) Christ's divinity was veiled under the form of flesh, but (3) in such a way as yet to be revealed.

In what way can he be said to be "emptied," while he, nevertheless, constantly proved himself by miracles and excellencies, to be the Son of God, and in him, as John testifies, there was always to be seen a glory worthy of the Son of God? I answer that the abasement of the flesh was, notwithstanding, like a veil, by which his divine majesty was concealed. . . . Finally, the image of God shone forth in Christ in such a manner that he was at the same time abased in his outward appearance and brought down to nothing in the estimation of men.[57]

The majesty of God was not annihilated, although it was surrounded by flesh; it was indeed concealed under the low condition of the flesh, but so as to cause its splendor to be seen.

It was only a few, whose eyes the Holy Spirit opened, that saw this manifestation of glory.[58]

In this concealing-revealing quality of the person of Christ, the divine incognito, we perceive at its sharpest and most paradoxical

[55] (CO L.51d); cf. II.vi.4, throughout. [56] II.xiii.4 (OS III.458.8–13).
[57] Com. Philip. 2:7 (CO LII.26c–d). [58] Com. Jn. 1:14 (CO XLVII.15b).

the double aspect of accommodation already pointed out. It is God's deepest condescension or descent from his own mysterious being, and at the same time it is both the high point of man's knowledge and the limit of it. "God is not to be sought out in his unsearchable height, but is to be known by us in so far as he manifests himself in Christ."[59] "If God, then, has spoken now for the last time, it is right to advance thus far; so also when you come to him [Christ], you ought not to go farther."[60]

To conclude, this concept of accommodation with respect to all knowledge of God, whether meant in principle for man as creature or as sinner, is the horizon of Calvin's theology. He never ventured to attach anything but the name of incomprehensible mystery to what lay beyond that horizon, yet he maintained stoutly that it is God's mystery, not an abyss of nothingness. The mystery belongs to the unknowable side of the known God. Such a phenomenalism in the hands of a speculative thinker could lead as easily to skepticism as to faith. But this is true always in a Christian theology, that is to say, any theology which recognizes that God meets man in revelation, rather than one which tries to produce Him out of an a priori system that, by its abstractness, allows for neither skepticism nor faith. We can call this a symbolic conception of religious knowledge only with greatest caution,[61] for its essence is not man's choosing the most adequate symbols for the great Unknown—as is implied in the term symbol—but rather it begins and ends with the self-revelation of God, the Known, before whom the creature in pious agnosticism confesses his inadequacy to comprehend the Infinite, except in so far as He actively approaches and makes himself known.

[59] Com. II Cor. 4:6 (CO L.53c).

[60] Com. Heb. 1:1 (CO LV.10b).

[61] Lobstein praises Calvin's appreciation of the "inadequate and essentially symbolic nature of our conceptions" of God, "La Connaissance réligieuse," p. 96, without, to my view, sufficiently emphasizing Calvin's objections to a merely symbolic view. E.g., in Com. Isa. 6:1, while the robe, throne, and bodily appearance of God are forms of revelation accommodated to human incapacities, still "lest we should suppose that the Prophet contrived the manner in which he would paint God, we ought to know that he faithfully describes the very form in which God was represented and exhibited to him." (CO XXXVI.126d).

The Correlative Character of the Knowledge of God and Man

Closely allied with the principle of accommodation, by which we learn that all our knowledge of God comes to us in a condition reduced to our capacities, is the principle of correlation,[62] by which we learn the intimate connection that exists between the knowledge of God and of ourselves. The first words of the *Institutes* describe this double relationship in all knowledge, which is one of the fundamentals of Calvin's conception of the knowledge of God.

> Almost the whole of all our wisdom, in so far as it ought to be deemed true and solid wisdom, consists of two parts, the knowledge of God and of ourselves. But as these are connected by many ties, it is not easy to determine which of the two precedes and produces the other. For in the first place no man can look at himself but he must immediately turn to the contemplation of God in whom he lives and moves.[63] . . . Again, it is plain that no man can arrive at the true knowledge of himself without having first contemplated the face of God and then descended to the examination of himself.[64]

The knowledge of ourselves drives us to look at God, and it presupposes that we have already contemplated him. Yet we never contemplate God prior to ourselves, "because, as we observed in the beginning, we cannot obtain to a clear and solid knowledge of God, without a mutual acquaintance with ourselves." [65]

One would hardly expect the opening words of such a careful work as the *Institutes* to have been carelessly chosen, and indeed they were not. The words of the edition of 1536, "The sum of almost all sacred doctrine consists in two parts, the knowledge of God and of ourselves," [66] were expanded already in the edition of 1539 to include "almost the whole of all our wisdom." [67] The second sentence about the difficulty of distinguishing between the two was present also in 1539, but was brought forward and joined to the other in the final Latin rewriting of 1559. In the

[62] I first heard this term applied to Calvin in a seminar by Professor Paul Tillich, at Union Theological Seminary. I shall use his language repeatedly.

[63] I.i.1 (OS III.31.6–11).

[64] I.i.2 (OS III.32.10–12).

[65] I.xv.1 (OS III.173.29–31).

[66] (OS I.37).

[67] (CO I.279b).

French edition of 1560, Calvin goes even further in binding the two elements together: "in knowing God each of us also knows himself." [68] There is a correspondingly closer intermingling of the two in the arrangements of the successive editions. In the edition of 1536, the first two paragraphs are respectively about God and "ourselves," and from 1539 to 1554 the first two chapters are entitled, respectively, "On the Knowledge of God . . ." and "On the Knowledge of Man . . ." But in the definitive form of 1559 Calvin is satisfied only by devoting the whole introductory chapter to the subject: "The Knowledge of God and of Ourselves Mutually Connected, and the Nature of this Connection."

Not only the titles but also the actual development of the material of the first two books of the *Institutes* adheres to this principle stated at the outset. In Book I the knowledge of God the Creator as learned through creation and Scripture leads to the revelation of how the world came to be, what is the nature of man, and a description of the providential relation of God and man.[69] In Book II five chapters on the sinful state of man stand as an introduction to the knowledge of God the Redeemer. As man himself is "the most noble and remarkable specimen of the divine justice, wisdom, and goodness among all the works of God," [70] from the point of view of the revelation of God as Creator, so Christ, incarnate in the form of a man, is the clearest revelation of God as Redeemer. Man, the image of God, is the summit of the general revelation, and Christ the God-man is the brightest mirror of both God's self-revelation and man's essential nature.[71] The introductory words of the *Institutes,* both in their comprehensiveness and in their cautious openness, are to be understood as one of Calvin's basic epistemological propositions—one he

[68] ". . . c'est qu'en cognoissant Dieu, chacun de nous aussi se cognoisse." CO III.37b. "This," says Doumergue, "is more than a translation, it is a transformation [of the Latin] and we know it is attributable to Calvin himself," *Jean Calvin,* IV, 25*n.*

[69] An old outline of the *Institutes* from the Amsterdam edition of 1671 says, "what respects the Scripture and images may belong to the knowledge of God; what respects the formation of the world, the holy angels, and devils, to the knowledge of man; and what respects the manner in which God governs the world, to both." Allen ed., p. 45.

[70] I.xv.1 (OS III.173.29).

[71] II.xii.6 (OS III.444.9–36); or I.xv.3–4.

never violated. They are not, however, a systematic postulate, but an a posteriori principle true to the Biblical picture of God and man. For Calvin, God is never an abstraction to be related to an abstractly conceived humanity, but the God of man, whose face is turned "toward us" and whose name and person and will are known. And correspondingly, man is always described in terms of his relation to this known God: as created by God, separated from God, or redeemed by him. Thus, every theological statement has an anthropological correlate, and every anthropological statement, a theological correlate.

This co-relation of knowledge between God and man is of course not merely formal. It is shot through on every level with a two-sided personal relationship which expresses itself in religious and moral categories. This is the subject of our next section, but it must also be touched here. In fact, all these four sections are so closely related as to be partly falsified by separate analysis. Not only man, but the depraved state of man; not only God but also the goodness of God is part of the relation.

> It is evident that the talents which we possess are not from ourselves, and that our very existence is nothing but a subsistence in God alone. In the second place, these bounties, distilling to us by drops from heaven, form, as it were, so many streams conducting us to the fountain head.

But also,

> from our poverty the infinite good which resides in God becomes more apparent. . . . For since there exists in man a whole world of miseries, and ever since we were despoiled of our divine array, this our naked shame discovers an immense mass of deformity: everyone, therefore, stung with a consciousness of his own infelicity, must necessarily arrive at some knowledge of God. . . .[72]

Both the bounties and poverties of existence drive us to look beyond ourselves to the Source. "Every person, therefore, by the knowledge of himself, is not only urged to seek God but also is led as it were by the hand to find him." [73]

[72] I.i.1 (OS III.31.15–26).
[73] *Ibid.* (32.7–9); cf. Com. Jn. 4:10 (CO XLVII.79c).

Correspondingly, the contemplation of God is never unrelated to the contemplator, but leads to a realization of the flaws and iniquity in even the apparent righteousness of sinful man.

> Hence that horror and amazement with which the Scripture always represents the saints to have been struck and overwhelmed whenever they beheld the presence of God. . . . We must infer that man is never sufficiently touched and impressed with a knowledge of his own meanness, till he has compared himself with the majesty of God.[74]

The knowledge "of ourselves" is a term which Calvin uses by synecdoche for all man's knowledge of creation. Man is a microcosm of the universe in which are to be found in unusual concentration and in higher quality than in other forms of life the marks of God's creative activity.[75] Actually the knowledge of man and of other parts of the created world form a single category which stands in correlation with knowledge that specifically concerns God. Thus, by correlation, we do not mean that Calvin finds two classes of objects of knowledge in the world, some of which pertain solely to ourselves, and some to God.[76] Nor, on the contrary do we mean that knowledge of ourselves and of the world is identical with knowledge of God, for creation is not God. Calvin recognizes other pursuits of learning besides theology and willingly refers questions of natural science or human psychology to the decisions of the special disciplines under which they fall.[77] However, he left no branch of knowledge completely autonomous, because, just as we know God only through his creative activity,

[74] I.i.3 (OS XXXIII.13–20). Warfield describes the "mode of implication of the knowledge of God in the knowledge of self" as that "Calvin lays stress upon our nature as dependent, derived, imperfect, and responsible beings . . . as over against that Being on whom we are dependent, to whom we owe our being, over against whom our imperfection is manifest, and to whom we are responsible." *Calvin and Calvinism,* p. 35.

[75] I.v.3 (OS III.46.32–47.3).

[76] Calvin's division of all knowledge into "things terrestrial" and "things celestial," II.ii.13 (OS III.256.22), and par. ff., is not relevant here, because we are discussing the deeper level on which the knowledge of "things celestial" is mediated under the forms of the things that we experience. In this respect Bauke is correct in classifying Scripture as a part of experience, *Die Probleme der Theologie Calvins,* pp. 43 f., although Calvin often refers to Scripture and experience as two separate sources of knowledge.

[77] I.xv.6; II.ii.13–15; Com. Gen. 1:15, 16.

so every part of that activity is a witness to its maker. "Whithersoever you turn your eyes, there is not a particle of the world in which you cannot behold at least some sparks of his glory." [78] "There are as many miracles of divine power, as many marks of divine goodness, as many proofs of divine wisdom as there are species of things in the world, and even as there are individual things, either great or small." [79] Thus, everything in creation stands in a double epistemological context: as knowledge within the world ("of ourselves") and as revelation of God.[80]

By the mere fact of knowing, man is driven to look beyond both himself and the object of his perception. When, as a result of sin, man does not look toward God he nonetheless stands in this correlation with some idol, as the universality of religion and religious philosophy demonstrates.[81] Religion, whether true or false, is coextensive with beings who know. Calvin can with perfect consistency call either the worship of God or human reason the quality of humanity which distinguishes man from brute creation.[82] The fact that he does both serves to illustrate that all knowledge implies God, that is to say, is theonomous.

Sin itself, which is farthest from God of all aspects of creation, is not an utter and complete separation from God. It takes place in the presence of God and even at its worst finally redounds to his glorification by means of the condemnation of the lost.[83] Satan and all sinners, although they have revolted against God, stand in a relation to God that is not entirely negative. If sin implied utter ignorance of God, man would not be "without excuse." Even hypocrisy cannot go so far "as that the mind would have no consciousness of its guilt in the presence of God." [84] If sin caused an utterly negative relation between God and the creature, the result would be autonomy: man would no longer be mere man,

[78] I.v.1 (OS III.45.19–21).

[79] I.xiv.21 (OS III.172.18–21).

[80] *Infra*, pp. 72 ff.

[81] *Infra*, pp. 24 ff.

[82] "The worship of God is therefore the only thing which renders men superior to the brutes and makes them aspire to immortality." I.iii.3 (OS III.40.27). "Let us conclude, therefore that it is evident in all mankind, that reason is a peculiar property of our nature, which distinguishes us from the brute animals, as sense constitutes the difference between them and things inanimate." II.ii.17 (OS III.259.29–32).

[83] E.g., III.xxiv.14.

[84] II.ii.22 (OS III.265.16), and *passim*.

and Satan would be a second God. But all revolt against God occurs both within the divine omnipotence and within the realm of creaturely responsibility which is based on knowledge. While sin in the unrepentant increases the separation from God, among the faithful the melancholy spectacle of our disgrace and ignominy issues in "disapprobation and abhorrence of ourselves, and true humility; and we are inflamed with a fresh ardor to seek after God, to recover in him those excellences of which we find ourselves utterly destitute."[85]

It is not surprising, in view of double-sided relation between the knowledge of God and of ourselves, that diverse opinions of Calvin have been expressed concerning the relative subjectivity and objectivity of his theology. Doumergue reviews some of these interpretations, among which the most interesting is that of Alexander Schweizer, who for a time regarded Lutheran theology as objective, Reformed as subjective, then later reversed his position.[86] Doumergue suggests experimentally that the opening passages of the *Institutes* represent two theological methods, a dogmatic and a priori method which proceeds from God to man, and an apologetic method from man to God. Then he rightly denies both possibilities as foreign to Calvin's whole mentality, because we are here not in the realm of dialectic, abstraction, postulate, and deduction, but "two realities, two beings, two persons, in the intimate rapport of Creator and creature, of Father and child."[87]

Köstlin finds it a false emphasis that would place objective rather than anthropological motifs in the foreground of Calvin's theology. "We must give attention to the fact that although according to its contents the Calvinistic teaching about God and man is absolutely determined by the former, yet for the *knowledge* of religious truth, the contemplation of God and man's self-contemplation, according to Calvin, emphatically go hand in hand from the very beginning. Thus, we must note that in the development of his doctrinal material, the statements about the Creator stand beside those about man as creature, the presentation of God

[85] II.i.1 (OS III.229.5–8). [86] *Jean Calvin*, IV, 29 ff.
[87] *Ibid.*, p. 26.

the Redeemer is preceded by that of man as needing redemption, and in the doctrine of the appropriation of salvation, the divine factor is only mentioned at all in so far as it is active in the moral awakening and moving of the individual person."[88]

It cannot be too strongly urged—in spite of the title of the present dissertation, and in spite of the titles of Books I and II of the *Institutes*—that we are speaking elliptically when we use the phrase "knowledge of God" in reference to Calvin's theology. The words are in fact an abbreviation for the whole complicated interrelation which we have been describing. God did not accommodate himself to man's capacities as a funnel accommodates a stream of fluid to a small opening, but in such a way that the instrument of accommodation (creation, "ourselves") is implicated in what is transmitted. The "knowledge of God" is therefore always man's knowledge of God's revelation (according to the principle of accommodation) and the very revelation of God always in a radical way implies man's self-knowledge (according to the principle of correlation).

The Existential Character of All Our Knowledge of God

The knowledge of God in Calvin's theology is never separated from religious and moral concern. More exactly, it is never separated from the answer that man gives through worship and obedience when God reveals himself. Whether discussing the encounter with God in creation or Scripture, Calvin always uses the term "knowledge" in conjunction with the love or hatred, mercy or wrath of God, as well as man's total response in trust or fear, obedience or disobedience.

Since Calvin speaks incessantly of knowledge and has used the word in the titles of the first two books of his *Institutes,* we might well expect that he has a distinguishable and definable concept of knowledge as such, apart from these religious, ethical, and psychological colorings, as the common denominator among the various uses he makes of the term. What, for example, is the common element between the knowledge of ourselves, which in

[88] "Calvins Institutio nach Form und Inhalt," p. 55, italics added.

so many respects is a matter of simple perception, and the knowledge of God and his will, which, in no respect is a matter of simple perception? But this question lies outside Calvin's interest. Chenevière's effort to distinguish between the human reason, which he calls an "organ of the experimental knowledge of the exterior world," and conscience, which is the seat of moral judgment, is labored and unsuccessful because Calvin's theology is not amenable to such speculative, formal analysis.[89] He is concerned solely with such distinctions as contribute to man's correct understanding of the central truths of the revelation of God. Other exercises in description, although "agreeable," "useful to be known," and even "true," [90] he leaves to the philosophers. He gives no philosophical or scientific epistemology, presumably because it does not fall within the theological task.

It is the custom of many writers to call this characteristic of the knowledge of God in Calvin's theology, its "practicality," meaning its quality of being nonspeculative, and useful to the believer.[91] Lobstein has a particularly good discussion of the subject. He writes, "the knowledge of God is not something purely theoretical, but a practical experience, engaging the whole human personality, soliciting all the energies of the conscience and heart, putting in motion all the spiritual faculties." [92] A more adequate term, it seems to me, is that current in both philosophy and theology under

[89] *La Pensée politique de Calvin,* pp. 46, 48–50. Chenevière's principle point might have been made without resort to this forcing of a distinction upon Calvin. That is, that in distinction from many medieval thinkers Calvin's idea of reason does not imply an ability a priori to deduce a natural ethic based solely on axioms of reason, apart from experience, p. 55. However, the tenuous separation Chenevière has made between reason and conscience causes him finally to claim that all positive law for the Christian is learned by reason's reading of the Decalogue with no participation whatsoever by the conscience! Pp. 83, 85, 99 ff.

[90] I.xv.6 (OS III.183.21).

[91] Cf. Doumergue, *Jean Calvin,* IV, 14, 16, 22, 28 f. He calls Calvin's theology "une doctrine de pratique." "Finally Calvin explains that a doctrine is true in the same measure that it is practical; the rule of orthodoxy is utility for salvation," p. 24. He rightly notes the practical character of even Calvin's doctrine of the Trinity, p. 102. The term is constantly in use by Pannier, *Témoignage de Saint-Esprit,* pp. 53–59; Clavier, *Etudes,* pp. 12 f.; and in Warfield, "Doctrine of the Knowledge . . ." *Calvin and Calvinism,* p. 256, and throughout.

[92] "La Connaissance réligieuse," p. 58, also pp. 58–59, 78, 87.

the influence of Kierkegaard, the word "existential." By this, we mean knowledge that determines the existence of the knower.[93]

H. R. Mackintosh describes existential thinking as

a mode of thought which concerns not the intellect merely, but the whole personality of the man who awakens to it and adopts it. To think existentially, therefore, is to think not as a spectator of the ultimate issues of life and death, but as one who is committed to a decision upon them. "This concerns *me* infinitely, now and here," is its pervading tone, all that is purely theoretical or academic falling away.[94]

Paul Tillich also stresses the aspect of decision, calling existential knowledge "deciding knowledge," and the existential thinker the "interested or passionate thinker."[95] F. W. Camfield writes, "The uniqueness of the knowledge of God of whom revelation speaks is that it is knowledge which wholly determines the knower."[96] One needs scarcely to prove that Calvin's concept of religious knowledge belongs to those that can be classified as existential. There is scarcely to be found a more passionate thinker than Calvin or one more completely controlled by his knowledge of God. For him the religious or existential response is not something that may or may not come in addition to knowledge of God, but is part of its very definition.

By the knowledge of God, I understand, of course, that we not merely conceive that some God exists, but also grasp what it is about him that is important for us to know, what is suitable to his glory, what, in short, is profitable. *For we cannot, properly speaking, say that God is known where there is no religion or piety.*[97]

[93] Cf. Erich Frank, "Religious faith expresses our essential relation to God, the presence by whom our entire existence is determined," *Philosophical Understanding and Religious Truth,* p. 100. Frank, however, drops completely the element of cognition from "existential truth." Instead he substitutes the "religious imagination," which tries to express the relation of man to God without anything like ordinary knowing, a relation of complete determination in freedom. Pp. 97–101, 114 f., 130 ff.

[94] *Types of Modern Theology,* p. 219.

[95] "Existential Philosophy," p. 53. The term "deciding knowledge" is from unpublished lectures.

[96] *Reformation Old and New,* p. 39.

[97] I.ii.1 (OS III.34.6–10), italics added.

And more emphatically,

If the conscience reflect on God, it must either enjoy a solid peace with his judgement, or be surrounded with the terrors of hell.[98]

Calvin criticizes the neutral or disinterested knowledge of God both objectively and subjectively. Objectively, he condemns any concept of God that imagines God to be unconcerned with the world or not active in it. His favorite target is Epicurus: "For what end is reached by acknowledging with Epicurus some God, who, throwing off all concern about the world, delights himself in inactivity? In short what profit is there in knowing a God with whom we have no intercourse?" [99] "Those who feign him to be a vain and lifeless image are truly said to deny God." [100] Subjectively, that is, in terms of man's actual response to God, Calvin's teaching is clear. "The knowledge [of God] ought to take effect in this way: first, to teach us fear and reverence; and secondly, to instruct us under its guidance and teaching to implore every good thing from him and when it is received, ascribe it to him." [101] The "pious mind" will know that it ought to "revere his majesty, endeavor to promote his glory and obey his commands. . . . See then, what is pure and genuine religion, namely, faith, united with a serious fear of God—fear which both includes in itself voluntary reverence, and brings along with it legitimate worship such as is prescribed in the law." [102] "By piety, I mean that union of reverence and love of God which a knowledge of his benefits causes." [103]

For Calvin the "sophists" are those schoolmen and philosophers who speculate about God, forming concepts that are not "useful." The very opposite of Biblical theology is speculative theology, "the science of wind," practiced in the schools. "And even if there were in the papacy a doctrine not bad and fully false of itself, it would nonetheless be necessary to detest such a style as they have invented, because by this means they have perverted the true and

[98] III.xiii.3 (OS IV.217.22–24).

[99] I.ii.2 (OS III.35.14–17); also Com. Ps. 10:5 (CO XXXI.112c), 33:13 (p. 331b); Com. Isa. 5:19 (CO XXXVI.116a), etc.

[100] I.iv.2 (OS III.42.15–16).

[101] I.ii.2 (OS III.35.17–20).

[102] *Ibid.* (36.19 and 37.7–10).

[103] I.ii.1 (OS III.35.3–5).

natural use of the word of God."[104] "We are invited to a knowledge of God, not such as, content with empty speculation, merely flutters in the brain, but such as will be solid and fruitful, if rightly received, and rooted in our hearts. For the Lord is manifested by his works and properties (*virtutibus;* French of 1541, *œuvres* and of 1560, *vertus*). When we feel their efficacy within us and enjoy their benefits, the knowledge must impress us more vividly than if we imagined a God of whom nothing penetrated to our feeling."[105] To know God disinterestedly is, for Calvin, a contradiction in terms. It is also, as we shall see in the next chapter, because of the "sense of divinity" in all men, an impossibility.

We can go into somewhat more detail concerning the existential character of the knowledge of God for Calvin by reference to two of the necessary accompanying phenomena, respectively, worship and obedience. "For our mind cannot conceive of God, without yielding some worship to him."[106] "For how can a thought of God enter your mind, without immediately giving rise to the thought that since you are his workmanship, you are bound by the very law of creation to be subject to his authority."[107] All knowledge of God involves these two elements and/or, of course, their sinful perversions, idolatry and disobedience.

The first echo of the knowledge of God in man is the fear of God expressed in worship. "Now in giving a summary of those things which are requisite to the true knowledge of God, we have shown [I.i&ii.] that we can form no conceptions of his greatness, but that his majesty immediately discovers itself to us to constrain us to worship him."[108] Correspondingly, in the first table of the Decalogue the Lord "claiming to himself the legitimate authority to command . . . calls us to revere his divinity, and prescribes the parts in which this reverence consists."[109] Here man is blinder than in the realm of ethics, for with reference to the first table of the law, "man, involved as he is in a cloud of errors, scarcely obtains from this law of nature the smallest idea

[104] Sermon on Job 15:2 (CO XXXIII.709d), cited by Doumergue *Jean Calvin,* IV, 22.

[105] I.v.9 (OS III.53.10–18).

[106] I.ii.1 (OS III.34.26 f.).

[107] I.ii.2 (OS III.35.20–23).

[108] II.xiii.1 (OS III.343.31–35).

[109] *Ibid.* (344.4–6).

of what worship is."[110] And this is all-important, for Calvin constantly reiterates the need for proper instruction in worship. Vague pious feeling implimented by haphazardly chosen forms is not acceptable to God. The difference between worship that is acceptable to God and that which is not, is not a matter simply of the intentions of the worshiper, but of the revealed character of the forms used. God prescribes the cult and man must neither add to it nor take away from it.[111] Calvin industriously shows that when Abel, Jacob, and other Old Testament characters erect altars, they do not do so on their own authority, but in accordance with special revelations.[112]

The prime importance of worship is strikingly shown in Book I of the *Institutes.* Not only is the necessity of worship introduced at the outset (chapter ii) and constantly in view throughout the whole discussion of natural knowledge of God (chapters iii–v), but before the doctrines of the Trinity, Creation, and Providence come two chapters on the proper worship of God (chapters xi–xii). Calvin is not first preoccupied with formulating correct propositions about God as if this need be or could be perfected prior to a subsequent expression of it in worship. First he concerns himself to show the proper worship relationship in this two-chapter critique of idolatry. Even in writing theology, which is primarily an intellectual effort, he puts this expression of the existential character of the knowledge of God before the doctrine of God proper. To do this, in the edition of 1559 he removed most of his comment upon the Second Commandment from its previous location in the Decalogue analysis, where it was in the editions of 1536 to 1554, and set it as an admonition to reverence before the study of what is usually called his doctrine of God. As he points out elsewhere, the "papists" have in a sense the "truth" about God, for they call him Creator of heaven and earth and even recognize Christ as the only begotten Son and Redeemer, yet by

[110] *Ibid.* (344.17–19).

[111] Warfield makes much of this "puritan principle" of "absolute dependence on the Word of God as the source of knowledge of his will, and exclusive limitation to its prescriptions of doctrine, life, and even form of church government and worship." *Calvin and Calvinism,* p. 38.

[112] E.g., Com. Gen. 4:2 (CO XXIII.83d–84b) and 28:18 (p. 395b).

contaminating the worship of God, they cause stupidity and blindness and turn that truth into a lie.[113]

Worship belongs primarily to man's apprehension of and reaction to God's numen. The reaction is twofold: man stands awe-stricken in fear, and yet is drawn in love. These two responses are not antithetical, but belong side by side in the pious heart.

Whence he [the Psalmist] appropriately connects the boldness of faith (*fidei audaciam*), which relies on the mercy of God, with that religious fear (*religioso timore*) by which we ought to be affected whenever we come into the presence of the divine majesty, and from its splendor discover our extreme impurity.[114]

For the abundance of happiness, which God has reserved for those who fear him, cannot be truly known without influencing them powerfully. And those whom it has once affected, it draws and elevates entirely towards itself.[115]

For not only piety produces a reverence of God but also the sweetness and agreeability of grace fills a man that is dejected in himself with fear and admiration, causing him to depend on God and humbly submit himself to his power.[116]

This knowledge produces in us at once confidence in him and fear of him.[117]

And on Romans 8:34, concerning the intercessory office of Christ, Calvin adds,

It was necessary expressly to add this [concerning intercession] lest the divine majesty of Christ should terrify us. Although, then, from his elevated throne he holds all things in subjection under his feet, yet Paul represents him as the Mediator whose presence it would be absurd for us to dread, since he not only kindly invites us to himself, but also appears as an intercessor for us before the Father.[118]

This all comports well with Otto's celebrated analysis of God as *mysterium tremendum* and *fascinosum*.[119]

[113] Com. Deut. 12:32 (CO XXIV.284b); Com. Acts 14:15 (CO XLVIII.325d–326a).

[114] III.ii.23 (OS IV.33.19–23).

[115] III.ii.41 (OS IV.51.34–52.3).

[116] *Ibid.*, par. 23 (34.4–7).

[117] Com. I Cor. 1:31 (CO XLIX.332c).

[118] (CO XLIX.165b).

[119] *The Idea of the Holy*, pp. 12 ff., 31 ff.

The same analysis holds in the realm of the ethical. Man is shaken to the depths of his existence by the ethical demands of God's will. Again it is the absoluteness or holiness or divinity of God that gives the character of unavoidable imperative to the commands. "Therefore the commencement and the fountain of that good and honest conscience, whereby we cultivate justice and fidelity towards men, is the fear of God." [120] "For whatever there is of rectitude or justice in the world, Joseph comprised in this short sentence, when he said that he feared God." [121] "Piety," for Calvin, is basic to "charity," that is to say, the first table of the Decalogue to the second, or worship to obedience.[122] Yet the second is a necessary part of the relationship. "It is certain that in the law and the prophets faith and all that pertains to the legitimate worship of God hold the principal place, and that love occupies an inferior station; but our Lord intends that the observance of justice and equity among men is only prescribed to us in the law that our pious fear of him, if we really possess it, may be proved by our actions." [123] We shall see below in more detail the existential importance of the Moral Law for Calvin, whether revealed in conscience or the Decalogue, or as the standard against which men are finally judged,[124] and against the background of which justification by faith has its meaning.[125]

The Clarity and Comprehensibility of Our Knowledge of God

Having already observed that the revelation of God is accommodated to human categories of understanding, that it stands inextricably in correlation with the knowledge of ourselves, and that it is a part of the total existential relation of man to God—it now remains to mention a characteristic of our knowledge of God that is much less subtle and everywhere obvious in Calvin's theology: its clarity and comprehensibility. This characteristic simply points to the objective success of God's accommodation to

[120] Com. Gen. 42:17 (CO XXIII.533a).
[121] *Ibid.* (533b).
[122] I.viii.11–12, 51–53, and III.vii, *passim*.
[123] II.viii.53 (OS III.392.20–25).
[124] *Infra,* Chapter III.
[125] *Infra,* Chapter V.

our limited abilities (clarity), and the resultant definite knowledge that we have of God (comprehensibility). Still, there are problems involved, for these two characteristics are conditioned by various factors.

Calvin never for a moment doubts the objective clarity of God's revelation, whether in creation [126] or in Scripture.[127] It is the noetic effect of sin, not the inadequacy of revelation, that causes errors of understanding. "The manifestation of God by which he makes known his glory in creation is, with regard to the light itself, clear enough; but on account of our blindness it is not sufficient." [128] Some say that the Bible is a "nose of wax" easily twisted by interpreters, but

> we reply with Isaiah and the rest of the prophets, that the Lord has taught nothing that is obscure, ambiguous, or false (*nihil obscurum, ambiguum aut fallax*). . . . [Heathen prophecies] were uncertain and deceitful, but nothing of this kind is found in God's answers, for he speaks openly and utters nothing that is fallacious or ambiguous (*aut fallax aut flexiloquum*). Nevertheless, experience teaches us that Scripture is difficult and somewhat obscure (*difficilem et subobscurum*). This is indeed true, but ought to be ascribed to the dullness and slowness of our apprehension, not to Scripture; for blind or weak-sighted men have no right to accuse the sun, because they cannot look at it.[129]

The obscurity of our knowledge of which Paul speaks in I Cor. 13, has to do with our subjective imperfection and with a comparison of our present state with the future—not an intrinsic obscurity of revelation.

> The knowledge of God which we now have from the word is indeed certain and true, and nothing in it is confused or perplexed or dark, but it is called comparatively obscure because it comes far short of that clear manifestation to which we look forward; for then we shall see face to face. . . . For we have an open and naked revelation of

[126] I.vi.1 (OS III.60.11–15); I.v, *passim*. It is upon the basis of the clarity of the revelation in creation that the heathen are declared inexcusable.

[127] I.vii.2 (OS III.67.5–7); I.viii, *passim*.

[128] Com. Rm. 1:20 (CO XLIX.24a).

[129] Com. Isa. 45:19 (CO XXXVII.145a–c); also I.vii.5 (OS III.71.7). On the greater clarity of the New Testament as against the Old; see, e.g., Com. Rm. 16:21 ff. (CO XLIX.289d ff.), and *infra*, pp. 164 ff.

God in the word (in so far as is expedient for us), and it has nothing intricate in it, as the wicked imagine, to hold us in suspense.[130]

If it be objected that the Scriptures do not contain everything and that they do not give special answers on those points of which we are in doubt, I reply, that everything that relates to the guidance of life is contained in them abundantly. If, therefore, we have resolved to allow ourselves to be directed by the word of God, and always seek in it the rule of life, God will never suffer us to remain in doubt, but in all transactions and difficulties will point out to us the conclusion. Sometimes, perhaps, we shall have to wait long, but at length the Lord will rescue and deliver us, if we are ready to obey him.[131]

The Christian, having a clear revelation can boldly claim to know the will of God:

But they allege that it is presumptuous boldness to arrogate to oneself an indubitable knowledge of the divine will. This, indeed, I would concede to them, if we pretended to subject the incomprehensible counsel of God to our feeble intellect. But when we simply assert with Paul, "we have received, not the spirit of this world but the Spirit which is of God, that we might know the things that are freely given to us of God," what opposition can they make against us, without offering insult to the Spirit of God? But if it is sacrilege to accuse the revelation which proceeds from him of either falsehood or uncertainty or ambiguity, how can we be wrong in maintaining its certainty? [132]

Thus Calvin expresses the clarity of revelation.

[130] Com. I Cor. 13:12 (CO XLIX.514d). "It is worthy of note what he [Peter] pronounces concerning the clarity (*claritate*) of Scripture. For it would be a false encomium were not the Scripture fit and suitable to show us with certainty the right way. Therefore, whoever will open his eyes through the obedience of faith, shall know by experience that Scripture is not in vain called a light. It is, indeed, obscure to the unbelieving, but they who are given up for destruction are willfully blind. Therefore the blasphemy of the papists is execrable, who pretend that the light of Scripture does nothing but dazzle the eyes in order to keep the simple from reading it. But it is no wonder that proud and perverse men, inflated with the wind of confidence do not see that light with which the Lord favors only the little children and the humble." Com. II Pet. 2:19 (CO XLV.457b–c). Again, "if there were such obscurity in the word as that of which the papists babble, it would be a false and artificial commendation with which the prophet here praises the law. Let us know, therefore, that an unerring light is shown to us, provided we open our eyes." Com. Ps. 119:105 (CO XXXII.260a).

[131] Com. Isa. 30:1 (CO XXXVI.507d).

[132] III.ii.39 (OS IV.48.31–49.9).

The comprehensibility of the revelation in creation is the subject of a later chapter. Suffice to say, the mind of man is an active, not a passive, recipient of it. Calvin's exegetical work will serve here as an illustration of his conception of the comprehensibility of the revelation in Scripture. Here the meanings of the loftiest mysteries of God are mingled constantly with problems of grammar, style, and context. Comprehensibility is a matter not only of illumination of the Spirit but also of sound learning. His method, so far as conscious purposes is concerned, is a posteriori. Calvin does not hesitate to surrender tradition-hallowed proof-texts on behalf of honest reading and to leave the interpretation of many passages undecided. To choose just a few examples from the commentary on Psalm 119, such mild and open-minded expressions as "the latter exposition [of several cited] agrees best with the context," [133] "the latter interpretation is preferable," [134] "if anyone prefer to extend the passage to include both meanings, I do not object," [135] "the meaning of these words is ambiguous," [136] or "I am rather inclined to follow the first opinion [of two cited]," [137]—such expressions as these occur on page after page of his comments and show a scholarly, open approach, leaving room for both individual opinions and future progress. Although the Bible is clear, the comprehension of what it clearly says is not a matter of simple mechanical reading, but is an accomplishment, under the guidance of the Holy Spirit, of thorough, patient scholarship. One of Calvin's favorite arguments against the church of Rome's claim to the exclusive right of interpretation of Scripture was the impure translation that it had made sacrosanct.[138]

Other difficulties in comprehension result from God's having placed some things beyond our reach to promote humility.[139] The challenge of these difficulties, however, must also be answered.

[133] Com. Ps. 119:8 (CO XXXII.217d).
[134] *Ibid.*, 119:17 (221c).
[135] *Ibid.*, 119:41 (232d).
[136] *Ibid.*, 119:57 (239a).
[137] *Ibid.*, 119:108 (261b).
[138] "So far is there from being an entire page, that there are scarcely three continuous verses without some noted blunder." Then he illustrates with numerous examples. "Acts of the Council of Trent, with Antidote," 4th session (CO VII.414d).
[139] III.ii.4 (OS IV.11.34–41).

The Christian has a duty to be ever increasing in knowledge and therefore must continually assault problems to that end. Refusal to investigate what God has put before us is no more a virtue than to try to penetrate beyond what he would have us know. Before analyzing Ezekiel's vision, Calvin writes:

A vision is now to occupy our attention, of which the obscurity so deterred the Jews that they forbad every effort to explain it. But God either appeared to his prophet in vain or with some fruit. To suppose the former is absurd beyond measure. Then, if the vision is useful to us, it is necessary for us to attain at least a partial understanding of it. If anyone object that it was intended exclusively for the prophet, this cavil is easily answered, because what the prophet wrote was clearly intended for the whole church. Now if anyone ask if the vision is lucid, I readily confess to its obscurity, and that I can scarcely understand it; however, it is not only lawful and useful, but necessary to inquire into what God has proposed to us. Base, indeed, would be our sloth should we willingly close our eyes and not attend to the vision. Although we shall only taste something of all that God wills, yet this is of no small moment, and not only a moderate but even a slight degree of understanding may suffice for this.[140]

Some depths of revelation are, of course, entirely incommunicable, thus Paul, who maintains silence about the "third heaven" he saw, is to be preferred to Dionysius, who showed less modesty.[141] Yet no one may keep silent about what God has publicly set out in his word. Calvin's principle is moderate and entirely defensible: "We should neither scrutinize those things which the Lord has left concealed nor neglect those he has openly exhibited." [142] One of the great goals of Calvin's life—one to which he referred shortly before his death in his farewell to the Genevan pastors—was purity of doctrine, and this was primarily right understanding of Scripture. "Concerning my doctrine, I have taught faithfully and God has given me the grace to

[140] Com. Ez. 1: preface to verses 4 ff. (CO XL.29b–c). One wonders why Calvin did not on this basis attempt a commentary upon the Apocalypse, but there is no answer, except what Jean Bodin remembers him as saying, *infra*, p. 122.

[141] I.xiv.4 (OS III.157.8–18); Com. II Cor. 12:4 (CO L.138a–b).

[142] III.xxi.4 (OS IV.373.19–21).

write. I have done this as faithfully as possible and have not corrupted a single passage of Scripture or knowingly twisted it."[143]

On the basis of the clarity and comprehensibility of the Scriptures Calvin defended his views against both anti-Protestants and ultra-Protestants.[144] Against the Roman esoteric concept of the Scriptures as a riddle solvable only by the clergy and presented to the people largely in pageant and image, and against the Protestant enthusiasts' scorn of sound learning and clear doctrine Calvin exalted the place of the teacher.[145] The teacher was not an inspired or infallible interpreter, but a believer more learned than the rest and therefore capable of exegesis and ready application of the teachings of Scripture. The teacher had no right of "private" interpretation, but rather the duty of constantly re-examining the church's doctrines in the light of Scripture, and vice versa. No one valued more highly than did Calvin the support of the early fathers and councils for his views, but always with the reservation that both had made errors.[146] A counsel of scholars assembled under the guidance of the Holy Spirit is the best way of solving difficulties, but its decisions are not to be taken as on a par with Scripture itself.[147]

143 (CO IX.893b).

144 Cf. Doumergue, *Jean Calvin,* IV, 79 f.

145 For example, IV.i.5, and iii.4–6. Pastors and teachers are the two "ordinary" officers of the church, from the list given in Eph. 4:11.

146 "But here a difficult question arises, because if everyone has the right and liberty to judge, nothing can be settled as certain, but on the contrary the whole of religion will be vacillating. I reply, there is a twofold test of doctrine: private and public. The private test is that in which every individual establishes his own faith, when he wholly acquiesces in that doctrine which he knows has come from God. For conscience will never find a safe and tranquil anchorage except in God. The public test refers to the common consensus and polity (πολιτείαν) of the church. For as there is danger that fanatical men may rise up who may presumptuously boast that they are endued with the Spirit of God, it is a necessary remedy that the faithful should meet together and seek a basis of agreement in a holy and pure manner. But as the old proverb is true, "So many heads, so many opinions," it is doubtless a singular work of God when he subdues all our perverseness, makes us to agree to one thing, and unites us in the pure unity of faith." Com. I Jn. 4:1 (CO XLV.348b–c). The remainder of the passage deals briefly with the authority of councils.

147 *Ibid.,* and "Acts of the Council of Trent" (CO VII.416c), "In case of an obscure passage, when it is doubtful what sense ought to be adopted, there is no better way of arriving at the true meaning than for pious doctors to make a common inquiry by engaging in religious discussion."

There were daily Bible studies for the populace in Geneva. The Academy and all its store of learning was directed toward Bible study.[148] The sermons in Geneva were Bible studies.[149] Calvin's *Institutes* is a Bible study—an aid to students in reading Scripture.[150] All these aids to comprehension where the clarity of Scripture was a by-word! The situation is typically Calvinistic—it involves a paradox that issues in a dynamic. The Scripture is clear, but it is "sufficiently," not "absolutely," clear.[151] And the clarity is comprehensible, but to the diligent and humble believer, not to any and every reader. The simplest mind can know all that is necessary for saving faith and ethical living because the Bible is sufficiently clear, yet the most learned scholar can never fully understand all problematic passages or plumb the depths of all the mysteries because it is not absolutely clear.

One of the most interesting and striking general features of Calvin's work, both systematic and exegetical, arises with regard to the problems of the limited clarity of the revelation in Scripture, and the limited powers of comprehension of the believer. This feature is the predominance of single themes which stand out in their individual clarity, as over against numerous systematic inconsistencies that arise because the systematic interrelationship of the themes is relegated by Calvin to the status of incomprehensibility. Doctrines that are clear in themselves, but logically incompatible with one another, are placed side by side because Calvin finds them so in Scripture. He developed each doctrine as he found it to its logical end, no matter how violently the conclusion might be controverted by some other theme similarly developed. In this pursuit Calvin was one of the most relentless of theologians and was sometimes called upon to borrow words from Augustine or Bernard to express his own wonderment before these antinomies of his thought that were to him none other than the mysteries of God's will.

When Calvin's theology is looked at as a logical system, he is seen to have developed the doctrine of the omnipotence of God

[148] Kampschulte, *Johann Calvin, seine Kirche und sein Staat in Genf.* II, 334 f.

[149] Parker, *The Oracles of God,* pp. 65 ff.

[150] "To the Readers," *Institutes* '39–'59 (OS III.6.18–25).

[151] Doumergue says, "une clarté suffisante," but not "une clarté absolue." *Jean Calvin,* IV, 80.

into a complete determinism, while at the same time maintaining with equal vigor a contradictory doctrine of the responsibility of the individual. Thus, he held that the fall of man and his subsequent damnation occurred by man's own fault, although it resulted from a decree of God's eternal, unchanging will; and while holding a doctrine of the instrumental function of Satan, he finds Satan justly condemned. On the other hand, within the concept of election, the individual is not a whit responsible for his having been chosen by God, and Christ's work is the "material," not the "instrument," of salvation. Justification is a completed matter, yet the process of sanctification by the Spirit must go on, and while the individual can contribute nothing to either, he must hear sermons inviting him to accept the call of God and urging him to put forth every effort to live a moral life. No man can merit God's favor, yet God freely rewards the good and justly metes out to the wicked their deserved punishment. Such logical inconsequences are the main basis of Hermann Bauke's conception of Calvin's theology as a *complexio oppositorum*.[152] Whether or not Bauke has discovered the secret of it in attributing it to the work of a "formal" rationalist "French" mind, which combined dialectically opposites that are a scandal to a "material" rationalist "German" mind, is beyond us here.[153] But certainly he is right in attributing this characteristic at least partially to Calvin's Biblicism. Calvin reads the Bible, however, according to a scheme.

Calvin is not an irresponsible and careless combiner of ir-

[152] *Die Probleme der Theologie Calvins,* pp. 16 ff.

[153] Calvin's rationalism, says Bauke, is a "purely formal rationalism which has no influence at all on the contents of his theology, on either its principles or the contents of single doctrines." *Ibid.,* p. 14. The French, he continues, cannot recognize this way of thinking in Calvin because it is so immediately their own, and the Germans because it is so completely different. *Ibid.,* p. 15. "I would call Calvin a dialectician rather than a systematic thinker, or at best a dialectic systematizer." *Ibid.,* p. 16. "The single basic elements of dogmatic stand [for Calvin] side by side and are bound together dialectically; they are not deductively derived from one or two basic principles." *Ibid.,* p. 32. "Calvin is, from the material point of view, completely independent of philosophy, but he works formally with philosophy's rational-dialectic method. He is by no means a speculative philosopher or theologian, but throughout a theologian of experience; at the same time he is a trained dialectician, a theologian who uses philosophical methods *(der "philosophisch arbeitende" Theologe)." Ibid.,* p. 43.

rationalities; he is no Biblical positivist unwilling to search for the deeper meanings wherever they exist. Logical contradiction is for him only apparent contradiction to sinful reason, it is always assumed to be resolved on the level of God's mystery and then only when human efforts to understand have been exhausted. He, further, will not stand for inconsistency on the surface of Scripture. For example, he will not leave unexplained the inclusive phrase "He loved their fathers and chose their seed after them" (Deuteronomy 4:37) and the exclusive one, "He . . . chose not the tribe of Ephraim, but chose the tribe of Judah" (Psalm 78:67). The incongruence of these two statements is not an ultimate mystery, but a proximate contradiction. To resolve it, Calvin will neither say that God changed his mind nor admit inconsistency in Scripture, nor will he claim that the contradiction is God's mystery. Rather, he introduces the descriptive classification of the "degrees" of election, showing that the choosing of the whole people was for one purpose, and the subsequent differentiation within the first chosen group for another.[154] Similarly, in the doctrine of the "universal" and the "special" calls, the former call is offered to all, and the latter to the elect only, to whom it imparts the illumination of faith and perseverance. Scripture teaches this. Again, however, the orderly scheme is marred by elements of both Scripture and experience, and Calvin is too vigorous an exegete, too honest an observer, and too little a lover of logical symmetry to maintain the pattern unblemished. He adds, that God "also communicates it [the special call] to those whom he enlightens for a season, and afterwards forsakes an account of their ingratitude and strikes with greater blindness."[155] That God does all this is clear from Scripture. Why he does it is incomprehensible and belongs to the mysteries implicit in his secret will. We must carefully study what is written, but halt before the mysteries, "lest we be condemned for excessive curiosity on the one hand or for ingratitude on the other."[156]

Calvin, then, was completely convinced of a high degree of

[154] III.xxi.5, ff; *infra*, p. 212.
[155] III.xxiv.8 (OS IV.419.23–25).
[156] III.xxi.4 (OS IV.373.18–21).

clarity and comprehensibility of individual themes of the Bible, but he was also so utterly submissive before divine mystery as to create a theology containing many logical inconsistencies rather than a rationally coherent whole. While Calvin as an exegete was a virtuoso at harmonizing surface inconsistencies in Scripture, he never conceived of his theological task as an effort to harmonize the deeper paradoxes of Scripture or to explain what he regarded as its central mysteries. Clarity of individual themes, incomprehensibility of their interrelations—this is a hallmark of Calvin's theology. The various motifs are like islands protruding from the sea which one knows are joined together by a subterranean land mass, even though the juncture is invisible. Later we shall suggest that the peculiar character of God and the Redeemer for Calvin, the God of "gratuitous mercy," may be an adequate principle for seeing the unity of Calvin's thought, stronger than the opposition of the various themes he derived from the Scriptures.

·II·

THE DUPLEX COGNITIO DOMINI

THE MOST PROMINENT CHANGE that took place when Calvin revised his *Institutes* for the last time was the reordering of the material. Ostensibly the new arrangement was a grouping of themes under what Calvin considered the four parts of the Apostle's Creed: God the Creator, God the Redeemer, God the Holy Spirit, and the Church and Sacraments.[1] Although much new material was added and many changes of style were made, most of the material in the edition of 1559 had already stood in earlier editions and was simply reshuffled, often with units many paragraphs long suffering no internal revision. The division into four books, however—in spite of the praise it has justly inspired [2]—is as misleading as the respective lengths of the books in judging the actual subordination of the material, indeed, almost as misleading as judging the importance of political thought and action to Calvin by the place it occupies in the *Institutes.* From the point of view of the knowledge of God, which is the foundation of Calvin's theological writing, Calvin's *Institutes* of 1559 contains two, not four, divisions. Further, the first and much the smaller of the two is the more general and inclusive, setting the context and proposing the categories within which the latter is to be grasped. This division corresponds to what Calvin conceived of as the two kinds of revelation: the revelation of God as Creator, and as Redeemer. The short Book I of the 1559 edition represents the former, and the whole remainder of the work represents the latter. If the Trinitarian titles of the first three books are thought to imply that they somehow belong together

[1] Calvin not only follows this order but also specifically claims to be doing so in I.xvi.18, although the title of Book III makes no mention of the Spirit, and the doctrine of the Spirit proper is divided between Books I and III.

[2] Cf. Warfield's "Literary History of Calvin's Institutes," Allen ed., *Institutes,* p. xix.

in a way in which Book IV does not participate, the implication is wholly false and is quickly banished by the contents.

Köstlin clearly perceives the real ordering and subordering of Calvin's material within the symmetrical external form.

In fact, one can summarize the course that Calvin really took, instead of identifying it with the Creed, rather, in the following way:

1. The doctrines of God the Father, Son, and Spirit, and his creation and world government in general, apart from sin and the redemptive revelation and redemptive activity that sin makes necessary—and similarly of mankind, apart from sin and the necessity for salvation. (Book I).
2. The historical revelation and activity of God for the salvation of the sinner, as follows:
   a. The establishing of salvation through the incarnate Son, for which preparation had already been made under the Old Covenant. (Book II).
   b. The application through the Holy Spirit of the salvation given in Christ, as follows:
      (1) The process of salvation which is realized inwardly by the Spirit in individuals, extending until the perfection of these persons in the resurrection. (Book III).
      (2) The outer means which God uses in this activity of the Spirit. (Book IV).

Köstlin continues, "We are here presenting an ordering [of the material], clear in itself, of which Calvin's own four-part division and its expressed relation to the Creed is a less clear and sharp presentation than the praise of it by many would seem to indicate."[3] I wish to maintain with Köstlin, although in greater detail and with more emphasis upon its importance, what was clear to me before consulting Köstlin: that the really significant ordering principle of the *Institutes* in the 1559 edition is the *duplex cognitio Domini,* not the Apostles' Creed.[4]

[3] Köstlin, "Calvins Institutio nach Form und Inhalt," pp. 57 f. Cf. O. Ritschl, *Dogmengeschichte,* III.161 ff.

[4] This is not to overlook the excellence and even beauty of Calvin's final arrangement in terms of the creed. It rather suggests that such a richness of thought as Calvin was trying to express is more than any one form of presentation could adequately show.

The *locus classicus* of the "twofold knowledge of God" is the following:

Therefore, since the Lord first appears, both in the formation of the world and in the general doctrine of Scripture (*in generali Scripturae doctrina*) simply as the Creator, and afterwards as the Redeemer in the person of Christ—from this arises *a twofold knowledge of him* (*hinc duplex emergit eius cognitio*), of which the former is first to be considered, and the other will follow in its proper order.[5]

From the start we must make perfectly clear what Calvin means by the twofoldness of this knowledge. It is not identical with the distinction between general and special revelation, that is, with the revelation in creation and in Scripture.[6] Rather, the first element crosses the border of the special revelation. The knowledge of the Creator has two sources: creation and the "general doctrine" of Scripture; and the knowledge of the Redeemer has one source, Christ.[7] Nor does it conform to the division of the Bible into the Old and New Testaments. Within each of the Testaments is to be found both orders of the knowledge of God. This distinction is nowhere clearly stated by Calvin before the 1559 edition of the *Institutes,* in which the above statement appears for the first time. That Calvin was fully conscious of the scope of the sentence is shown by a whole row of references to it, also inserted in 1559, which are designed to keep the fact of the twofold knowledge before the mind of the reader.

To keep his appeal to Scripture in I.vi.1 from being misunderstood as a change of subject to the redemptive revelation, Calvin states in some detail what he is doing.

I am not yet speaking of the peculiar doctrine of faith by which they [the patriarchs] were illuminated into the hope of eternal life—although in order for them to pass from death to life it was necessary that they know God not only as Creator but also as Redeemer, and

[5] I.ii.1 (OS III.34.21–25, italics added).

[6] It is therefore not congruent with the distinction made at the outset of Chapter I.

[7] Karl Barth states it wrongly in *No! Answer to Emil Brunner:* "It is true that Calvin spoke of a *Duplex cognitio Domini,* from creation and in Christ." P. 105. Wilhelm Niesel makes the same mistake, *Die Theologie Calvins,* p. 40. Cf. Appendix III.

indeed they did obtain both kinds of knowledge from the word. For that species of knowledge (*notitiae species*) which was given that he might be known as God who created and governs the world, in order preceded the other. Then, afterwards was added that other interior knowledge which alone vivifies dead souls, and by which God is known not only as the Creator of the world and as the sole author and arbiter of all events but also as the Redeemer in the person of the Mediator. But being not yet come to the fall of man and the corruption of nature, I also forbear to treat of the remedy.[8]

Then, exercising double caution, Calvin continues by delimiting this "species of knowledge," first in the Old Testament, then in the New.

Let the reader therefore remember that I am not yet speaking of the covenant by which God adopted the children of Abraham and of that branch of doctrine by which, properly speaking, believers have always been separated from profane nations, because it is founded in Christ. I am only showing how we must come to Scripture to learn to distinguish God who is the Creator of the world by definite characteristics from the whole herd of false gods. This course will in time lead us to redemption. But, though we shall adduce many references from the New Testament and some also from the Law and the Prophets in which express mention is made of Christ, nevertheless, all will tend to this end, to show that God the Creator of the world is manifested to us in Scripture, which exhibits what we should know of him, that we may not seek in obscurity after some doubtful deity.[9]

This one long passage might be thought sufficient instruction for the reader, but Calvin returns to the issue many times. "Yet again I repeat, besides the peculiar doctrine of faith and repentance which proposes Christ as the Mediator, the Scripture distinguishes the only true God, considered as Creator and Governor of the world, that he may not be confounded with the multitude of false deities." [10] Again, after he has completed his long discourse on Scripture, Calvin returns to the theme:

I am not yet referring to the peculiar covenant by which God distinguished the people of Abraham from the rest of the nations . . . we are still considering that knowledge which stops with the creation

[8] I.vi.1 (OS III.61.10–22). [9] *Ibid.* (lines 22–34).
[10] I.vi.2 (OS III.62.16–20).

of the world, without ascending to Christ the Mediator. But although it will soon be worthwhile to cite some passages from the New Testament (since there also is demonstrated both the power of God the Creator and his providence in conserving original nature), yet I wish to give the readers this reminder of my present intention that they may not transgress the boundaries prescribed.[11]

Again, in the Doctrine of the Trinity, Calvin guards carefully against confusing the two orders of knowledge by showing that he writes only of the Eternal Son, not yet in his office of Mediator, even though some passages with soteriological content are used as evidence for the deity of the Son.

Although I am not yet referring to the office of the Mediator, but defer it until the place where redemption is considered, still, because it ought to be held without controversy by all that Christ is that Word clothed in flesh, it is most suitable here to introduce such passages as assert the deity of Christ.[12]

Although the Apostles spoke of him after he had appeared in the flesh as Mediator, yet all that I shall adduce will be adopted to prove his eternal deity.[13]

Let us look at just one more passage, the last to occur in the *Institutes,* which alludes to the separate treatment of the two species of knowledge of God. This is the main transitional passage between Books I and II, therefore between the two great divisions of the *Institutes* as set forth by Köstlin's outline. Book II really begins only in chapter vi, after Calvin has completed his analysis of sin, which is the occasion for the redemptive revelation. Before proceeding to the *cognitio Dei redemptoris,* he takes one last look at *cognitio Dei creatoris* and utters a short, final verdict: "Therefore, since we are fallen from life to death, all that knowledge of God the Creator of which we have discoursed would be useless unless it were succeeded by faith exhibiting God to us as the Father in Christ."[14] From this transitional point

[11] I.x.1 (OS III.85.16–25).

[12] I.xiii.9 (OS III.119.16–20).

[13] I.xiii.11 (OS III.123.12–14); cf. also I.xiii.23 (OS III.140.14–15, and 141.22–24); I.xiii.24 (OS III.142.31–143.1); I.xiv.20 (OS III.170.25–29), and par. 21 (OS III.171.34 ff.).

[14] II.vi.1 (OS III.320.10–13). The remainder of this paragraph is an elucidation of this sentence.

Calvin's doctrine has a whole new orientation. All that he says subsequently lies within the vast background he has given of the Trinitarian God, his creation of the universe and of man in a state of perfection and his providential care of that creation. Yet, while this background is a frame of reference and a presupposition of the redemptive revelation—it is not even known apart from the redemptive revelation which Calvin has yet to discuss. Thus, from another point of view the redemptive revelation is actually the presupposition of the knowledge of the Creator which in Calvin's treatment precedes it. It is as background for discussing the problems that arise in this double presupposition that we are emphasizing the clarity with which Calvin distinguished between the two orders of the knowledge of God. Rather than discuss the problems further just now, however, we must turn back to the distinction itself. Obviously, the differentiation of the two orders needed no further emphasis than we have already displayed in the *Institutes* of 1559. Let us see where else it is found.

The *duplex cognitio Domini* was not clearly formulated by Calvin before 1559. All the citations we have made were added to the *Institutes* in the final Latin edition. They are largely methodological statements rather than theological propositions. Some were inserted for the sake of helping the reader follow the discussion in passages otherwise unchanged since the edition of 1539. There is, however, ample ground for saying that this was no new idea for Calvin and that the 1559 redaction was simply the first time that he had used this fundamental distinction of his thought as a formal principle in the expression of it. The make-up of Book I in 1559 is not merely "eine gewaltsame Abstraktion," [15] but an appropriate grouping of elements that had formerly been inappropriately interspersed among purely soteriological material.

As early as the 1539 edition there was a clear distinction between the knowledge of God as Creator and God as Redeemer, even within the scriptural revelation.[16] This carries through editions

[15] Wernle, *Der evangelische Glaube nach den Hauptschriften der Reformatoren*, III, 394.

[16] To become familiar with the arrangement of material in ed. '39, I used the French of '41 in the edition prepared by Jacques Pannier. While the text of ed. '39

from 1539 to 1554. First of all, this is observable in the ordering of the material. Throughout these editions, Chapter I (*De cognitione Dei . . .*) contains Calvin's doctrine of the religion of creation in its subjective and objective aspects, which is summarized in a definition of true religion,[17] and a list of the attributes of God.[18] Scripture is introduced when the failure of the revelation in the heart of man and the world at large has been shown [19] and even then only to emphasize that the God of Scripture is exactly the same as the God of creation [20]—with no reference yet to Christ. Even the doctrine of the "internal testimony of the Holy Spirit," by which the Scripture is accredited, is presented with no reference to Christ and Faith.[21] This is a chapter "Concerning the Knowledge of God," which shows God's "power," "eternity," "wisdom," "justice," "mercy," and "bounty," as well as his "final judgment" and gives the hope of a future life, all within the knowledge taught in common by creation [22] and Scripture [23]—with no reference to Christ. What Wernle says of Book I of the 1559 edition is equally true of Chapter I of all editions from 1539 on: ". . . the Creator and Father, the Provider, the faithful and merciful One, who deserves our deepest trust. And all that in the beginning without a word about Jesus Christ!" [24] Clearly, the entire soteriological revelation is purposely put off to a later chapter because it is a different kind of thing from the persent subject. This chapter in all editions closes with the same sentence: *Duplex cognitio Domini!*

---

is clearly marked out in CO Vol. I and OS Vols. III–V, both show the material as it was redistributed in the editions of '54 and '59, respectively. With one exception, a change in the position of the chapter on false sacraments, the order of '39 was preserved in the French of '41. Hence, I shall here cite the disposition of ed. '39 from the Pannier edition.

17 Pannier ed., p. 50.

18 *Ibid.*, pp. 50–58.

19 *Ibid.*, p. 63, exactly as in ed. '59.

20 *Ibid.*, pp. 76 ff.

21 Those who have "special knowledge of God" are called the "faithful," *ibid.*, p. 49, and "faith" is part of the definition of true religion, *ibid.*, p. 50, so there is no doubt that Calvin is talking of the elect. Yet here Calvin does not speak of Christ or of faith in the narrower sense in which he defines it later (same ed., Chapter IV). He is concerned exclusively with the knowledge of God as Creator.

22 Pannier ed., pp. 51–58.

23 Pannier ed., pp. 77–79.

24 *Op. cit.*, p. 394.

Nevertheless, since God does not show himself rightly and to intimate contemplation except in the face of his Christ, which can be regarded only with the eyes of faith, that which remains to be said of the knowledge of God can best be deferred to the place where we have to speak of the knowledge of faith.[25]

In addition to the evidence given by this general view, the edition of 1539 contains also some specific statements that foreshadow the concept of the *duplex cognitio Domini*. The clearest is the long passage that is exactly reproduced in 1559 as I.x.2,[26] which shows the agreement between the attributes of God revealed in creation and Scripture, with no mention of Christ or salvation. After a summary of the biblical view of God:

This description agrees very well with that which we have said appears in the universal figure of the world.[27]

But it is not necessary to collect a large number of passages,—for the present, one psalm [Psalm 145] will suffice, in which the whole sum of his properties is so thoroughly recited that nothing is left out. And nevertheless there is nothing named that one cannot contemplate in the creatures—so God gives himself to be known by experience, just as he shows himself to be in his word.[28]

Again, the correspondence of the God of creation and Scripture, with no allusion to redemption.

Although the *duplex cognitio Domini* is thus clearly a theological principle with Calvin as early as 1539, as is shown by our references to Chapter I, the succeeding chapters show that it was not yet strictly adhered to in the ordering of the system. Chapter II (*De cognitione hominis*) treats of the *imago Dei*, sin, and the grace of Christ all together, as Calvin had to do also, despite his circumspectness, in the final edition. Chapter III (*De lege*) is a return to the original theme of the Creator and his will for the creatures. Christ is mentioned only briefly in discussion of the "third office" of the moral law, and the abrogation of the cere-

[25] Pannier ed., p. 79; cf. CO I.304d and OS III.87.36–40.
[26] Pannier ed., pp. 76–79. [27] *Ibid.*, p. 77.
[28] Pannier ed., p. 78; cf. p. 63.

monial law—thus maintaining the separation. Chapter IV (*De Fide*)[29] gives exclusive attention to the "gratuitous promise in Christ" quite apart from the description of God given in creation and Scripture at large.[30] This is a conscious turning from one element of the "twofold knowledge" to the other. Very striking in the Apostle's Creed analysis, which makes up Chapter IV, is the place of the Doctrine of the Trinity, which falls, not as we might expect in the Christology, but completely outside the Creed, where it serves as a prologue.[31] This was true even in the edition of 1536.[32] Thus, it was easy for Calvin to "abstract" it, as Wernle says, in arriving at a final disposition. After Chapter IV the discourse keeps to the redemptive revelation except for the examination of civil government, which is a special case even in 1559. Is is clear, then, that the two parts of the knowledge of God, although not collected into separate "books" until the last edition, were always distinct in Calvin's mind. His method intermingled, but did not confuse them. Chapters I and IV of the 1539 edition bear to one another the same relation, except for the Doctrine of the Trinity, as Book I to Books II and III in 1559, a relation to which Calvin has carefully and repeatedly pointed in methodological assertions.

Calvin's final plan, which from the epistemological point of view follows the *duplex cognitio* and not the Creed, is simply the systematic arrangement most compatible with his concept of the knowledge of God. We shall now examine this twofold concept, considering the origin and contents of the parts and their mutual relation. First, the knowledge of God the Creator, in Chapter III, then the knowledge of God the Redeemer in Chapter IV, followed by an analysis of their systematic relationship in Chapter V.

[29] This is Chapters V-VII in eds. '41-'54.
[30] Pannier ed., II, 26.
[31] *Ibid.*, pp. 49-76.
[32] (CO I.59-62).

·III·
THE KNOWLEDGE OF GOD THE CREATOR

THE KNOWLEDGE of God the Creator has two sources: creation itself, and Scripture. The first of these, which we are now to consider, corresponds to the accommodation of God to human finiteness, the second, to the accommodation to human sinfulness discussed above in our Chapter I.

THE KNOWLEDGE OF GOD THE CREATOR DERIVED FROM CREATION

By creation we do not mean only the external world, or "nature," as something upon which man looks from inside out to garner knowledge of God. Man himself, including his inner mental life, his subjectivity, is a part of creation. Calvin's conception of the revelation in creation corresponds to the doubleness, the subjectivity and objectivity, which is one of the elemental characteristics of mental life. In fact, it is the subjective element of the revelation in creation that receives his first attention in the *Institutes,*[1] although the objective receives more detailed attention.[2] God reveals himself to man internally by a direct perception of which Calvin distinguishes two elements: the sense of divinity, and the conscience. These correspond to worship and obedience, or the numinous and the moral, which we referred to in Chapter I, as existential aspects of the knowledge of God. God also reveals himself externally in nature and history, and this revelation comes to man through experience.

THE SENSUS DIVINITATIS.—The *sensus divinitatis* in man is not very closely defined in Calvin's thought, although he uses it widely, and with much dependence on Cicero.[3] Let us note first what it is not.

Clearly Calvin does not mean by the term a special organ or

[1] I.iii and iv. [2] I.v.

[3] The phrases in I.iii and iv which are reminiscent of Cicero are noted in OS III.37–44.

faculty of the soul,[4] but a *sensus* which is a perception or sensation, an *intelligentia numinis,*[5] and elsewhere a *gustus divinitatis.*[6] Nor does the term "religious a priori" seem an adequate description, because it implies something formal rather than material, and Calvin does not represent this as a formal possibility or precondition of knowing God.[7] This is already *notitia,* knowledge,[8] and indeed religious knowledge. It is a material and existential concept describing an actual, vital knowing relationship of the human mind with God. The *sensus divinitatis,* or *deitatis,* is not the product of ratiocination, such as we shall find in Calvin's analysis of the knowledge of God derived from external nature. Closely related as the two concepts seem to be at first glance, the *sensus divinitatis* of I.iii is by no means to be confused with the *semen divinitatis*[9] and the *insignia divinitatis in homine*[10] of I.v.4–5. The latter refer to the signs or evidences within us of God having made us—the complicated functioning of body and soul[11]—which stand in the same relation to our subjectivity as the rest of the external world: we observe them, both microcosm and macrocosm, and then look to their Source. From the latter evidences of God, as we shall see, Calvin deduces a whole list of attributes of God; from the *sensus divinitatis,* none.

Having indicated what this *sensus* is not, we yet face real difficulties in describing what it is. Calvin's terminology is not of much help. He sometimes varies his technical term *sensus divi-*

[4] As, e.g., is maintained by Riissen: "Some recent writers explained the natural sense of deity as an idea (*ideam*) of God impressed on our minds. If this idea is understood as an innate faculty (*facultate*) for knowing God after some fashion, it should not be denied; but if it expresses an actual and adequate representation of God from our birth, it is to be entirely rejected." Quoted by Warfield, *Calvin and Calvinism,* p. 34.

[5] I.iii.1 (OS III.37.19).

[6] II.ii.18 (OS III.260.37).

[7] Cf. Peter Brunner and Seeberg, *infra,* p. 56; also Engelland, *Gott und Mensch bei Calvin,* pp. 16, 7–32, *passim.*

[8] *Dei notitiam hominum mentibus naturaliter esse inditam.* Title to I.iii; cf. title I.iv. *Notitia* is Calvin's favorite word for knowledge of God. He uses it three times more frequently in I.i–x than *cognitio,* which he dignifies by a place in titles of Books I and II. Both words are translated by Calvin into French as *cognoissance.*

[9] (OS III.47.38).

[10] (OS III.49.10).

[11] Cf. *infra,* p. 79.

nitatis with the metaphor *semen religionis* [12] (seed of religion), and elsewhere he uses words of quite indefinite noetic value, *persuasio,*[13] *impressio,*[14] and others. Yet, in spite of the varied terminology, we must insist again that the noetic element does exist. This is knowledge of God. It is not a mere notion, or presentiment, and it does not originate from within us. Were the knowledge element not clearly present, this primitive feeling might be interpreted in terms of mere subjectivity and by its vagueness might be said to have some other source than God. Although at one point Calvin does say that this "doctrine" is self-taught,[15] it is quite clear that *"God himself* has endued all men with some knowledge of his deity." [16] This knowledge issues in a proposition: "God exists,[17] or "some God exists." [18] And "God" means the One God Himself, for this revelation is not so vague as to allow polytheistic interpretation. "Those who worshiped a great multitude of gods, whenever they spoke according to the genuine sense of nature used simply the name of God, as if they were contented with one God." Justin Martyr is correct when he "demonstrates from numerous testimonies that *the unity of God is engraved on the hearts of all men."* [19] Hence, the intellectual element, formulable in the necessary proposition one God exists, is part of the primitive *sensus,* which thereby has a brief but extremely important knowledge content. But we cannot go further. Calvin's major occupation with the *sensus divinitatis* is not in analyzing the how and what of its knowledge content, but with its empirical effects.

The empirical effects of the *sensus divinitatis* are (1) the uni-

[12] I.iii.1 and I.v.1, though the two do not mean exactly the same thing. He combines the two in his summary, I.v.15, "Semen notitiae Dei" (OS III.59.37). Cf. *Dei sensu,* Com. Acts. 17:28 (CO XLVIII.417d). Outside the *Institutes, semen religionis* is more widely used.

[13] I.iii.2, 3 (OS III.38.28; 39.24). [14] I.iii.1 (OS III.38.16).

[15] I.iii.3 (OS III.40.10–12). In "Allgemeine und besondere Offenbarung in Calvins Institutio," Peter Brunner emphasizes that the *sensus* is self-taught in a way that would destroy its revelatory character. "I need no one to tell me that God is Creator and that I am his creature. This I can say fundamentally to myself, here I am my own teacher to myself," p. 199.

[16] I.iii.1 (OS III.37.19, italics added). [17] I.iii.1 (OS III.38.3).

[18] I.iii.3 (OS III.39.24), and I.iv.2, *passim.*

[19] I.x.3 (OS III.87.25–30, italics added).

versality of religion, which because of sin means the universality of idolatry,[20] accompanied by (2) the servile fear of God[21] and (3) the troubled conscience.[22] These three together are implicated in the inexcusability of all men,[23] which will occupy us later. At present they are a clue that we have not yet discussed the real nature of this *sensus*. A mere wrong proposition about God, a denial or misconstruction of bare knowledge, could scarcely work the havoc of idolatry. The explanation of these undertones of our existence—the servile fear of God and the troubled conscience—is found in a quality of the internal revelation which is much more prominent in Calvin's analysis and much more adequate as a basis for understanding the universality of religion, than the intellectual perception of God to which we have referred. The "knowledge" or "persuasion" that God exists, which man receives internally by "natural instinct," causes him to react religiously.[24] In it the glory and majesty of God, by which he inspires fear and worship, are given directly to the mind. This powerful persuasion penetrates even the benumbed receptivity of sinful man so forcefully that it breaks down his usual self-exaltation. See proud man at idol worship.

[20] I.iii.1. I shall not labor the point of universality, as material on it is common. Gloede, *Theologia Naturalis bei Calvin,* pp. 282–292, is particularly good. Yet Gloede concentrates so much on this aspect of the "natural disposition (*natürliche Anlage*) toward religion" that one might think the *sensus divinitatis* a mere working hypothesis by which Calvin explains the universality of religion. He calls it "knowledge (*Wissen*) of the existence of a divine Being," but a knowledge of which the content is lost, pp. 300–302. Peter Barth gives very peremptory treatment of I.iii and iv in his article, "Die fünf Einleitungskapitel von Calvins Institutio." He, too, regards these chapters as primarily a note on the general history of religions. It is only when he discusses the revelation in the external world as "also" a "corresponding" revelation that one realizes that the *sensus divinitatis* is also for him a separate source of knowledge of God, p. 46, col. 2. Doumergue, similarly, sees the *sensus divinitatis* as Calvin's method of stating the universality of religion. He does not call it a revelation. In fact, in Doumergue's treatment the concept seems to hang in the air, insufficiently related to either the revelation in nature or conscience. *Jean Calvin,* IV, 41–43.

[21] I.iv.4.

[22] I.iii.2, 3. The conscience is treated separately below, in the next section.

[23] I.v.15.

[24] "In other words, our native endowment is not merely a *sensus deitatis* but also a *semen religionis*. For what we call religion is just the reaction of the human soul to what it perceives God to be." Warfield, *Calvin and Calvinism,* p. 37.

For we know how reluctantly man would degrade himself in order to exalt other creatures above him. Therefore, when he chooses to worship wood and stone rather than be thought to have no God, it is evident how very powerful is the impression of deity, which is much more difficult to obliterate from the human mind than to break down its natural disposition—and this is certainly broken down when man, descending from his natural pride, spontaneously lowers himself before the meanest object as an act of reverence to God.[25]

No man ever showed more audacious and unbridled contempt of God than Caligula, "and yet none trembled more miserably when any instance of divine wrath offered itself; thus against his will he shook with terror before the God he professedly studied to despise."[26]

Calvin uses the term "conscience," with its inevitable moral coloring in this connection, but he goes beyond moral categories when he describes others of Caligula's stamp trying to hide from the awful majesty of God. "For the most audacious despiser of God is frightened in the highest degree even at the sound of a falling leaf. How so, unless in vindication of divine majesty, which smites their consciences more violently the more they try to flee from it."[27] This is not only disobedience of the Will but also recoil before the Presence.

All, indeed, seek out hiding places in which to conceal themselves from the presence of the Lord and efface it from their minds, but they avail nothing, they are always held fast. Although it may seem at times to vanish for a moment, it immediately returns and rushes in with new vigor, so that any remission of the anxiety of conscience is not unlike the slumber of the intoxicated or the insane who do not rest placidly in sleep, but are continually vexed by fearful and horrific dreams. Therefore even the wicked themselves exemplify the fact that some idea of God always remains vivid in every human mind.[28]

When distorted by sin the *sensus divinitatis* issues in degrading and frightening inversions of true reverence, secret dread and open idolatry. This cannot be explained intellectualistically. These sinners have more than a wrong concept of God. They are stand-

[25] I.iii.1 (OS III.38.12–19).
[26] I.iii.2 (OS III.39.1–5).
[27] *Ibid.* (lines 6–10).
[28] I.iii.2 (OS III.39.10–20).

ing before the qualitatively Other One, and their sin is actual blasphemy in his presence. We have seen Calvin picture it vividly. If this *sensus* is a knowledge of God's existence, it is also an overwhelming and ineludible apprehension of his awfulness and majesty. It is the *mysterium tremendum*.

It is significant that Reinhold Seeberg says the "essence of religion" for Calvin is the same as for Schleiermacher, "absolute dependence" [29]—and further that Rudolph Otto chooses this same quality in Schleiermacher to illustrate the first element of the numinous "creature feeling." [30] We are here in the area of the truly numinous in Calvin's theology. This knowledge which is more than knowledge is a suprarational awareness of God's majesty to which man responds in fear. The terror of Caligula is the distortion by sin of that wholesome creature feeling, the religious dread and amazement, *horror et stupor*,[31] which Abraham and Job and Elias felt in the presence of God, and before which "even the cherubim themselves must veil their faces." [32] Calvin does not speculatively isolate the numinous from the moral as Otto does, nor does he subjectivize it with Schleiermacher.[33] Peter Brunner's judgment that for Calvin "'das Heilige' is in fact an 'a priori category,'" [34] is too abstract. But

[29] "Schlechthinige Abhängigkeit von Gott," *Lehrbuch der Dogmengeschichte*, p. 561. Seeberg attributes Schleiermacher's use of the formula to its presence, introduced by Calvin, in Reformed piety. He finds it in Calvin chiefly in I.i and ii. Heppe links Schleiermacher with Calvin in the same connection, but more cautiously as one who fixed conceptually under the idea of "essence of religion" (which had formerly received but little thought in reformed dogmatics) one of the ideas that was loosely present in the older theologians from Calvin on. Curiously, Heppe's "proof text" from Calvin is from I.v.9, which makes one wonder how he arrived at his conclusion. I suspect he had a somewhat rationalized concept of "absolute dependence," as he did of the *sensus divinitatis*. *Dogmatik der evangelischen-reformierten Kirche*, pp. 2, 6.

[30] *The Idea of the Holy*, pp. 8–11.

[31] I.i.3 (OS III.33.13). Note entire paragraph.

[32] *Ibid.* (line 33).

[33] Otto, *The Idea of the Holy*, pp. 9–11, 20. No one, of course, can accuse Calvin of subjectivizing religion here or elsewhere in his theology. He is more vulnerable to Otto's charge against moralizing it. However, this analysis of the *sensus divinitatis* shows, I believe, that the "holy" as such was a part of his own consciousness of God and his view of non-Christian as well as Christian religion.

[34] Peter Brunner, in "Allgemeine und besondere Offenbarung," pp. 198/99, implies more than once that the *sensus* is an a priori category in the bad sense we have rejected.

the allusions we have made show that the *sensus divinitatis,* the direct revelation of God to the soul of man as creature, is an intensely numinous awareness.

THE CONSCIENCE.—The *conscientia* takes its place next to the *sensus divinitatis* as part of the subjective revelation in creation.[35] "There are two principal parts of the light which still remains in corrupt nature: first, the seed of religion is implanted in all men; next, the distinction between good and evil is engraved on their consciences."[36] We have already seen that Calvin speaks of the fear of God and obedience together in the *Institutes,* I.iii and iv. We now have authority from his commentary on the fourth Gospel to separate out the moral element and treat it alone.

Since "conscience" is a term that comes from the pen of Calvin in peripheral and central usages almost as much as any other and is used just as frequently in the context of redemption as of creation,[37] we shall encounter some difficulty both in defining it and in keeping our discussion within the present bounds of the revelation in creation. There is no question, however, but that conscience is an element of the subjective revelation of God the Creator, given in the created order itself, not in Scripture. It is a universal endowment, part of man as man,[38] an element of the *imago Dei.*[39]

The specific area of human life with which conscience has to do is, of course, moral choice: "the distinction between good and evil."[40] We are now concerned with more than the holiness or majesty of God, we are dealing with his will. The response,

[35] Seeberg terms it the *"lex naturalis* in the soul," which together with the *sensus divinitatis* makes up the "natural knowledge of God." "As the latter constitutes the a priori element of consciousness by which revelation can be understood, so the former is the a priori of devotion to the divine command." *Lehrbuch der Dogmengeschichte,* p. 571.

[36] Com. Jn.1:5 (CO XLVII.6d); cf. 1:9 (9b).

[37] For example, III.xix; IV.x.

[38] Sermon on Job 33:14–17 (CO XXXV.74a–d).

[39] "A judgment had been given to him by which he might discriminate between virtues and vices. Nor could what Moses formerly related otherwise hold, that he was created in the image of God, since the image of God comprises in itself the knowledge of him who is the chief good." Com. Gen. 2:9 (CO XXIII.39c).

[40] V. *supra,* note 36.

correspondingly, is more than fear and reverence; these are combined with obedience. "Conscience," however, is a noetic term. It involves obedience only with regard to recognition and judgment, not execution. It shows man his responsibility, but only the will can carry it out.[41]

Conscience, too, like the other element of the subjective revelation in creation, is a *sensus,* the "sense of divine judgment," [42] or *cognoissance,* the "knowledge of the will of God." [43] But it is also many other things, if we take seriously Calvin's baffling variety of expressions. He refers to the conscience as the "knowledge of what is right and just," [44] "conceptions of justice and rectitude, which the Greeks called προλήψεις," [45] "the distinction and the power of judging, by which they distinguish between just and unjust, the honorable and the base," [46] which is "inscribed," [47] or "engraved," [48] or "implanted by nature" [49] variously in the "heart," [50] or "reason," [51] or "soul" [52] of man from his birth. In one instance Calvin refers within the same paragraph to conscience as the "internal law," [53] "conscience," [54] and twice as the

[41] "He [Paul] means not that it was so engraved on their wills that they sought and diligently pursued it, but that they were so mastered by the power of truth that they could not disapprove of it." Com. Rm. 2:15 (CO XLIX.38a), and *passim.*

[42] "Sensum habent divini iudicii . . ." IV.x.3 (OS V.166.10); "Ergo sensus hic, qui hominem sistit ad Dei iudicium . . ." *Ibid.* (line 19).

[43] "Si est-ce que desia nous serions assez advertis de la volonté de Dieu, et en aurions assez de cognoissance . . ." Sermons sur le livre de Job, 33:14–17 (CO XXXV.74d).

[44] Com. Rm. 2:14 (CO XLIX.37d) "notitia"; (p. 129d) "intelligentia." Cf. also "notitia" in II.ii.22 (OS III.264.34) and Com. Pent. (CO XXIV.725a).

[45] Com. Rm. 2:14 (CO XLIX.37d) "conceptiones."

[46] *Ibid.* 2:15, (p. 38a) "discrimen et iudicium"; (p. 129d) "differentiam." III.ii.24 (OS III.266.12) "iusti et iniusti delectu imbuta sunt corda hominum."

[47] II.viii.1 (OS III.344.13) "inscriptam."

[48] Com. Pent. (CO XXIV.725a) "insculpta est." Also Com. Gen. 26:10 (CO XXIII.361a). Sermons sur le livre de Job (CO XXXIII.571b) and II.ii.22 (OS III.264.30).

[49] Com. Rm. 2:14 (CO XLIX.37d) "naturaliter ingenitas."

[50] *Ibid.* (p. 38d); II.ii.24 (OS III.266.12).

[51] II.ii.12 (OS III.255.11) "ratio"; also II.i.24 (OS III.266.17).

[52] I.xv.8 (OS III.185.26) "animam."

[53] II.viii.1 (OS III.344.12) "lex illa interior."

[54] *Ibid.* (line 15) "conscientia."

"law of nature." [55] Similarly, elsewhere it is called "the righteousness of the law [of Moses] inscribed by nature on their [the Gentiles] minds," [56] the "law of nature," [57] "knowledge of the law," [58] the "knowledge of conscience sufficiently discerning between good and evil," as opposed to the "pretext of ignorance," [59] and the "judgment of good and evil impressed upon him." [60] He then repeats the latter as the "universal judgment distinguishing between good and evil." [61]

Calvin also refers to the moral judgment without any of the terms just given: "nature dictates," [62] the "perception of nature" convicts,[63] or he speaks of deeds that are approved "by the instinct of nature." [64] Again, conscience is called "a kind of medium between God and man," [65] and finally, "a good conscience is nothing else than inner purity of heart." [66]

Among these various phrases several lines of thought emerge. When we read them with the idea in mind of defining conscience psychologically, we see that it involves both the ability to know and actual knowledge, as well as the ability to judge and a criterion of judgment.[67] If we seek the origin of conscience, we find that the source of the knowledge as well as of the ability to receive it discriminatingly is called both "nature" and God. The object of it—that which is known and acted upon by human judgment—is variously called God's will, the difference between good and evil,

[55] II.viii.1 (line 18) "per legem illam naturalem," and (line 26) "quod in lege naturali nimis obscuram erat."

[56] II.ii.22 (OS III.264.29) "naturaliter Legis iustitiam habent mentibus suis insculptam."

[57] *Ibid.* (line 31) also (p. 265.7). [58] *Ibid.* (p. 264.34) "Legis notitia."

[59] *Ibid.* (p. 265.8–10) "conscientiae agnitio."

[60] *Ibid.* (line 18) "iudicium."

[61] II.ii.24 (OS III.266.10) "iudicium universale."

[62] Com. Lev. 18:6 (CO XXIV.662d) "natura dictat."

[63] Com. Pent., concluding summary (CO XXIV.726a) "naturae sensus."

[64] Com. Rm. 3:21 (CO XLIX.58b) "naturae instinctu."

[65] III.xix.15 (OS IV.295.15) "Est enim quiddam inter Deum et hominem medium"; also IV.x.3 (OS V.166.13).

[66] III.xix.16 (OS IV.295.32) "ut conscientia bona nihil aliud sit, quam interior cordis integritas"; also IV.x.4 (OS V.166.30).

[67] Concerning a more accurate psychological definition, v. *supra,* the comment on Chenevière, p. 25.

the law of God, and the law of nature. The latter categories may be said to make up the content of what conscience knows. The last three are indentical as to content and mark out a definite area within the first, God's will.

With these ideas in mind, we can appreciate better Calvin's formal definition of conscience, which taken alone gives neither the psychological implications nor the broad significance of the conception with regard to law, nature, and day-to-day moral distinctions. The definition serves the special purpose of accentuating the ultimacy of conscience, the absoluteness of what God reveals in it. Our course will now be to proceed by means of this definition to appreciate the life and death seriousness of the "court of conscience," [68] and then return to the problem of the content of conscience as moral knowledge in terms of the expressions just noted.

For a formal definition of conscience, which he repeats twice in the *Institutes,*[69] Calvin uses the etymology of the word:

For just as when men apprehend the knowledge of things by the mind and understanding they are said to know (*scire*) whence is derived the name science (*scientiae*), so when they have a sense of divine judgment (*sensum habent divini iudicii*), as it were an additional witness, which does not allow them to conceal their sins, but takes them forcibly before the tribunal of judgment, this sense (*sensus*) is called conscience (*conscientia*).[70]

Con-scientia is a knowing-with, or joint knowing. It cannot remain private.

Simple knowledge (*simplex notitia*) might remain as it were shut up in a man. Therefore this sense (*sensus*) which causes man to appear before the judgment of God, is as it were appointed sentinel to man, which observes and examines all his secrets that nothing may remain buried in darkness.[71]

[68] III.xix.15 (OS IV.295.2) "conscientiae forum."

[69] The whole section III.xix.15–16 distinguishing between conscience on the one hand and human laws on the other is repeated in IV.x.3–5. Some whole sentences are copied without change.

[70] III.xix.15 (OS IV.295.10–14); and IV.x.3 (OS V.166.7–13).

[71] III.xix.15 (OS IV.295.20–24).

The "sentinel" [72] reports only to God. "As works have respect to men, so conscience refers to God." [73] Although the "fruits" of conscience extend to men, "in strict propriety of speech, it has regard to God alone." [74]

Calvin boldly identifies conscience with God's judgment, both from day to day and in the Last Judgment. "For conscience sake, that is to say, before the judgment seat of God . . ." [75]

> Observe how learnedly he [Paul] describes conscience, when he says that reasons come to our minds by which we defend what is rightly done, and on the contrary also those which accuse and reprove us for our vices. These reasons, however, accusing and defending, he refers to the Day of the Lord, not because they then first emerge, which now are constantly active and exercise their function; but they will then also prevail—lest any should condemn them as vain and evanescent.[76]

> As often, then, as the secret compunctions of conscience invite us to reflect upon our sins, let us remember that God himself is speaking. For that interior perception (*interior sensus*) is the court of God where he exercises his jurisdiction. Let those beware, therefore, who are conscious of their wickedness, lest they confirm themselves in obstinacy after the example of Cain. For this is truly to kick against God and to resist his Spirit when we repel those thoughts which are nothing else but incentives to repentance.[77]

The wicked always try to conceal their evil deeds from other men.

> In this they show that there is a law in nature which cannot be abolished, that there is a distinction between good and evil. And when we say that, we must conclude that God is judge; otherwise who has impressed on the hearts of men such a perception (*sentiment*) that they feel shame and remorse for their sins? [78]

> Shall we think that he [God] is blind where we see clearly? Has he not more authority than our consciences can have? Thus, then, if a man condemns himself in a sin, we must conclude that he is certainly damnable before God . . . every time and insofar as we see a man who is

[72] Elsewhere "witness and monitor," I.viii.1 (OS III.344.15).
[73] III.xix.16 (OS IV.295.31–33).
[74] *Ibid.* (p. 296.10–11).
[75] Com. I. Cor. 10:25 (CO XLIX.469b).
[76] Com. Rm. 2:15 (CO XLIX.38d–39a).
[77] Com. Gen. 4:9 (CO XXIII. 91d–92a).
[78] Sermon on Job 24:10–17 (CO XXXIV.386d–387a).

obstinate to do evil, or rather when we feel our own sins, it is as if God summons us to his judgment, and forces us to think on it. And this is not once a year, but we must examine ourselves endlessly every day, as when we have failed in something and we are immediately remorseful, it affects us acutely. It is as if God had sent a sergeant to us to say, "You must come before me, I am your judge." We see many who have transgressed who try to cover their sins subtly. And why, if not that they know that sin is damnable? [79]

The conscience, a part of the original endowment of man, is one with that standard against which men are measured and against which they are finally either damned without excuse or justified by faith in Christ. "A bad conscience is, therefore, far from being only a sense of grief over an immanent wrong, rather a place where, to use Karl Heim's term—the last 'dimension' breaks through." [80]

The "dimension" that "breaks through" is the Lordship of God in terms of his eternal, unchanging, orderly rule in creation, that is to say, his government of creation according to his will. Not, however, by mere willing, but by revealing his will, does God govern that part of creation which is human history. Since man can and does disobey, a discrepancy arises between God's revelation, or the "precepts" [81] of his will, and what actually takes place in the world when God's omnipotence is exercised through human wills. Thus, the normative or ethical quality of his will as revealed. God's precepts, or what God "wants" remain the same regardless of man's disobedience.[82] God, however, in accommodating his revelation to man's condition has made known these same eternal precepts in various forms. The original form, according to Calvin, is conscience. Successive forms are, chiefly, the Mosaic Law as summarized in the Decalogue, the prophetic comment on the Mosaic Law, and the ethical teachings of Jesus and the

[79] *Ibid.* (p. 387c–388a). [80] Gloede, *op. cit.*, p. 123.

[81] I.xii.v (OS III.208.14) "praeceptum." Cf. I.xvii–xviii, *passim*.

[82] Calvin can say both that God wills man's disobedience and that he does not will (or want) it. The former is a corollary of God's omnipotence, the latter of his goodness. Calvin does not reconcile the two and does not feel called upon to do so. The Christian can make both statements, not because he can rationally solve the mystery of God's will, but because we know Him in faith as both sovereign and good; v. *infra*, pp. 185 ff.

Apostles. All these forms, however, have exactly the same content: God's eternal will for man.[83] Thus is grounded the transcendent, revelatory character that Calvin sees in conscience.

Protecting this eternal dimension of human life, which is conscience, or man's responsibility to God's revealed will, Calvin marks out rigorously two realms of jurisdiction: the spiritual and the political or temporal. The former is simply conscience. The latter finds its general basis in conscience, but can never be identified with it. The "spiritual" regimen is that "by which the conscience is trained to piety and the worship of God, and the other is political, by which man is instructed in the duties of humanity and civic responsibility, which are to be observed among men. These are commonly and not improperly called spiritual and temporal jurisdiction."[84] To the latter belong all "constitutions" or positive law, both ecclesiastical[85] and civil.[86] As such, no authority of church or state can bind the conscience, although conscience demands recognition of the legislation of church and state to the degree to which God confers their authority.

> Human laws, whether enacted by magistrates or by the Church, although they are necessary to be observed (I speak of such as are just and good), are not in themselves binding upon the conscience, because the whole necessity of observing them has respect to the general end [the French of 1551 adds "that there be good order and administration among us"] but does not consist in the things commanded.[87]

No earthly power can usurp the place of conscience. Thus, conscience, which has to do "not with men, but with God

[83] V. *infra,* pp. 229 ff.

[84] III.xix.15 (OS IV.294.5–10); cf. Com. Mt. 22:21 (CO XLV.601d–602).

[85] IV.x.1–6, and ff.

[86] IV.xx.1, and ff. This is not to be confused with the distinction between piety and charity (v. *infra,* 235), that is, between our relation to God and our relation to our fellow men—but between the law or eternal will of God of which the Decalogue and conscience are (under sin) partial expressions, as against positive law or all particular rules for ordering society according to the principles of the law.

[87] IV.x.5 (OS V.168.13–18). This is an excellent statement of the relation of the universal law of God to all positive law. It epitomizes Calvin's extensive treatment of the Decalogue in the Com. Pent., in which individual, temporal laws of the Jews, both religious and civil, are classified under appropriate "eternal precepts" of the Ten Commandments.

alone,"[88] is the ground for both conservative and revolutionary principles in society: since God has given a certain authority to church and state, the consciences of all men are responsible to God for respecting that authority;[89] yet since these human institutions have derived and not original authority, they dare not impose themeslves between men and God,[90] where conscience is the "medium" or middle term. Thus, God binds man by conscience to endure an unjust government and to remain affiliated with an impure church so long as the actual marks of church and state are on them.[91] At the same time, neither bishop nor magistrate can demand divine authority, binding consciences, for arbitrary and heteronomous legislation. A follower of Calvin's principle here can be, for conscience sake, depending upon the circumstances, either revolutionary or conservative, but never anarchistic or authoritarian with regard to human institutions which God has prescribed for the preservation of order.[92]

It is legitimate to have shown briefly a relationship between conscience and the institutions of church and state because both, in so far as they are human institutions, have a continuing relation to this original endowment in man, and the state, at least, belongs to human society as God created it, apart from the Fall of man and his redemption.[93]

[88] IV.x.5 (OS V.167.28).

[89] "We should obey them [magistrates], not so much because of human necessity, but that we thereby obey God . . . as conscience through God's work binds us." Com. Rm. 13:5 (CO XLIX.251d). The remainder of this paragraph shows the same distinction made in the citation *supra,* n. 86, which was added to the *Institutes* in 1550. Calvin points out twice in *Institutes* '59, that when Paul says to obey rulers "for conscience sake," that rulers do not thereby have authority over our consciences. We obey them because we are responsible to God.

[90] "If God is the sole Legislator, it is not lawful for men to assume this honor to themselves." IV.x.8 (OS V.170.13–14).

[91] IV.i.10 ff.; IV.xx.24 ff.

[92] Calvin's doctrine of the state is introduced to combat two opposite extremes: "on the one hand frantic and barbarous men are endeavoring furiously to overturn this divinely established order; and on the other, the flatterers of princes, extolling their power without measure, do not hesitate to oppose it to the rule of God himself." IV.xx.1 (OS V.471.21–24, and pp. ff.). Calvin was however, more than cautious about revolt. Cf. Com. Gen. 14:1, 13 (CO XXIII.197c, 198b) and Beyerhaus, *Studien zur Staatsanschauung Calvins,* pp. 97 ff.

[93] "Understand further, that the powers [magistrates] are from God, not as pestilence, famine, and war and other punishments of sins are said to be from

Having seen that conscience is man's knowledge of God's eternal will which both brings him before the tribunal of divine judgment and serves as a general basis for preserving order in human history, we can now put in their proper subordination some of the varied expressions we summarized above. We shall pay particular attention to the terms "nature," "order," and "law." Many have written and disagreed over the status of these terms and their precise interrelation in Calvin's theology. Bohatec surveys some of the arguments in *Calvin und das Recht,* beginning with Troeltsch's raising of the issue and the subsequent discussions.[94] It is beyond the scope of this dissertation on knowledge as well as the competence of the writer in the semi-theological field of the history of theories of law and nature, to study these issues fundamentally or to try to describe all the shades of meaning involved. However, I shall illustrate briefly the point of view taken in view of my own reading of Calvin, which causes me to follow, in general, Beyerhaus, Bohatec, Emil Brunner, Brunner's pupil Gloede, McNeill, and in some respects Doumergue,[95] as against Lang, Peter Barth, Niesel, Chenevière, and the recent English opinion expressed by T. H. L. Parker.[96] The special characteristic of my own presentation is the use of the term conscience, which is deeply imbedded both in Calvin's utterly nonredemptive "natural" theology and in the very heart of his conception of justification

him; but because he has instituted them for the legitimate and just government (*administrationem*) of the world. . . . For the punishments which God inflicts upon men for their sins, we cannot properly call ordinations, for these are the means which he designedly appoints for the preservation of legitimate order." Com. Rm. 13:1 (CO XLIX.249c–d).

[94] Pages 1 f.; also in Beyerhaus, *Studien zur Staatsanschauung Calvins,* p. 66, and Doumergue, *Jean Calvin,* V, 464 ff.

[95] Beyerhaus, *Studien zur Staatsanschauung Calvins,* pp. 66 ff.; Bohatec, *Calvin und das Recht,* pp. 3–12 and ff.; Brunner, *Nature and Grace,* pp. 35–50, *Man in Revolt,* pp. 516–541; Gloede, *Theologia Naturalis bei Calvin,* pp. 103–133; McNeill, "Natural Law in the Theology of the Reformers," 179 ff.; Doumergue, *Jean Calvin,* V., 454–475.

[96] Lang, "Die Reformation und das Naturrecht," pp. 302 ff.; Peter Barth, *Das Problem,* pp. 12 ff., 38–53; Chenevière, *La Pensée politique de Calvin,* pp. 61–75; Parker, *The Oracles of God,* p. 53. Parker's is an excellent book, but on this issue he is dependent on P. Barth, thus reflects the confusion that existed between him and Brunner at the time of writing on the meaning and legitimacy of the term "natural."

by faith and of sanctification, as a category which brings into proper focus the "natural" and the soteriological, the knowledge of the will of God the Creator in its relation to the will of God as Redeemer. Even the first group of writers mentioned above do this incompletely, although Brunner carries it through in his own theology by means of the central term of his anthropology, "responsibility." [97] "Conscience" is the term in Calvin's theology that equates the "natural" with the divine will and, because of sin, with divine judgment. It places all three in the God-man relationship in terms of man's responsibility as over against God's freely forgiving grace. This responsibility, because of sin, issues in inexcusability, and finally, for the elect, in justification. The manward side of justification can be expressed synonymously as Christian liberty or peace of conscience.[98]

Calvin uses the term "natural" in the traditional senses of, first, the proper or natural qualities of a thing—for example, a man is "by nature" a being with the ability to reason [99]—and secondly, to denote the substance or essence of anything as opposed to its accidental characteristics—the word of God is in its "nature" saving,[100] the fact that it blinds some arises "not from its nature," but "by accident." [101] The distinction between nature and accident has no metaphysical interest for Calvin. It is only an analogy drawn from the classics and often preceded by "so to speak," or "in a manner." Sin is for Calvin the only cause for a thing being other than what it should be, therefore, the only "accident." [102] Thus, "nature" refers to created perfection, or the state before the Fall. On the other hand, to emphasize the depths of sin, however "accidental" from the point of view of creation, Calvin speaks of "corrupt nature" [103] and "fallen nature," [104] and as often as not, simply "nature," [105] and allows the context to indicate that the

[97] *Man in Revolt*, pp. 155–163.
[98] III.xix; v. *infra*, p. 235.
[99] Com. Jn. 1:5 (CO XLVII.7a) "naturaliter."
[100] Com. Jn. 12:39 (CO XLVII.297c) "natura."
[101] Com. Jn. 12: 47 (CO XLVII.303b) "non ex eius natura . . . accidentale."
[102] Cf. *infra*, p. 225.
[103] Com. Jn. 1:5 (CO XLVII.6d) "corrupta natura."
[104] *Ibid.* (p. 7a) "naturam collapsam."
[105] Com. Lk. 1:6 (CO XLV.11c) "homines . . . qui natura prorsus aversi sunt a lege."

term means the opposite of created perfection, for example, "natural reason" will not lead men to Christ.[106] Here nature, or man's "natural gifts" in their sinful state are opposed to what comes by regeneration.[107] As a result of this dual usage, the "nature" of man is both his original, created goodness, from which any lapse is unnatural; and it is also the sinfulness or "natural" disposition of man as against his created goodness. The two occur in conscious juxtaposition: "We say therefore that man is corrupted by a natural wickedness, which however does not proceed from nature."[108] Thus, as Brunner says, "nature is for Calvin both a concept of being and a concept of a norm."[109] In the phrases "nature teaches," or "nature dictates,"[110] Calvin always speaks of the norm, which is essential, created "nature."

"Nature," in the term *ordo naturae,* refers to whatever God has created, the whole array of the physical world including human nature. In this bearing, it never means the fallen state. The "order of nature" refers to the orderliness and regularity of events within creation and implies proper interrelationships among all things, as well as the realization by every creature of its appropriate purpose.[111]

Calvin rejects the conception that nature can be understood as a mere order operating by "perpetual law"[112] or an "eternal command" of God,[113] which is immanent in the "natural inclinations"[114] of things. Nature is not only "order," but the field of God's special volitions. No two seasons or days, however orderly their procession in the series, are alike; and although rain proceeds from "natural causes,"[115] it always exhibits a special bless-

[106] Com. Jn. 1:5 (CO XLVII.6d) "ratio naturalis."

[107] *Ibid.* (p. 7a), "naturalibus donis."

[108] II.i.11 (OS III.240.16, and the entire paragraph).

[109] *Nature and Grace,* p. 37.

[110] Com. Lev. 18:6 (CO XXIV. 662d).

[111] Bohatec defines it as "the laws which rule and condition actual being and occurrences in the universe (*fabrica mundi, orbis machina, universitas mundi*) . . . as well as the unalterable necessities of social and political life." *Calvin und das Recht,* p. 4. Bohatec, however, does not relate this concept to *lex naturae,* although in his citations from Calvin the two terms overlap.

[112] I.xvi.3 (OS III.191.4).

[113] I.xvi.4 (OS III.194.14).

[114] I.xvi.5 (OS III.195.2, and p. 196.11).

[115] I.xvi.5 (OS III.195.11); Com. Ps. 147:7 (CO XXXII.428c).

ing or curse of God.[116] The *ordo naturae* is simply *the orderliness or constancy of God's will within nature.*[117] This is not an empirical orderliness pure and simple, but an order such that God can work miracles, which are a scandal from the point of view of empirical order, without breaking the order of nature.[118]

Human society is part of the order of nature. Because of human sin, however, the term *ordo naturae* is in this connection less a description of nature as it is and more a description of nature as it was originally and ought to be. In the area of human activity the *ordo naturae* is the pattern or norm for human relations, for example, between man and wife,[119] and in employment [120] as well

[116] I.xvi.5. Peter Barth is wrong in trying to identify Calvin's *ordo naturae* in any of the various uses of the term with what a scientist can learn about the world, *Das Problem,* pp. 12 f. It is exactly this view that Calvin is combatting in I.xvi, because this "very modest" (P.B.) view is so often pretended to be adequate. Calvin struggles against it while trying at the same time to include what the scientist can know of nature (natural causation), within his theological concept. Cf. Com. Ps. 148:5, 6 (CO XXXII.434a–b), and Ps. 147:7, *supra,* note 115. Peter Barth's zeal to exclude everything "natural"—learned from nature—from Calvin's theology causes him wrongly to try to isolate and detranscendentalize this term, at least "in this connection" with the physical world. It is only from this false point of view that Calvin's usage can be called "changeable" when he applies the term normatively to human society, *Das Problem,* p. 17. Cf. Gloede's criticism of Peter Barth, *Theologia Naturalis,* p. 333.

[117] "When we look at the world of natural events, it admits of no doubt that the *imperium maius* stands over the *causae naturales.* Not nature (*rerum series*), but God alone is the Lord!" God shows his free power in the variation of natural events. "As God created the whole world for the purpose *ut gloriae suae theatrum foret,* so the essence as well as the task of the *ordo naturae* consists exclusively in revealing the sovereignty of God." Beyerhaus, *Studien zur Staatsanschauung Calvins,* p. 71. Also Doumergue, *Jean Calvin,* V, 470 f.

[118] "When God would have Jonah thrown into the sea, he sent a wind to raise a tempest. Those who do not think that God holds the helm of the world will say that this is outside the ordinary practice (*praeter communem usum*). But I infer that no wind ever either arises or blows except by the special command of God." I.xvi.7 (OS III.197.18–22). "Hence we conclude that his general providence not only works in creatures, so that the order of nature continues, but adjusts them to a certain and special end by his wonderful counsel." I.xvi.7 (OS III.198.13–16). God does "not merely preserve the order of nature fixed by himself, but he exercises a peculiar care over every one of his works." I.xvi.4 (OS III.194.11–13).

[119] The relation of the woman as helper to her husband is called both the "order of nature" and the "divinely appointed order" in Com. Gen. 2:18 (CO XXIII. 47a–c). Cf. Com. Gen. 1:28 (CO XXIII.29a).

[120] Slavery corrupts the "order of nature," Com. Gen. 12:5 (CO XXIII. 179c); and work is prescribed as against gluttonous idleness by the same, Com. Gen.

as in the more general prescription "love thy neighbor." [121] But since the perfect *ordo naturae* in human history has been disturbed, it has continuing significance rather as precept, or law of God, than as a description of an existing order. Hence *lex naturae* and *ius naturae* are the more appropriate terms since the Fall for what God wills (wants) within creation.[122] Bohatec shows that these two terms are often interchangeable in Calvin, as throughout antiquity and the Middle Ages. Yet he describes a difference. He presents the *lex naturae* as "predominantly the content of the practical principle of morality and justice native to man," the court of God's judgment, a "psychic" reality involving knowledge and judgment.[123] That is to say, he treats *lex naturae* and what we have already called *conscientia* as the same thing. The *ius naturae* or *Naturrecht* (Bohatec) is the "justice offered through the *lex naturae*" in which life, freedom, and property are protected by God-given right.[124] Both are clearly nothing but the continuing expression, subsequent to sin, of the *ordo naturae*—nature as created, the "nature" of Nature—held up as a norm for human life.[125]

2:15 (CO XXIII.44b). P. Barth cites many references to this area of social ethics in reference to the *ordo naturae* in *Das Problem*, pp. 15 f., also Gloede, pp. 332 f. Yet Barth, as Gloede points out, denies the ethical significance of the *ordo naturae*.

[121] The "natural" plays a large part in Calvin's exegesis of the Sermon on the Mount. Under Com. Mt. 5:43 we learn that *natura ipsa dictat* universal love among men, and that man's failure to live up to this nonetheless does not profane the *naturae ordo* (CO XLV.187d).

[122] The closeness of the terms are shown by their appearance together: "For God had determined that they two should be one flesh, and that is the perpetual order of nature (*perpetuus . . . naturae ordo*). Lamech [by his polygamy] with brutal contempt of God corrupts the "right of nature (*naturae iura*)." Com. Gen. 4:19 (CO XXIII.99c). The same occurs again: Calvin first calls primogeniture the "right of honor (*ius honoris*) conferred by nature." When Jacob reverses this right and is reproached by Joseph, Calvin adds, "Yet he [Joseph] errs in binding the grace of God to the usual order of nature (*naturae ordinis*), as if God did not often change purposely the right of nature (*ius naturae*)" to show his freedom. Concluding, "God changed the accustomed order of nature (*naturae ordinem*)." Com. Gen. 48:17 (CO XXIII.585d–586a, d). In view of these citations, I think Bohatec's short definition of *ordo naturae*, requires further explanation. Cf. *Calvin und das Recht*, p. 4.

[123] *Ibid.*, pp. 4–8.

[124] *Ibid.*, pp. 10–12. See Appendix II.

[125] "The *ordo naturae* comprehends, on one hand, the world of natural events, the courses of the stars and the planets, and the alternation of the seasons. On the

Thus, we are brought back to the subject of conscience proper. For conscience is a native and irrepressible knowledge of God's will in the sense that these terms imply: that is, as the no longer actual (because of sin) and the not yet reconstituted (in the process of redemption) *ordo naturae*. Conscience is not contrary to the natural order or the law of nature. Rather, the innate knowledge and power of distinguishing between good and evil which is conscience, is precisely recognition of the "natural" as divine, as the expression of the will of the Creator. Further, it is no contradiction, but rather a repetition to say that conscience comes from "nature" and that it comes from God, or that it is a sense of divine judgment, a knowledge of the will or law of God, and at the same time a knowledge of the law of nature. For all these have identical content although individual connotations. "Now, as that *law of God* which we call *moral* consists of nothing other than the testimony of *natural law* and of that *conscience* which God has engraved on the minds of men, the whole principle of the *equity* of which we now speak is prescribed in it." [126]

The differentia of conscience, as against the law or right of nature, is found in its noetic character and the method by which it is given to man. These two qualifications must be kept in mind when Calvin interchanges the terms, as reported above. First, the noetic character of conscience makes it self-evidently a different thing from the *lex naturae*. It is not itself the law, but is knowledge of the law. Secondly, the method by which conscience is given to us—remember Calvin's metaphors of "inscribing," "engraving," or "implantation" in man—marks it off from all other kinds of knowledge of God's orderly will for creation, which come from without through experience, whether by observation or creation or listening to special revelation. Together these

---

other, it represents a complete body of regulations which are normative for earthly life, and which are implanted in man by God himself for the protection and maintainance of political society." Man is predisposed toward these by a natural drive. "So *ius naturale* is built upon the *ordo naturae*." Beyerhaus, *Studien zur Staatsanschauung Calvins*, p. 67.

[126] "Iam quum Dei Legem, quam moralem vocamus, constet non aliud esse quam naturalis legis testimonium, et eius conscientiae quae hominum animis a Deo insculpta est, tota huius de qua nunc loquimur, aequitatis ratio in ipsa praescripta est." IV.xx.16 (OS V.488.3–7).

qualities make up the subjectivity of conscience. This subjectivity does not imply individuality of content, but refers to the means by which the knowledge is given. It is the only guarantee that the content will not be individual. Were this knowledge socially mediated, it would be at the mercy of custom or mores which Scripture and experience both confirm to be corrupt and varying from age to age.[127] Rather, it is such a continually renewed knowledge that it acts even among the most corrupt heathen as a corrective against the general practice, thus functions as God intends it for the preservation of society.[128]

What, then, is the knowledge content of conscience? What kind of knowledge is "engraved" on the hearts of all men, so that if they lived by it there would be no sin? It is, as we have shown, the knowledge of God's regular and orderly will in creation, which because of sin is also the tribunal of judgment before which men are condemned. But what does this mean? Clearly Calvin has excluded from it all political "constitutions" or positive laws, although it does underlie their general authority. It is a knowledge of principles rather than detailed laws. But, is it a fund of moral maxims that men know from birth? This would be as much an overemphasis on the cognitive side as is the opinion that conscience is a structural faculty or ability to judge and nothing else, on the other side.

No expression of the intellectual element of conscience that is a true interpretation of Calvin can be either definite or definitive. Because of sin, we no longer have such knowledge completely, and reconstruction of it in terms of Adam's perfect endowment is not only purely theoretical but also impossible. Indeed, "God's own" formulation of it in the Decalogue is, in accommodation to our sinful incapacities, negative and fragmentary. Calvin must transpose each Commandment from negative to positive, then derive its "substance," and finally expand it synecdochically, before he can state what element of the universal and eternal will of God it teaches.[129] With conscience, the problem is still more com-

[127] II.ii.24 (OS III.267.1–19); Com. Lev. 18:6 (CO XXIV.662a, b) "nam quod naturale est, nullo consensu vel more potest deleri."

[128] Com. Lev. 18:6 (CO XXIV.662d).

[129] V. *infra*, pp. 226 ff.

plicated. The method of introspection to discover this "internal law" never comes into consideration.

The material Calvin works with consists of such expressions of this innate knowledge as are found in human society, specifically in the bodies of law of pagan cultures which he had learned to know as a law student in Paris. From these he infers that all men are taught from within that God is to be worshiped and obeyed rather than cursed or ignored,[130] that parents and rulers stand as the instruments of God for preserving order in society,[131] and that bisexual, nonconsanguinous, monogamous intercourse is the ordained method of propagating the race, to the exclusion of polygamy, homosexuality, or incestuous marriage.[132] These make up the orderly, revealed will of God in creation as distinct from his "secret" will or decrees.[133] It includes also regard for property rights,[134] helping the needy,[135] respecting the aged,[136] and preserving human life.[137] All these, and probably others within not exactly determinable bounds, are part of the natural piety and charity[138] with which God intended and still intends that man conduct his life within the created order.[139]

130 I.ii.2 (OS III.36.17–21).

131 Com. Ex. 20:12 (CO XXIV.605c), rulers and (603b), parents; Com. Num. 3:5 (CO XXIV.444d), order in general, here as basis for ecclesiastical order.

132 Com. Gen. 1:28 (CO XXIII.29a), monogamy. Com. Rm. 1:26 (CO XLIX.28b), bisexual relations. Com. Lev. 18:1 (CO XXIV.660b), consanguineous marriages.

133 Com. Deut. 29:29 (CO XXIV.255d–256).

134 Calvin points to an instance in Mosaic law in which this right takes precedence over marriage. A freeman married to a slave is told to leave his wife and children although it is "against nature" rather than rob the owner of his investment. "Thus the sanctity of marriage in this case gave way to private right (*iuri privato*)." Com. Ex. 21:1 (CO XXIV.701a).

135 Com. Isa. 58:7 (CO XXXVII.329d, 330a).

136 Com. Lev. 19:32 (CO XXIV.610c).

137 II.viii.39–40, *passim;* Com. Ex. 20:13 (CO XXIV.611–613 *passim*).

138 V. *infra,* p. 230, for these two terms as the summary of the Law. "Charity" is for Calvin, the same as "equity."

139 Doumergue gives a long list of the things "nature" teaches, in addition to those listed above: rejection of all kinds of magic and divining, simplicity in food and clothing, condemnation of counterfeiting, inviolability of boundary lines, and the wrong of drunkenness. *Jean Calvin,* V, 467–469. These are all, according to Doumergue, both the bases for social life and, negatively, the charges on which man's just damnation is based. One does not know exactly where to stop in attributing these to the innate knowledge of conscience as against those things learned

As the *sensus divinitatis* has for its intellectual content the proposition that One God is, so the *conscientia* has as its content the proposition that the will of God is to be obeyed—and the latter includes knowledge of the principles of piety and charity more or less as we have just enumerated them. Undoubtedly these things are also learned in experience. How this experience is related to what is internally revealed is no clearer here than in the instance of the *sensus divinitatis*. This is understandable because of the fact that Calvin places emphasis on the function of both rather than on a psychological analysis and that in both instances he is finally interested in the verdict "inexcusable," not in reconstructing theoretically the state before the Fall. It is only just to his theology, however, to note such positive elements of innate knowledge as he recognizes, particularly in relation to such an important concept as conscience. Although all these are to be evaluated, as we shall see below, as by no means adequate for or even contributory to salvation, they have a considerable place in Calvin's theology.

THE KNOWLEDGE OF GOD DERIVED FROM THE EXTERNAL WORLD.—We now leave the realm of the subjective in Calvin's theology and proceed to the second part of the revelation in creation, God's self-manifestation as mediated through man's experience of his works. God has "not only planted in the minds of men the seed of religion of which we have already spoken, but has manifested himself in the whole structure of the world and daily exhibits himself to public view so that we cannot open our eyes without being compelled to behold him." [140] While it is true that a negative sign stands over the whole revelation in creation in Calvin's theology, we must not allow this sign to erase from our minds the magnitude of the sum thus negatived. A negative sign is meaningless before a zero. Man's guilt is meaningless unless it is the persistent negation of the positive revelation which God per-

---

in experience over which conscience exercises judgment. Doumergue's treatment is of little help, because he does not connect his discussion of the "Droit naturel" in Vol. V, with any of his dogmatic discussions of conscience in IV, 46 ff., 268 ff., 326 ff., except to note (V, 470) that such a relation exists.

[140] I.v.i (OS III.45.1–4).

sistently offers him. God did not stop revealing himself in nature at the Fall. The actual guilt of man in Calvin's theology is the result of actual rejection of an actual revelation that remains clear.[141]

Had we not approached this subject through the preceding discussion, we might now think to find ourselves in the presence of some kind of rational theist. Calvin never forgets for a moment that sin has blinded man to the revelation in creation, but since *sin* does it, the revelation itself is not harmed. Man's receiving apparatus functions wrongly. In the description of how it should function Calvin uses in simplified form some arguments from nature that would do credit to Herbert of Cherbury.[142] Calvin steers consciously, carefully, and successfully between the rationalisms that lead to deism and pantheism. He cannot possibly be accused of either. But at the same time, the rational quality of the arguments we are about to analyze and the active contribution to them of the human mind on the level of ordinary logic are unmistakable. Calvin makes use of such truths as he finds in deism and pantheism in their contrary descriptions of the relation of God to the world, and in rational theism in general in its evaluation of logic in demonstrating the existence of God. In this sin-negated natural theology, the arguments from design and from sufficient cause are held up as norms for the mind, and the immortality of the soul is maintained in opposition to Aristotle on purely rational grounds.

Every single Scripture reference that Calvin uses in developing the theme "The Knowledge of God Conspicuous in the Formation and Continual Government of the World" (I.v.1–13) could be dropped out without in any way affecting the argument. Scripture, mostly from Psalms and the Acts, is not appealed to as the ground of the argument, but to show that what is written stands

[141] Com. Rom. 1:20 (CO XLIX.24a).

[142] "When we look at Calvin's consideration of nature nowadays, it is striking to us with what unrefracted self-evidence the theistic-optimistic explanation of nature remains in effect. Here we meet in its characteristic principles that theological understanding of nature that made up the undoubted background of the whole classic period of natural scientific-philosophical thought from Kepler, Galileo, and Descartes to Newton, Leibniz, and Kant." Peter Barth, "Die fünf Einleitungskapitel von Calvins Institutio," p. 49.

in confirmation of what all men should know of the revelation in creation by their own experience. In every relevant instance Calvin first cites the revelation in creation, then introduces the Scripture reference with *"therefore,* the prophet exclaims" or *"for this reason"* Paul or David says so and so.[143] The emphasis is thrown on experience. At this point in the *Institutes* no mention has yet been made of the "spectacles" of Scripture, nor have we come to the knowledge of creation by the man who has faith.

In the *Institutes* (I.v.) Calvin purposely omits the special Biblical revelation of creation and speaks exclusively of such knowledge as comes from the general revelation. As if it were not clear enough in earlier editions, he adds in 1559 the following:

> Here are pertinent those praises of the power of God from the testimonies of nature which occur throughout Scripture, but especially in the book of Job and that of Isaiah, *which I purposely omit,* as they will be more suitably introduced in another place when I come to treat of the Scriptural account of the creation of the world. *I wish here only to touch upon that way of seeking God which is common to aliens and to those who belong to his family* (*exteris et domesticis communem*) *by tracing the lineaments which both above and below us shadow forth his living image.*[144]

This clear-remaining general revelation is a norm for both Christian and pagan. What we are now about to point to is the philosophic and rational quality of the process by which man derives the content of the objective revelation from his experience of the world. Man empirically observes the order of nature and from this draws conclusions about its Maker and Governor. Rather than an immediate *sensus divinitatis,* we have immediate experience of the world as the raw material or sense data on the basis of which the mind of man says "therefore" about God. Thus, certain attributes of God appear in the form of predicates to human experience, so far as the knowing process is concerned. The fact that mental processes rather than immediacy are involved, seems in no way to detract in Calvin's mind from the revelatory character of what is known or to make it less compelling. The sin

[143] I.v.1–13 (OS III.45.8, 24, 25; 47.3, 9, 19; 52.8, 23, 24, 26).
[144] I.v.6 (OS III.51.13–21, italics added).

which negates the revelation in the external world is this rational process gone awry, whereby man denies God, refusing to see in him the sole explanation of the world process, and instead substitutes such concepts as "chance,"[145] "nature,"[146] "universal mind,"[147] or even cruder idolatries. The philosophers as well as the unlearned—even Plato, says Calvin—err in limiting their attention to the world of effects and second causes and not rising from it to the will of God which is the great cause.[148]

The objective revelation in creation falls within two general classifications, the "ordinary course of nature" and "human society" or history—corresponding roughly to God's creative and providential work.[149] The universe at large is a "book,"[150] "theater,"[151] or "mirror"[152] for the display of God's attributes. The God who is in himself invisible and incomprehensible makes himself known by appearing in the "garment" of creation.[153] Man in the universe receives this revelation through his own *experientia* and *usus*.[154] From experience man is compelled (except that he sinfully resists) a posteriori to draw conclusions concerning the One who thus is known. This is neither the immediacy of the *sensus divinitatis* nor the a priori reasoning of such a thinker as Anselm. It is a combination of empirical observation and ratiocination.

The commonest phenomena of the world are not self-explanatory, and we must rise above them to their Author. "David shows how it is that the heavens proclaim to us the glory of God, because they openly testify that they have not by chance produced themselves, but were fabricated wonderfully by the supreme artificer."[155] The regular succession of days and nights and their

145 I.v.11 (OS III.55.13).

146 I.v.4 (OS III.48.5). "For men are commonly subject to these two extremes of error: some, neglecting God, apply the whole force of their ability to the consideration of nature, while others, overlooking the works of God, aspire with foolish and insane curiosity to inquire into his essence." Com. Gen. Argument (CO XXIII.8b).

147 I.v.5 (OS III.50.18).

148 I.v.11 (OS III.55.6–11, 27–29).

149 I.v.7 (OS III.51.30–36).

150 Sermon on Job 9:7–15 (CO XXXIII.428d).

151 I.v.5 (OS III.50.6).

152 I.v.11 (OS III.55.4).

153 I.v.1 (OS III.45.11).

154 I.v.4 (OS III.47.33); I.v.5 (OS III.49.20); I.x.2 (OS III. 86.29–30).

155 Com. Ps. 19:1 (CO XXXI.195b).

variation through the seasons according to "uniform law," or even the event of a single night, are evidences of God's work. "Although God should not speak a word, the well-adapted series of days and nights eloquently proclaims the glory of God . . . for the days and nights perform the office of teacher so well that they [men] can obtain enough knowledge by their teaching."[156]

The wisdom of God is deduced by man from the evidences of it seen around him. Astronomy uncovers the vastness, regularity, and symmetry of the universe, and medicine the ingeniousness and intricacy of the human body. But even without these special sciences every man lives in the presence of natural phenomena which cannot but excite him to rise to consideration of the Creator's wisdom.[157] Calvin challenges the Epicureans to explain with their chance theory how food and drink in the body are distributed into blood and excrements,[158] or how a blind "nature" could distinguish man from the beasts by implanting in him the excellencies of the human soul.[159] Clearly such phenomena imply a wise Creator, and men sinfully "substitute nature in the place of God."[160]

God's power is shown in the strength required "to sustain with his word this immense fabric of heaven and earth," to shake the heavens with thunder and to restrain the sea which by its elevation seems to threaten the earth with devastation,[161] as well as in controlling the mighty powers of wickedness in history.[162] "Now he from whom all things derive their origin must be eternal and self-existent. Moreover, if the cause is sought for which he was induced once to create all these things and now inclines him to preserve them, we shall find the sole cause to be his own goodness."[163]

Paul and Barnabas "did not examine the secrets of nature subtly and after the manner of the philosophers," because they spoke to an ignorant mob.

[156] Com. Ps. 19:1 (CO XXXI.196a).
[157] I.v.2, throughout.
[158] I.v.4 (OS III.48.17–21).
[159] *Ibid.* (lines 1–6).
[160] *Ibid.* (line 8).
[161] I.v.6 (OS III.51.3–13).
[162] I.v.8 (OS III.52.32–53.5).
[163] I.v.6 (OS III.51.21–26); note 2 at this place in OS shows the classic origin of this argument in Plato and Cicero. Also Com. Rm. 1:20 (CO XLIX.23d).

Nevertheless, they cite this principle, that in the order of nature there is a certain and clear manifestation of God, in that the earth is watered by rain, the heat of the sun causes it to vegetate, and such an abundance of fruit is produced yearly that from this it is inferred that there is some God who governs all. For heaven and earth do not act by their own motion, much less by chance. It remains, therefore, that the admirable workmanship of nature displays publicly the providence of God, and those who say that the world is eternal do not speak from the observations of their own minds, but by malicious and barbarous ingratitude they wish to suppress the glory of God—by which they betray their impudence.[164]

These "natural arguments"[165] exhibit a highly inductive character. Man first observes the phenomenon then proceeds to the explanation. Calvin's point is that God is the only adequate explanation as against the false hypotheses of chance or nature. Here he sides with Plato and Cicero against the Greek naturalists.[166] Clearly this explanation of the world in terms of cause, design, and order differs from the immediacy of the *sensus divinitatis,* although it does bear some relation to conscience

[164] Com. Acts 14:17 (CO XLVIII.328a-b).

[165] *Ibid.* (p. 328a) "naturalibus argumentis"; also 17:22 (p. 408b).

[166] Peter Barth correctly emphasizes the simplicity of Calvin's view of God in nature, but overstates the case when he refers to the "immediacy" of it. However simple, in contrast to other forms of rational theism, the view is not "immediate" as long as the inferential step remains. It is nature, not God, that is given immediately, and from nature, the "work" of God, man infers certain attributes of God himself. With this clarification, P. Barth's observations are very enlightening: "It is further striking with what immediacy Calvin sees the proof for the omnipresence and omniscience of divine wisdom break forth in nature. Who has eyes to see recognizes at first glance everywhere the *specimina sapientiae Dei,* the traces of the almighty and merciful God and Governor of the world." There is no trace, he continues, of the minute thought work which the scholastic expended on a theologically rooted view of nature, and the graduated teleological superstructure of churchly Aristotelianism seems not to exist for Calvin. "With astonishing sovereignty Calvin goes back into Christian antiquity and the Christian humanism domiciled in Plato, passing by the Middle Ages." Therefore, he is different from German-Lutheran (via Melancthon) Aristotelianism leading up to Leibniz and his theodicy. Calvin makes no effort to give a totality of teleological relationships. He simply looks at the infinite variety of single *specimina* of divine wisdom. "It is rewarding to take note of the line which binds together the Biblical knowledge of God, Plato, and Calvin, passing by the Catholic, as well as the Melancthonian-Leibnizian Aristotelianism." "Die fünf Einleitungskapitel," pp. 49 f.

through the connection of conscience with the concepts of order as well as experience.

In his analysis of the knowledge of God gained from human history, "the second species of his works," Calvin is equally inductive. God's power is recognized when the apparently insuperable ferocity of the impious is brought to nothing, the oppressed and afflicted raised up to good hope, and the unarmed, the few, and the weak, are given victory over the many armed and strong.[167] The wisdom of God is shown in "arranging all things most opportunely, confounding at will the perspicacity of the world and taking the wise in their own craftiness, so that, in short, there is nothing but what is adjusted to highest reason."[168] Calvin outdoes himself in deriving the justice and mercy of God from history. His justice is clear in the punishment of the wicked and the clemency exercised toward the pious.[169] The punishment of one sin is evidence enough for this, and the conclusion is not overturned when the wicked are rampant and prosperous and the good are harrassed.[170] God's mercy and patience are shown in the "paternal indulgence" with which he tirelessly woos to himself the wretched sinners and delays the punishment of the wicked.[171] The imbalance of justice and mercy in history must not, however, lead us to despair. Rather, this is ground for seeing that God has only begun to reveal his clemency and severity.

> Conversely, when we see the pious burdened with afflictions by the impious, troubled with injuries, oppressed with calumnies, tortured by insult and contumely, while on the contrary the wicked flourish, prosper, obtain ease and dignity, all with impunity—we should immediately infer that there is another life to which is reserved the punishment of iniquity and the reward of righteousness.[172]

Having drawn these conclusions and cited Augustine in support,[173] Calvin turns again to man as the center of the historical process. For although God's perfections are delineated in his works "as in a picture, by which the whole human race is invited

[167] I.v.8 (OS III.52.14–31).
[168] I.v.8 (OS III.53.2–5).
[169] I.v.7 (OS III.51.32–36).
[170] *Ibid.* (p. 52.1–8) and Com. Rm. 1:21 (CO XLIX.24d).
[171] I.v.7 (OS III.52.9–13).
[172] I.v.10 (OS III.54.7–13).
[173] *Ibid.* (line 15).

and enticed to the knowledge of him, and thence to complete felicity," yet their true meaning and use is discovered only when "we descend into ourselves and consider how God displays in us his life, wisdom, and power, and exercises towards us his righteousness, goodness and mercy." [174]

The soul of man is, for Calvin, even more than the body, a marvel that cannot be accounted for by mere nature or chance. Merely to consider it is to deny at once Aristotle's doctrine that the soul is bound to the body and therefore dies with the body, and Virgil's like pantheistic notion of a God who is mere world soul. Calvin argues—not from Scripture [175]—first that the human soul, although it indwells and directs all the organs of the body (an Aristotelian idea that he accepts),[176] also transcends the body in functions peculiar to itself in such a way that we must conclude that it is capable of a separate, immortal existence; secondly, by analogy he draws exactly the same conclusion concerning the transcendence of God over the created world.[177]

Indeed the manifold agility of the soul by which it surveys heaven and earth, joins past to future, retains the memory of that which it heard long before, pictures to itself whatever it will; its skill by which it conceives incredible things and which is the mother of so many wonderful arts—these are certain signs of the divinity in man. What of the fact that although sleeping, it not only moves itself around and turns, but conceives many useful ideas, reasons about many things, and even divines the future? What shall we say, but that marks of immortality are impressed upon man which cannot be effaced? Now what reason could be given that although man is divine, he should not acknowledge his Creator? [178]

Then the analogy:

Shall we, indeed, by the judgment which has been given us, discern between right and wrong, and there be no judge in heaven? Shall some

[174] *Ibid.* (lines 19–29).

[175] Rather in direct dependence upon Cicero. Cf. OS III.49, note 2.

[176] I.v.4 (OS III.48.15–17).

[177] I.v.5, *passim.* This is clearly observable in spite of the "literary rather than scholastic form he gives his treatise," as Warfield observes in another connection, "Calvin's Doctrine of God," *Calvin and Calvinism,* p. 172.

[178] I.v.5 (OS III.49.5–15).

remains of intelligence continue with us even in sleep, and no God keep watch in the government of the world? Shall we be deemed the inventors of so many arts and useful things in order to defraud God of his praise—although experience teaches abundantly that what we have is variously distributed to us by someone other than ourselves? [179]

The meaning of Virgil's pantheism is "that the world which was made as a display of the glory of God, is its own creator," [180] God being simply the "universal mind." [181] Calvin recognizes such truth as there is in this, in the same way that he assented to Aristotle's idea of the ubiquity of the soul in the body. He even cautiously permits the term "nature is God." [182] But he maintains that limiting God to this is to introduce the impossible concept of a self-created world, and such an idea could come only from the sinful ambitions of men to be free from true worship and fear of God and to set up instead a shadowy deity of their own invention.[183]

Thus, from the immediate experience of the world and the observation of the structure of the human mind and body, as well as from the course of history, a number of attributes of God are known to men. Calvin summarizes them in Commentary on Romans 1:21. The Apostle

plainly testifies that God introduces the knowledge of himself into the minds of all, *that is, he so points to himself through his works* that they must necessarily see what of their own accord they do not seek, that there is some God, because the world does not exist by chance, nor could it have proceeded from itself. . . . It is not possible to conceive of God without including his eternity, power, wisdom, goodness, truth, righteousness, and mercy: his eternity is apparent, because he is the creator of all things; his power, because he holds all things in his hand and causes them to continue to exist; his wisdom, from the most orderly disposition of things; his goodness, because there is no other cause why he should make all things and no other reason could move him to preserve them, except this alone; his righteousness, because in his management of affairs he punishes the guilty and defends the innocent; his mercy, because he tolerates with so much

[179] I.v.5 (OS III.49.15–21).
[180] *Ibid.* (p. 50.6–7).
[181] *Ibid.* (line 18).
[182] *Ibid.* (line 24).
[183] *Ibid.* (lines 19–22).

patience the perversity of men; his truth, because he is unchangable. Therefore, whoever has received the knowledge of God ought to praise him for his eternity, wisdom, goodness, and righteousness. Since men have not recognized these attributes (*virtutes*) in God, but have dreamed of him as an empty phantom, they are deservedly said to have impiously robbed God of his glory.[184]

In summary and criticism, we must note that the nonambiguity of both the universe at large and the exigencies of history as read by Calvin ostensibly from experience "common both to aliens and those of his family" appears to bear the imprint of Calvin's own faith rather than an independent natural theology. His arguments are too easy, not considerate enough of the problems of the searching mind. The arguments that he introduces so quickly—"We see that there is no need of long and laborious argumentation . . . to produce testimonies of the divine majesty . . . which are so evident and obvious that they are easily distinguished with the eye or pointed to with the finger" [185]—may not be so compelling as Calvin thinks. At the very least Calvin's derivation of God's justice and mercy from history seems not so much rational argument as an ex post facto delineation derived from his own believing interpretation of history. It can more easily be understood and justified in terms of Calvin's Biblically derived doctrine of providence than an unbiased reading from nature.

CALVIN'S EVALUATION OF THE REVELATION IN CREATION.—There is a "great gulf fixed" in Calvin's theology between the *original purpose* of the revelation in creation and its *actual function*. As for the purpose, he teaches everywhere that God not only revealed himself, but still reveals himself in creation solely for the purpose of bringing about the eternal felicity of man in glorifying God. "The natural order (*genuinus ordo*) certainly was that the fabric of the world should be a school in which we might learn piety and by that means pass to eternal life and perfect felicity." [186] All the qualities of the natural man which led to awareness of God originally, "not only sufficed for the government of earthly life,

[184] (CO XLIX.24c–d, italics added); cf. I.x.2.
[185] I.v.9 (OS III.53.6–10).
[186] II.vi.1 (OS III.320.13–15); cf., I.x.2 (OS III.87.14–16).

but enabled him to ascend even to God and eternal felicity."[187] God made himself known in creation "that no one might be precluded from attaining felicity."[188] In his primitive condition man possessed everything needful to the full realization of the purpose of his creation. God's revelation is always for the purpose of man's salvation, and it is only accidentally that it has any other function.

But this accidental function of the revelation in creation is in fact, under the conditions of sin, its actual function. It no longer achieves its original purpose, but it operates only to involve "the whole human race in the same condemnation."[189] "Men who are taught only by nature, have no certain, sound or distinct knowledge, but are confined to confused principles, so that they worship an unknown God."[190] "It is no trivial fault to worship haphazardly an unknown God; however, Christ pronounces all to be thus guilty who have not been taught by the law what God they ought to worship."[191] "Vain, therefore, is the light afforded us in the formation of the world to illustrate the glory of its Author, which though its rays be diffused all around us, is insufficient to conduct us unto the right way. Some sparks, indeed, are kindled, but they are smothered before they have emitted any great degree of light."[192] "But whatever deficiency of natural ability prevents us from attaining the pure and clear knowledge of God, yet, since that deficiency arises from our own fault, we are left without any excuse."[193] "Wherefore we are justly excluded from all excuse for our uncertain and extravagant deviations, since all things conspire to show us the right way."[194] *"Si integer stetisset Adam* . . . that is the sign under which the knowability of God on the basis of his original revelation must be understood. Had man not fallen, then would the *genuinus ordo naturae* have led us immediately to the recognition of our Creator."[195] The revelation in creation, then, serves the formal purpose of preserving responsibility before God, which is one of the essential characteristics of man, endued as he is with an internal sense of divinity,

[187] I.xv.8 (OS III.185.32–34).
[188] I.v.1 (OS III.44.31).
[189] I.vi.1 (OS III.60.13 f.).
[190] I.v.12 (OS III.57.22–24).
[191] *Ibid.*, par. 13 (p. 58.19–22).
[192] *Ibid.*, par. 14 (p. 58.35–59.3).
[193] *Ibid.*, par. 15 (p. 59.24–26).
[194] *Ibid.* (lines 34–36).
[195] Peter Brunner, "Allgemeine und besondere Offenbarung," p. 197.

a conscience, and the ability to see the revelation God has given of himself in nature and history.[196]

Strictly speaking, Calvin's evaluation of these elements of the revelation in creation do not belong to his "natural" theology. It is only from the standpoint of special revelation that one can judge properly the revelation in creation, since the fall of man. Here Calvin can no longer use even the positive things he finds in Cicero or Plato, for these at their best come under the verdict of Paul. Appropriately, after paragraph 13 of I.v, Scripture references are appealed to as authority, whereas before they were used as confirmation for arguments derived from experience. At the same time, as the whole course of the argument has thus far shown, Calvin does not allow the Pauline verdict to stand solely as a judgment from above, but tries to give it understandable content by insisting upon the continuing existence and adequate clarity of the revelation in creation. His doctrine of the secret decrees of God which are the causes of all things does not obviate the necessity of his investigating what is knowable concerning man's guilt by means of the revelation in creation.

Calvin's negative evaluation of the revelation in creation, however, does not mean that it is to be completely ignored. We shall see below to what degree it is rehabilitated through the Biblical revelation. But even its negative function is to be made use of. It has a teaching value, just as the law does in its function of "schoolmaster." It heightens the conviction of sin and brings to consciousness the state of inexcusability. The comments to the sermons of Paul in Acts 14 and 17 make this even clearer than the argument of I.v.

We know that the order of teaching (*docendi ordinem*) requires that we begin with things that are better known. Since Paul and Barnabas spoke among the gentiles, they would have tried in vain to bring

[196] Emil Brunner's conception of responsibility as the essence of man agrees well with Calvin. It must be remembered, however, that in both cases this formal element is not speculatively separated from the material, which is man's actual relation to God. The material is "lost" in the sense that it is negated or negatived. Man still stands in a relationship of responsibility to God, but of unfulfilled responsibility, of guilt or inexcusability. This is not a purely formal possibility, but an actuality which has been wrongly actualized. Cf., *Man in Revolt*, pp. 155 ff.

them immediately to Christ. Therefore it was necessary for them to begin at some other point less remote from common perception (*communi sensu*) so that after that was confessed they might pass over to Christ (*ad Christum transirent*).[197]

This is not only a point of pedagogic or homiletical strategy, a trick to gain a hearing, but also has a definite eristic function. Wrong ideas must be cleared away to make room for the truth.

The minds of the men of Lystra were possessed with that error, that there are many gods. Paul and Barnabas, on the contrary, show that there is but one Creator of the world. After that fictitious multitude of gods was taken away, passage was now made to the second part, that they might teach of what character is that God (*qualis esset Deus ille*) who is Creator of heaven and earth.[198]

Calvin goes on to explain that such attack is not necessary in his own day because the "papists" confess the one God and admit the Scriptures. "It remains therefore that we prove to them from Scripture *qualis sit Deus* and how he wills to be worshiped by men."[199] Again: "There is no express mention made of the word, because he spoke to the gentiles."[200] And in the sermon at Athens "Paul's plan is to teach *qualis sit Deus*. Furthermore, because he dealt with profane men, he draws proofs from nature itself; for he would have contended with them in vain by citing Scripture."[201]

Two observations are in order at this point. First, Calvin favored the use in preaching (Commentary on Acts 14 and 17) and writing (I.v) of an enlightened view of the revelation in creation. He did not care whether the enlightenment came from Cicero or Plato or Aratus for use against "gentile" polytheism and idolatry, or from

[197] Com. Acts 14:15 (CO XLVIII.326a).

[198] *Ibid.* (p. 326a–b).

[199] *Ibid.* (p. 326c).

[200] Com. Acts 14:15 (CO XLVIII.325b).

[201] Com. Acts 17:24 (CO XLVIII.410b). The comments on the Athens sermon are particularly detailed (CO XLVIII.408–423). It is very interesting to compare Karl Barth's analysis of the same passage, *Dogmatik*, II/1, pp. 134 ff. Calvin blames the unreceptive Athenians for being unconverted by a good sermon; Barth regards the whole incident as a failure to be expected from a bad method. Barth hastens to point out at the beginning that the crowd is later going to laugh and depart when the resurrection is mentioned.

the psalms and prophets for use against the errors of the "papists." The latter was for the most part appropriate to Calvin's own quarrel with Rome, although what he has written on the former gives ample reason to suspect that we would have a much larger proportion of "natural arguments" in his theology were Calvin alive in the present secularized world. The second point is that Calvin does not regard this approach as a positive contribution to faith, a foundation for it or a base under it, but he attributes to it an exclusively negative function agreeable to the negative verdict he derived from Romans 1:18–21. It is not a bridge to true faith, but a battering ram against false "faiths." The way to preach to idolaters or philosophers is not to quote Scripture verses, he says, but to show them the foolishness of idolatry and philosophy—that is to say, to make clear to them that they are not living up to the light that they already have: that they are guilty of "suppressing the truth." Then, after this clearing away of the bad, the gospel is to be preached. Thus:

> Here Paul and Barnabas take away the pretext of ignorance from the gentiles. For however greatly men please themselves in their own inventions, at last, being convicted of errors, they flee to this asylum: that they ought to bear no blame, but rather that God was cruel who did not deign so much as a hiss to recall those whom he saw perishing. Paul and Barnabas anticipate this frivolous objection when they admonish that God lay hid in such a way that he still bore witness of himself and his divinity. Nevertheless, we must see how these two things agree, for if God bear witness of himself, he did not (as far as it lay with him) suffer the world to err. I answer, this kind of testimony of which mention is made, is such that men are deprived of excuse and yet it was not sufficient to salvation. For the Apostle has truly said: "by faith it is known that the worlds were made by the word of God" (Heb. 11:3). *But faith is not conceived by the bare beholding of heaven and earth but by the hearing of the word. Whence it follows that men cannot be led to a saving knowledge of God except by the direction of the word.* And yet this does not prevent but that *they may be made inexcusable without the word,* who although they be naturally deprived of light, are yet blind through their own malice, as Paul teaches in the first chapter of Romans.[202]

[202] Com. Acts 14:17 (CO XLVIII.327d–328a, italics added).

Again:

Indeed, seeing that the true knowledge of God is a singular gift of his, and faith, by which alone he is rightly known, comes only from the illumination of the Spirit, it follows that our minds cannot pierce so far, having nature only for our guide. And Paul does not discuss in this place the ability of men, but only shows that they are without excuse.[203]

The man of faith, then, who knows from the word the inexcusability of mankind, can bring that consciousness to the pagan unbeliever by argumentation based on the revelation in creation. This does not lead directly to faith, but to awareness of the insufficiency of this or that heathen creed. After this, the gospel is introduced.

The Knowledge of God the Creator Derived from Scripture

Parallel to the knowledge of God the Creator learned from creation (*Institutes* I.ii–v), Calvin sets forth the knowledge of God the Creator learned from special revelation (I.vi–ix), then he compares the two (I.x.1–2) and finds that God has been perfectly consistent in revealing himself identically in both places.[204] In the remainder of Book I he then goes on to elaborate what Scripture teaches of the Creator over and above what can be learned (at least under the conditions of sin) from creation itself. The latter section includes the Biblical doctrines of the Trinity, Creation, and Providence. Just as Calvin appealed before to the universality of the phenomena of religion, morality, and philosophy to point back to the subjective and objective revelation in creation, he now must find evidence to show that the Bible is a valid special revelation. This he does in *Institutes,* I.vii–ix.

The three all-important chapters on Scripture (I.vii–ix) appear, so far as the drift of the argument of the *Institutes* is concerned,

[203] Com. Acts 17:27 (CO XLVIII.416b).

[204] "Thus, by the teaching of experience we perceive God to be just what he declares himself in his word." I.x.2 (OS III.86.29–30).

as an excursus or a footnote to chapter vi.[205] They could be dropped, assuming that the problem of the authority of Scripture were dealt with elsewhere, without affecting the course of the argument between vi and x. The actual progression of the *Institutes* is as follows:

Chapters i-v: the knowledge of God the Creator revealed in creation.

Chapter vi: the knowledge of God the Creator revealed, because of sin, in Scripture.

(Chapters vii-ix: the validity of Scripture.)

Chapter x: the agreement of the knowledge of the Creator revealed in creation with that revealed in Scripture.

The misleading title of chapter x,[206] which applies really only to the final paragraph of the chapter, tends to obscure this parallel development and comparison.

Since the Scriptures contain not only the revelation of the Creator but also the redemptive Word, this section is fundamental, one of the most fundamental, of the whole *Institutes*. The implications of it are not fully in view until the doctrine of faith in III.ii. In spite of this the doctrine of Scripture is discussed at this point in terms circumscribed by the problem at hand: the validity of the Biblical statements about God the Creator. That this is entirely obvious to the reader and is noted by Calvin[207] does not prevent the confusion which develops in relating this insert about Scripture to the whole doctrine of faith to which it properly belongs. The Biblical theologian par excellence has unfortunately separated the problem of the authority of the book from that of "the assimilation of its revelatory contents," as Warfield notes in short-lived disappointment.[208] Further, we are suddenly within a discussion of a kind of knowledge of God known

[205] "Before I proceed further, it is worth while to introduce some observations concerning the authority of Scripture, which will not only prepare our minds with reverence for it, but also will remove all doubt." I.vii.1 (OS III.65.5–8).

[206] "In Scripture the true God is opposed exclusively to all the gods of the heathen, in order to correct all superstitions."

[207] I.vii.5 (OS III.71.14–17).

[208] *Calvin and Calvinism*, p. 71.

only to the Christian man in faith through the testimony of the Holy Spirit—and the doctrines of Christ, Faith, and the Spirit are still a long way off in the disposition.[209] The difficulties that follow from this method will occupy us from time to time in the following pages. My own method will be to follow Calvin's lead and to treat separately the doctrine of Scripture, seeing it for the present as an authoritative book in its supporting role for the revelation of the Creator, and in Chapter IV I shall endeavor to set it in the context of the redemptive revelation and the doctrine of faith.

Calvin's arguments in defense of Scripture are in several respects not to be likened to his method with respect to the revelation in creation. First, this is a much more vital problem to him. The Bible is the sole norm of his faith and theology. True enough, he felt he could confound Aristotle and the Epicureans without the aid of Scripture, but even while about that, what finally mattered to his faith was the judgment of the Bible on them. Secondly, he now moves into the realm of positive teaching, of the true content of the revelation in creation. Formerly he was content to confound the philosophers and idolaters. Now he makes positive theological capital out of the revelation in creation as known by "those of His family." Thirdly, since the present subject is a special, supernatural revelation Calvin is bereft of universal and, so to speak, "natural" evidence. Formerly he was in the area of what men can observe commonly and demonstrate to one another. Now he deals with a proof that God alone can give. In the very nature of the case, Calvin cannot be described as validating to us the Scripture as the word of God, since God alone can do that. Rather he is analyzing in our presence the place of Scripture in his own faith, which is by implication important for the

[209] This is true of all editions of the *Institutes* except '36, where there is not as yet a developed doctrine of Scripture. Also in the catechisms and confessions, the doctrine of Scripture is separated from that of faith. Köstlin notes that the doctrine of the testimony of the Spirit appears abruptly in ed. '59 without any systematic ground, since the Spirit is not introduced until the doctrine of the Trinity, I.xiii, "Form und Inhalt," p. 414; cf. Otto Ritschl, *Dogmengeschichte des Protestantismus,* p. 162.

whole church. The demonstrable, rational proofs, which are available to all mankind, play only a secondary role.

THE AUTHORITY OF SCRIPTURE.—Calvin recognizes two problems with reference to Scripture, first, the problem of the original giving of the sacred oracles by which their objective validity was acquired, and secondly, the subjective recognition by the believer of their divine authority. In terminology to which Calvin does not adhere strictly, these are the problems of inspiration and revelation, respectively.[210] These are separate problems in Calvin's theology, but they are not of equal significance. Their separation is shown in that, according to Calvin, it is possible for a person to receive inspiration without revelation (for example, Balaam who prophesied, but was not a believer),[211] and it is the common order of the day to receive the revelation in faith without inspiration (for example, the ordinary believer who, with no special messages from God, accepts what the prophet teaches as revealed). The relative evaluation of these two problems, however, shows the question of inspiration to be much the subordinate issue. In-

[210] Calvin uses these terms in exactly this way in Com. II Tim. 3:16 "Ut scripturae autoritatem asserat, divinitus esse inspiratam docet. . . . Si quis obiiciat, undenam id sciri possit: respondeo, eiusdem spiritus revelatione tam discipulus quam doctoribus Deum patefieri autorem." (CO LII.383a–b). It might seem more appropriate to call this second problem the problem of faith. But that would be to gloss over the real difficulty which we are now approaching in Calvin's theology, the incongruity between the doctrines of revelation and of faith. Calvin's doctrine of revelation concerns itself wholly with the recognition by the believer of the authority of Scripture, while his doctrine of faith concerns the believer's appropriation of Christ. The correlate elements of the first are word and Spirit; of the second, Christ and faith, *infra,* p. 158.

[211] "God claims to himself the glory of foretelling events, which does not at all prevent him from conferring the office of prophecy from time to time upon the ministers of Satan. Balaam was worse than a hireling crier, who wished to frustrate the eternal decrees of God, and yet we know his tongue was directed by the inspiration of the divine Spirit so as to be the proclaimer of that grace which he had been hired to quench. . . . All true prophecies come from God, yet the same prophet who has predicted the truth may, in other respects be a deceiver." Com. Deut. 13:1 (CO XXIV.276b, d, 277a). Calvin is much interested in the case of Balaam and other gentile prophets who occasionally predicted the future by divine inspiration as compared with true prophets whose gift was life-long. Cf. Com. Num. 22:8 and 23:4 (CO XXV.267 f., and 278); also, the case of Caiaphas, Com. Jn. 11:49 (CO XLVII.274b).

spiration has independent status only as an answer to "how." The "what" and the "that" of it are identical with revelation. There is, strictly speaking, no independent doctrine of inspiration in Calvin's *Institutes.* His teaching about the historical origin and providential preservation of the sacred books is carried along by his doctrine of the living and present witness of the Spirit to the truth of the contemporary Bible. Calvin does not accept the Bible as revelation because it has somehow objectively been proved to be inspired. On the contrary, he finds the Bible to be a revelation of God, then he makes the corollary assertion that its writers were inspired, as they asserted, by God. "Corollary assertion" is not an exact term here, because it denotes subsequence and inference. This corollary is neither subsequential nor inferential. It refers to a prior event which is a presupposition of the revelation, and it is said simultaneously when one speaks of revelation. Yet we use the word "corollary" to show that the inspiration of Scripture does not stand alone and cannot, in Calvin's theology. Revelation, the present revelation in the life of the believer, is the theological peg upon which the teaching about inspiration hangs. Hence, the "proofs" of inspiration, such as predictive prophecy, which are so important in Calvinistic orthodoxy, do not exist for Calvin as independent proofs, but can be found among the "secondary aids to our weakness."[212] It is only in answering the question "how?" of the Bible, in scattered references throughout his writings, that Calvin gives us observations on its inspiration. That these are by no means rare shows Calvin's interest in the problem, but for all their frequency, their importance remains derivative and corollary.

The Inspiration of the Writers of the Bible

Granting that we shall not have reached the fundamental issue until we discuss the believer's recognition of the authority of Scripture, it will be instructive to look first through Calvin's eyes at the process by which we got our Bible and by which the Bible was endowed with objective validity as the word of God. The Bible is not invested with validity by the believer or by the inner

[212] I.viii.7–8.

testimony of the Holy Spirit within the believer, but by special works of the Spirit in the chosen men to whom the divine oracles were originally given. This process is inspiration. As a result of it the Bible is an objective revelation of God which comes to man from without, in the same way that the objective revelation in creation is mediated to him by experience. It is man's sinful blindness, a subjective disability, that keeps him from recognizing the Bible as the word of God and thus submitting to its authority.

The Biblical writers are the instruments or organs [213] or amanuenses [214] of the Holy Spirit. Their mouths are "the mouth of the one God"; [215] their writing style is the style of the Holy Spirit.[216] When we turn to them, we may say, "Now let us hear God himself speaking in his own words." [217] We owe their writings in Scripture "the same reverence which we owe to God, because it has proceeded from him alone and has nothing human mixed in." [218] Calvin has no hesitation in citing the Bible thus: "the Holy Spirit . . . announces and repeats in innumerable forms of expression," [219] or "we see that the Spirit is not less diligent in narrating burials than the principal mysteries of faith." [220] We "ought to embrace with mild docility, and *without any exception, whatever* is delivered in the Holy Scriptures." [221] "For Scripture is the school of the Holy Spirit in which as *nothing useful and necessary is omitted, so nothing is taught which is not profitable to know*." [222]

The most extreme of these expressions for the divine origin and complete objective validity of Scripture is found in the word "dictation," *dictante spiritu sancto*.[223] "Whoever wishes to profit in the Scripture, let him first agree to this, that the law and the prophets are not a doctrine delivered at the discretion of men,

[213] Com. II Tim. 3:16 (CO LII.383a). [214] IV.viii.9 (OS V.141.13).

[215] Com. I Pet. 1:25 (CO LV.230d).

[216] I.vii.2 (OS III.73.1–3). Elsewhere Calvin distinguishes between the style of Scripture as "human eloquence" and as the work of the Spirit, Com. Rm. 5:15 (CO XLIX.98b). [217] III.viii.12 (OS III.354.19).

[218] Com. II Tim. 3:16 (CO LII.383c); also I.vii.1 (OS III.65.11–16).

[219] I.xvii.2 (OS III.204.6). [220] III.xxv.8 (OS IV.449.6–8).

[221] I.xviii.4 (OS III.227.27–30, italics added).

[222] III.xxi.3 (OS IV.372.1–3, italics added).

[223] IV.viii.6 (OS V.138.12).

but are dictated by the Holy Spirit."[224] And "nothing else was permitted the Apostles than the prophets formerly had," which was to expound the Scriptures and show their fulfillment in Christ; "and this they could not do except from the Lord, that is, without the Spirit of Christ going before and in a manner (*quodammodo*) dictating the words."[225] Each of the gospel writers told the story of Christ differently, and John apparently wrote in opposition to the Ebionite heresy, but whatever their individual motives, God "so dictated to the four Evangelists what they should write, that the parts distributed among them might be related in a single whole. It now therefore falls to us mutually to join together the four so that we may allow ourselves to be taught by all of them as by one mouth."[226] To take exception to Scripture is to quarrel with the Holy Spirit who "dictated" it.[227]

In two instances where the text gives him occasion Calvin describes the actual mechanics of inspiration in terms of dictation.

> Here the prophet declares that he dictated to Baruch, a servant of God, what he had previously taught. But there is no doubt that God suggested (*suggeserit*) to the prophet what might have been effaced from his memory; for not all things which we have formerly said always occur to us: therefore the greater part of so many words must have escaped the prophet had not God dictated them again to him (*rursum illi dictasset*). Jeremiah, then, stood between God and Baruch, for God, by his Spirit, presided over and guided the mind and tongue of the prophet. Now the prophet, the Spirit being his guide and teacher, recited what God had commanded. . . . Jeremiah repeats again that nothing came from himself (*ex sensu suo*). We see, hence, that he did not dictate according to his own will what came to his mind, but that God suggested whatever he wished to be written by Baruch.[228]

Further on, "the words which God dictated to his servant were called the words of Jeremiah; yet, properly speaking, they were not the words of man, for they did not proceed from a mortal man but from the only God."[229] After King Jehoiakim had burned the roll which Jeremiah had dictated to Baruch, and Jeremiah

[224] Com. II Tim. 3:16 (CO LII.383a).
[225] IV.viii.8 (OS V.140.1–6).
[226] Com. Jn. "Argument" (CO XLVII.p.viiia).
[227] I.xviii.3 (OS III.224.6–8).
[228] Com. Jer. 36:4–6 (CO XXXIX.118c–d).
[229] *Ibid.*, verse 8 (p. 121c).

is commanded to write again in the same words, Calvin paraphrases: "As though he said, 'Let not a syllable be omitted, but let that which I once proclaimed by thy mouth, remain unchanged.'"[230] In commenting on the giving of the Decalogue, Calvin does not use such passages as "And God spoke all these words" (Exodus 20:1) or "And the Lord said to Moses, write thou these words" (Exodus 34:27) to press the idea of dictation. Yet in the Commentary on Deuteronomy 5:4, "the Lord talked with you face to face in the mount, out of the midst of the fire," he conceives of a literal voice and literal fire. Paying due respect to the Mediator as the transmitter of all oracles, Calvin nontheless says, "To speak face to face is equivalent to conferring personally and familiarly in words. And indeed God has spoken thus with them, as mortals and companions converse with one another."[231]

The oracle, or direct verbal communication, was in Calvin's view the fundamental form of revelation before Moses, who was the first to write it down. This concerns in part not only central revelatory truths but also guidance in answer to individual prayers.[232] Unusual and miraculous manifestations often accompanied it and were of great importance in confirming its authority, but the message or knowledge communicated was always of central importance. "Mute visions are cold, therefore the word of the Lord is as the soul which quickens them. . . . We may therefore observe, that whenever God manifested himself to the fathers, he also *spoke,* lest a mute vision should have held them in suspense."[233] A vision and a voice came to Moses, but "the chief thing was the voice, because true knowledge of God is perceived more by the ears than by the eyes. . . . For speechless visions could be cold and altogether evanescent, did they not bor-

[230] Com. Jer. 36:28 (CO XXXIX.133d). I have never seen the above-mentioned passages from Jeremiah cited in other studies of the subject. The commentaries on Jeremiah are the recorded lectures of Calvin rather than his own writing, yet he approved their publication and wrote a dedicatory epistle to the Elector Frederick with no more than his usual protestations of unworthiness, assuring the Elector that Jeremiah himself would approve of everything said. Calvin's Letters (CO XX.72 ff., 76d, and 77).

[231] (CO XXIV.211b).

[232] Com. Gen. 25:22 (CO XXIII.349a).

[233] Com. Gen. 28:13 (CO XXIII.392b, italics added).

row efficacy from words. . . . The soul of a vision is the doctrine itself, from whence faith takes its rise."[234] In the incident of the burning bush, "it was not a voiceless spectacle to alarm the holy man, but that instruction accompanied it by which his mind might comprehend."[235] What was important in Jacob's famous dream was the "promise," which is the object of faith in all ages. The figure of the ladder "was the inferior appendage of this promise, just as God illustrates and adorns his word by external symbols, that both greater clearness and authority may be added to it."[236] The importance of this motif to Calvin is revealed by his inclusion here of a criticism of the frivolity of papal sacraments, "because no voice of God is heard in them to edify the soul."[237] Of God's appearance to Abraham in the Commentary on Genesis 71:1, similarly, Calvin says: "Besides, the vision was not speechless, but had the word annexed, from which the faith of Abraham might receive profit."[238]

In spite of this emphasis on the transmission of the message, Calvin shows considerable interest in the various accompaniments of the oracles. Dreams and visions were the "two ordinary methods of revelation,"[239] of which the latter were the less common. By virtue of these there was added to the word "a kind of symbol of the Divine presence,"[240] or a "visible symbol of the Divine glory."[241] But even these phenomena needed special marks, because a dream is a very ordinary thing that cannot always be taken seriously, and because Satan is equipped to use dreams and visions for his purposes. Thus, "whenever God intends to make known his counsel by dreams, he engraves on them certain marks which distinguish them from passing and frivolous imaginations, in order that their credibility and authority may stand firm."[242] "Since Satan is a wonderful adept at deceiving . . . it was necessary that some sure and notable distinction should

[234] Com. Ex. 33:19 (CO XXV.109a–b).
[235] Com. Ex. 3:4 (CO XXIV.36d).
[236] Com. Gen. 28:13 (CO XXIII.392b).
[237] *Ibid.* [238] (CO XXIII.234b).
[239] Com. Isa. 1:1 (CO XXXVI.27b); Com. Gen. 26:24 (CO XXIII.365a–b).
[240] Com. Gen. 26:24 (CO XXIII.365a); cf. Com. Acts 9:10 (CO XLVIII.205d).
[241] Com. Gen. 15:1 (CO XXIII.207d).
[242] Com. Gen. 37:5 (CO XXIII.482d).

appear in true and heavenly oracles which would not suffer the faith and the minds of the holy fathers to waver."[243] Yet, for all his investigation of these phenomena Calvin never tries to fix the "mark" by which the visions from God are distinguishable from those of Satan.[244] It seems that a subjective illumination of the mind of the recipient causes him to recognize who speaks in a revelatory dream or vision. A voice came to Ezekiel, "but nothing was effected by this voice until the Spirit was added. God indeed works efficaciously by his words, but the efficacity is not included in the sound itself, but proceeds from the secret instinct of the Spirit. The prophet therefore shows us both sides: on the one hand he says that he heard the voice of God so that he stood on his feet, God in this wished to animate his confidence; but at the same time he adds that he was not raised up by the voice until the Spirit placed him on his feet. The work of the Spirit therefore is joined with the word of God. But a distinction is proposed that we may know that the external word is of no avail by itself, unless animated by the power of the Spirit."[245] Nebuchadnezzar knew what dream to take seriously "because God had inscribed in his heart a distinct mark by which he had denoted this dream."[246]

The oracle preserves the vision from indefiniteness, the vision prepares the mind for and confirms it in the oracular message—but the peculiar mark of divinity is a mystery of God. Two examples will illustrate this summary statement and show Calvin's thoroughgoing interest in the phenomena which accompany the inspiration of the Old Testament. Note also Calvin's careful attention to the concept of accommodation.

The vision (as I have elsewhere said) was to prepare him to listen more attentively to God and to convince him that it was God with whom he had to deal, for a voice alone would have had less energy. Therefore God appears in order to produce confidence in and reverence towards his word. In short, visions were a kind of symbol of the

[243] Com. Gen. 15:2 (CO XXIII.209a).

[244] For example, Com. Gen. 15:2 (CO XXIII.209b); 40:5 (p. 511d); Com. Ez. 8:3 (CO XL.179c–d).

[245] Com. Ez. 2:1–2 (CO XL.61d–62a, and *passim*).

[246] Com. Dan. 4:4–6 (CO XL.652c); cf. Com. Acts 9:10 (CO XLVIII.205d).

divine presence, that the holy fathers might not doubt that it was God who spoke the word. Should it be objected that this was not sufficiently sure, since Satan often deludes by similiar deception, being, as it were, the ape of God, we must keep in mind what has been said before, that a clear and unambiguous mark was engraven on the visions of God by which the faithful might certainly distinguish them from those that were fallacious, so that their faith should not be kept in suspense: and certainly, since Satan can only delude us in the dark, God exempts his children from this danger by illuminating their eyes with his own splendor. Yet God did not fully manifest his glory to the holy fathers, but assumed a form by means of which they might apprehend him according to the measure of their capacities; for, as the majesty of God is infinite, it cannot be comprehended by the human mind, and by its magnitude it absorbs the whole world. Besides, it follows of necessity that men, on account of their infirmity, must not only melt, but be altogether annihilated in the presence of God. Wherefore Moses does not mean that God was seen in his true nature and greatness, but in such a manner as Isaac was able to bear the sight. But what we have said, namely, that the vision was a testimony of Deity, for the purpose of giving credibility to the oracle, will more fully appear from the context; for this appearance was not a mute specter, but the word immediately followed, which confirmed in the mind of Isaac faith in gratuitous adoption and salvation.[247]

The vision by night availed for the purpose of giving greater authority (*majestas*) to the oracle. . . . It was profitable for him [Jacob] that he should be affected as with the glory of the presence of God, in order that the word might penetrate more effectually in his heart. It is, however, proper to recall to memory what I have said before, that the word was joined with it because a silent vision would have profited little or nothing. We know that superstition eagerly snatches at bare specters by which means it presents God in a form of its own. But since no living image of God can exist without the word, whenever God has appeared to his servants, he has also spoken. Wherefore in all outward signs, let us be ever attentive to his voice if we would not be deluded by the wiles of Satan. But if those visions in which the majesty of God shines require to be animated by the word, then they who obtrude signs invented at the will of men, upon the Church, exhibit nothing else than the empty pomps of a profane theater. . . . Let this mutual connection then be observed, that the vision which

[247] Com. Gen. 26:24 (CO XXXIII.364d, 365a–b).

gives greater dignity to the word, precedes it, and that the word follows immediately as if it were the soul of the vision. And there is no question that this was an appearance of the visible glory of God, which did not leave Jacob in suspense and hesitation, but which, by removing his doubt, firmly sustained him, so that he confidently embraced the oracle.[248]

Unusual natural phenomena, such as the ten plagues and the blossoming of Aaron's rod, serve the same supporting function for the word as do visions and dreams. Since they are objective physical manifestations, they have a public character not attributable to visions and dreams. Thus, miracles, particularly in the New Testament, have to do with confirming the word, not so much to the chosen individual, as to the common believer. They are thereby generally more closely related to revelation in faith than to the process of inspiration, which is our problem at hand.

Calvin points to the preparatory and confirmatory function of miracles in commenting on the incident in which Moses' rod was turned into a serpent and his hand made temporarily leprous.

We see an example of both [preparation and confirmation] in the change of the rod by which Moses was increasingly animated and encouraged to gather strength, although he already had faith in the promise of God; but the Israelites, who were both incredulous and unteachable, were both prepared and compelled to believe. Moreover, the miracle opened the door of faith for the Israelites, that being persuaded of his prophetical office, they might submit to be taught, while he himself was led on to greater assurance and perseverance.[249]

Even such miracles as might appear useful and self-explanatory Calvin shows to be empty apart from the accompanying word. The children of Israel did not recognize the significance of the mana until Moses explained it, "for the power of God was manifest to the eye, but the veil of unbelief prevented them from apprehending God's promised bounty."[250] So also,

[248] Com. Gen. 46:2 (CO XXIII.559d, 560a).

[249] Com. Ex. 4:5 (CO XXIV.52d). "But faith cannot be acquired by any miracle or any perception of divine power; it requires instruction also. The miracles avail only to prepare for piety or for its confirmation." Com. Dan. 3:28 (CO XL.643b).

[250] Com. Ex. 16:15 (CO XXIV.171a, and 170 *passim*).

it was not in vain that Paul sought in miracles of this kind [the cloud that guided the Israelites and the parting of the Red Sea] something more than the mere outward advantage of the flesh. For although God designed to serve his people's advantage in respect to the present life, what he mainly had in view was to declare and manifest himself to be their God, and under that eternal salvation is comprehended.[251]

All is subordinate to the revelation of God's purpose.

Apart from the word that accompanies it and apart from a reception of this word in faith, a miracle is a sheer demonstration of extraordinary power and may be the work of Satan rather than of God. Miracles as an external evidence of divine inspiration are not sufficient to produce faith. Calvin notes that Pharaoh's magicians repeated some of Moses' miracles at the time of the ten plagues[252] and that the anti-Christ himself is to be attested by miracles.[253] The only protection for the elect in such instances is to have heard the word in faith. The Jews were not deceived by the Egyptian magicians, because they had already received a measure of the knowledge of faith through the promise to Moses.[254] Given the word, their faith was strengthened by resisting the lures which God permitted the devil to show them in the work of the heathen magicians. On the other hand, both the miracles of Moses and the heathen magicians served to drive Pharaoh more and more against God, because he lacked the faith through which alone these displays of power could be interpreted.[255] Correspondingly, in the *Institutes* miracles, insofar as they stand alone, apart from faith, as independent evidences of the inspiration of Scripture, are relegated to the level of rational evidences, or "secondary aids to our weakness."[256]

Two other peculiar manifestations which accompanied the

[251] Com. I Cor. 10:2 (CO XLIX.452c). In this passage Calvin goes on, following Paul, with an explanation of the sacramental character of the miracle, whereby word and external sign are inseparably connected, although not identified.

[252] Com. Ex. 7:11–12 (CO XXIV.91).

[253] Com. Ex. 7:10 (CO XXIV.90a, b), 7:12 (p. 91c); Com. Mt. 24:24 (CO XLV.663 f., *passim*).

[254] Com. Ex. 7:22 (CO XXIV.96a).

[255] Com. Ex. 7:12 (CO XXIV.91d, 92a), 7:22 (CO XXIV.95d).

[256] I.viii.6–7.

giving of divine oracles deserve mention, angelic messengers and theophany. The latter, however, has already been considered in another connection, and the former adds nothing to what has been said. It is enough to note here that they serve the same functions as those just discussed: preparation for and confirmation in the truth of the transmitted oracle.

We must now consider briefly whether Calvin's teaching about inspiration as so far presented requires the interpretation that Calvin held a mechanical or literal dictation theory of the writing of the Bible. He incontrovertibly did mean literal dictation in his description of Jeremiah's inspiration, cited above.[257] His emphasis as seen throughout our study of the miraculous accompaniments of inspiration upon the transmission of the message, in my opinion adds weight to the claim that he conceived the Scriptures as literally dictated by God. All attention is focused upon what he said. Further, the utter seriousness with which he takes every word of the text is an indication that he believes the revelation to have been given word for word by the Spirit.[258] Most of what today are recognized as idiosyncrasies in style and even mistakes in the text are attributed to the purposes of the Holy Spirit. To this end, the principle of accommodation is for Calvin a common exegetical device for explaining away irregularities that might otherwise, with a less rigorous view of the perfection of the text,

[257] *Supra,* pp. 92 f. In view of this, Pannier's statement is rash and careless: "In any case, Calvin has not written a single word that one can invoke in favor of literal inspiration." *Le Témoinage du Saint-Esprit,* p. 200. So also Heppe, "Of a real inspiration of the recording process (*Aufzeichnung*), there is no mention." *Dogmatik der Evangelischen-reformierten Kirche,* p. 17, and Peter Barth's article on "Calvin" in *R.G.G.,* Vol. I/2, p. 1430. Fuhrmann, *God-Centered Religion,* p. 85, simply quotes Pannier.

[258] For example, the word "blameless" applied to the parents of John the Baptist is explained by Calvin in the light of the whole doctrine of forgiveness, Com. Lk. 1:6 (CO XLV.10/11); when an angel addresses Hagar as "Sarah's maidservant" and tells her to return home, Calvin finds that "by this word God shows that he approves political order and that the violation of it is inexcusable," and he enters into a brief discussion of slavery, Com. Gen. 16:8 (CO XXIII.227c); the plural form of Elohim in Gen. 1:1 is scrutinized, then construed as denoting the plurality of powers in God's acts of creation rather than the Trinity, while "Let us make . . ." in 1:26 is taken as trinitarian (CO XXIII.15b–c and 25 ff.). Cf. *infra,* p. 167.

be simply attributed to inaccuracies.[259] When he does admit an undeniable error of grammar or of fact, without exception he attributes it to copyists, never to the inspired writer.[260] There is no hint anywhere in Calvin's writings that the original text contained any flaws at all.

At the same time, one cannot deny some cogency to Doumergue's case for the figurative use of the term in many instances. "Clerk" and "amanuensis" are figures, the term "mouth of God" is applied to Old Testament priests and to all pastors, as well as to the specially chosen instruments of inspiration, and the term "dictate" is changed to "inspire" in certain instances in the original French translations.[261] Certainly the phrase "nature dictates" is metaphoric. As O. Ritschl shows, the verb *dictare* did not always mean "to articulate words" among writers of theology of Calvin's time, although its use with reference to Scripture was generally a clue to someone who believed in verbal inspiration.[262] A further argument of Doumergue and Clavier is that according to Calvin's terminology the "doctrine," rather than the words, is most frequently referred to as inspired.[263] Pannier subscribes to this in claiming that for Calvin, Scripture is the *verbum Dei* not the *verba Dei*.[264] He distinguishes between the "contents" (the message of grace) and the "container" (Scripture),[265] although

[259] Why are angels and Satan not mentioned in the Genesis account of creation? I.xiv.3 (OS III.154.27–32), and Com. Gen. 3:1 (CO XXIII.53c). Why is the moon represented as larger than Saturn, when astronomy proves the contrary? Com. Gen. 1:15–16 (CO XXIII.21d–22). Why has the Nile river not dried up as predicted by Isaiah? Com. Isa. 19:5, 6 (CO XXXVI.332b–c). What of passages of Scripture that imply salvation to be partly dependent on merit? Or that God's will is changeable? III.xxiv.9 (OS IV.420.20–421.16, esp. p. 421.8), and par. 17 (pp. 430.22 ff., esp. lines 35 f.). The one answer to all these questions is the accommodation of the writer, simplifying or exaggerating his material to fit the needs of those for whom it is intended.

[260] *Infra*, pp. 104 f.

[261] Doumergue, *Jean Calvin*, IV, 72–74.

[262] *Dogmengeschichte des Protestantismus*, pp. 59 ff.

[263] Doumergue, *Jean Calvin*, IV, 78 f.; Clavier, "In spite of the first appearance, an extreme literalism is not implied in these [dictation] passages, where it is a question of inspired doctrine. If the letter does not escape the control of the Spirit, it is for its contents alone, its spiritual contents, that divine infallibility is claimed." *Etudes sur le Calvinisme*, p. 27; also pp. 81–84, and 110 f.

[264] Pannier, *Le Témoignage du Saint-Esprit*, p. 203; cf. pp. 197 ff.

[265] *Ibid.*, p. 198.

"practically [Calvin] did not feel the need of the distinction." [266] Heppe, too, regards the identification of the "word of God" and "Scriptures" as arising in reformed theology after Calvin.[267]

All of these writers except Ritschl are trying to state Calvin's doctrine of inspiration so as to leave room for the testimony of the Spirit in the heart of the reader of Scripture and to allow theologically for Calvin's critical approach in exegesis. None of them has been willing to face candidly the clearly stated dictation theory where it occurs, even to the extent of granting that Calvin sometimes taught it.

Against the foregoing stand R. Seeberg,[268] O. Ritschl,[269] and A. M. Hunter,[270] who attribute unambiguously a dictation theory to Calvin. These are closer to the truth, but probably the solution of Warfield, curious as it appears at first glance, is the best formulation for doing justice to a certain lack of clarity or variation in Calvin himself. Concerning "dictation," Warfield comments,

> It is not unfair to urge, however, that this language is figurative and that what Calvin has in mind, is, not to insist that the mode of inspiration was dictation, but that the result of inspiration is as if it were by dictation, viz., the production of a pure word of God free from all human admixtures.[271]

Dictation describes "the effects rather than the mode of inspiration." [272] The important thing to realize is that according to

[266] *Ibid.*, p. 199.

[267] "At the basis of the original [Calvin's] reformed doctrine of inspiration lay the differentiation between the concepts of 'Word of God' and 'Holy Scripture,' while these were identified in the late doctrine of the church." *Dogmatik der Evangelischen-reformierten Kirche*, p. 16. "But by the end of the sixteenth century the view of inspiration was entirely different. . . . The Scriptures were valued as inspired because they were dictated by God to the Biblical authors." *Ibid.*, p. 17, cf. pp. 15–18. Heppe's one reference to Calvin is erroneous (should be I.vi.1–2) and not relevant to the problem.

Assenting to the identification of Scripture and the word of God in Calvin are Peter Brunner, *Vom Glauben*, p. 95, and Lobstein, "La Conaissance religieuse," p. 29. The latter calls it one of the guiding ideas of his whole theology. Others are cited by Peter Brunner, *Vom Glauben*, p. 95, n. 2.

[268] *Lehrbuch der Dogmengeschichte*, pp. 566–569.

[269] *Dogmengeschichte des Protestantismus*, pp. 63 f.

[270] *The Teaching of Calvin*, pp. 68 ff.

[271] "Calvin's Doctrine of the Knowledge of God," *Calvin and Calvinism*, p. 63.

[272] *Ibid.*, p. 64.

Calvin the Scriptures were so given that—whether by "literal" or "figurative" dictation—the result was a series of documents errorless in their original form.

Closely connected with the process of the original inspiration of the Scriptures is their providential preservation. This is a necessary corollary—since it would profit little were the given oracles either lost or allowed to become impure. Calvin recognizes and states the fact of the providential preservation of Scripture. In I.viii.9–10 he mentions some great crises in the history of the sacred book, its neglect prior to the time of Josiah, and the efforts of Antiochus to have it burned, in showing that it was preserved "rather by the providence of heaven than by the zeal of men."[273] Further, the Septuagint was prepared for the Greek world as the Hebrew language was disappearing,[274] although God also kept that language alive for the sake of his revelation;[275] and even the Jews themselves by preserving the book, participated in God's protection of his word.[276] Twice in this connection Calvin quotes Isaiah 59:21, "My Spirit that is upon thee and my words which I have put in thy mouth shall not depart out of thy mouth, or out of the mouth of thy seed, or out of the mouth of thy seed's seed forever."[277] Aside from this, however, the theme is almost untouched by Calvin. It is notably lacking in IV.viii.3–10, where he reviews the whole history of revelation in introducing his attack upon the power of the Roman church to promulgate dogma. Abruptly in the middle of IV.viii.9 he makes the transition from Apostles, who are "authentic amanuenses of the Holy Spirit," to other ministers and the church at large whose office is solely to teach what is recorded in Scripture.[278] The same occurs in the "Acts of the Council of Trent, with Antidote," where Calvin slips from praise of the original Hebrew and Greek to scorn of the Vulgate with no remarks about providential preservation.[279] At one point he does say that blunders by translators are excusable.[280]

[273] (OS III.77.34–35).

[274] *Ibid.* (p.79.4 ff.).

[275] *Ibid.* (p. 79.10 ff.).

[276] *Ibid.* (p. 79.16 ff.).

[277] I.viii.4 (OS III.70.9 ff.) and I.ix.1 (OS III.82.13 ff.).

[278] (OS V.141.11–16).

[279] "Acts of Council of Trent, with Antidote," (CO VII.414).

[280] *Ibid.* (415c).

Neither in these places nor anywhere else does Calvin discuss in detail the method by which the Scripture was preserved. This leaves an interesting hiatus in his doctrine. It is interesting precisely because it is always to the text before him, never to the original text of Scripture, that Calvin attributes such errors as his exegesis discovers.[281]

Doumergue, Clavier, and others are wrong to introduce Calvin's free a posteriori exegetical method as evidence against his holding a dictation theory concerning the origin of Scripture.[282] They are wrong simply because they are relating two issues which Calvin himself never related and could not relate while a hiatus remained in his doctrine concerning the identification of the original text of the Bible and any given copy. Here we find Calvin the theologian and Calvin the humanist scholar side by side, co-operating, but unreconciled in principle. When he writes as a theologian about the inspiration (and rarely the preservation) of Scripture, there is not the least hint that Calvin the scholar ever has found or ever may find an error in the text before him. Why is this, if not because he is writing of the original Scriptures, not as rendered by Erasmus, Jerome, the Septuagint or even by copyists of the original manuscripts? On the other hand, when he sees an obvious error in the text before him, there is no indication that it makes any *theological* impression on him at all. It never causes him to retract or to qualify or generally even to mention his general position of verbal inerrancy. Again, why, if not because the error is a trivial copyist's blunder, not a misunderstanding of divine "dictation" by an apostle or prophet?

The openness of Calvin's exegesis, by which he leaves points undecided, which is so highly prized as evidence by those who think Calvin no verbal inspirationist, actually is evidence to the contrary. The obscurities in the text are allowed for theologically, as we showed above.[283] They are designed by the Spirit to promote humility. But neither these obscurities nor obvious mistakes are

[281] Warfield, "Doctrine of the Knowledge," *Calvin and Calvinism,* pp. 65 ff. *infra,* p. 105.

[282] Doumergue, *Jean Calvin,* IV, 76–78 and 456–458; Clavier, *Etudes sur le Calvinisme,* p. 84.

[283] *Supra,* p. 35.

ever explained in a way that would imply any admixture of human fallibility in Scripture, as if the inspired writer were not a perfect instrument of transmission for the message he received.

To Calvin the theologian an error in Scripture is unthinkable. Hence the endless harmonizing, the explaining and interpreting of passages that seem to contradict or to be inaccurate.[284] But Calvin the critical scholar recognizes mistakes with a disarming ingenuousness. The mistake or the gloss is simply a blunder made by an ignorant copyist. The criterion by which he judges it is simple grammar, arithmetic, and common sense.[285] I know of no instance in which Calvin draws any theological conclusions from the existence of error in the text or asks why the providence of God let it happen. He does not, like Luther, hold some other theological criterion higher than the canon itself. It is clearly a mild form of the "lower," not the "higher," criticism that he exercises. If Calvin has not seen fit to relate his doctrine of Scripture to his exegetical technique at this point, it would seem that Doumergue and the others should not do it for him, particularly not so as to modify another strand of his teaching where he himself did not appreciate the interrelation. This appears to be an instance of the incomplete assimilation of a traditional doctrine with the new manner of approaching the text. Suffice it to say—the discovery of occasional grammatical and even historical errors in the text plays no role in Calvin's view of the verbal inspiration of Scripture.

The two Calvins, theologian and humanist scholar, come closest to quarreling in the passages where New Testament writers misquote and even change the meaning of Old Testament passages. Calvin is sensitive to the slightest alterations, but never once does he admit a "mistake" at this level, for this would impugn the correctness of the Holy Spirit. Rather, the discrepancies are

[284] Hunter lists some of these, *The Teaching of Calvin*, pp. 72–74.

[285] Com. Gen. 46:9 (CO XXIII.561d–562a); Com. Acts 7:14 (CO XLVIII.137); Com. Mt. 1:6 (CO XLV.60d), 27:9 (749a), 23:35 (641a); Com. Eph. 2:5 (CO LII.164a); Com. Heb. 9:1 (CO LV.105d); Com. James 4:7 (CO LV.417b). Doumergue has collected numerous other examples, *Jean Calvin,* IV, 76–78, but only to conclude speciously that such errors attributed to transcribers are evidence against Calvin having conceived of the original inspiration as dictated and inerrant.

"accommodations" or simplifications, repeating the "substance" of the passage, or even changing it completely to accord with the purposes of revelation.[286] They are never inadvertencies. Thus, concretely even in these crucial passages Calvin never has to choose between his critical technique and his doctrine of inspiration, and he never has to state explicitly their interrelation. If he betrays his position at all, it is in apparently assuming a priori that no errors can be allowed to reflect upon the inerrancy of the original documents. If the latter be the case, the conclusions drawn by Doumergue and Clavier at this point do not hold.

The special revelation of God the Creator, then, was given by inspiration of God. This means by the dictation to prophets and apostles of sacred oracles which were often accompanied by visions, dreams, physical miracles, angelic messengers, and even theophany. It was the message transmitted that was central in this process. The accompanying phenomena were to prepare the mind to hear and to confirm it in the truth of the communications by showing that it was God who spoke. Because of the human tendency to forget and distort and invent, the oracles had to be recorded. "For if we consider how slippery is the human mind, sliding into forgetfulness of God, how prone to all kinds of error, how desirous of continually fabricating new and false religions, we can perceive how necessary is such a repository of heavenly doctrine, that it will neither perish by forgetfulness, nor vanish in error, nor be corrupted by the audacity of men." [287] This repository of doctrine is the Holy Scriptures. It is not, however, any given, specific and sacrosanct edition or translation of the Bible, but a hypothetical original document that is inerrantly inspired.

[286] Com. Ps. 8:3, 6 (CO XXXI.90c, 92d, 93c–d), 22:16 (228c–d), 68:19 (628a–629a); Com. Isa. 28:16 (CO XXXVI.474a–b), 64:3 (CO XXXVII.409a–c); Com. Mt. 8:17 (CO XLV.155d); Com. Rm. 3:4 (CO XLIX.48d–49a), 10:6 (199c–200a); Com. I Cor. 1:19 (CO XLIX.322d–324a), 2:9 (339, 340), the latter is especially good; Com. Eph. 4:8 (CO LI.194a–b); Com. Heb. 4:3 (CO LV. 46c). A perusal of these passages will show that for Calvin even the repetition of an error from the Septuagint by the New Testament writer is credited as conscious accommodation, not as failure to recognize the error.

[287] I.vi.3 (OS III.63.15–20).

The Witness of the Spirit to the Authority of the Bible

It is not with an alleged process of the inerrant transmission of oracles long ago from God to prophets and apostles that Calvin's doctrine of the authority of Scripture properly begins. This would be foreign to the whole genius of his thought, which is intensely living, present, and personal. This would be to depend for the certainty of faith upon the testimonies of men—albeit prophets and apostles—and God has made this forever suspect by arming even false prophets with miracles and warning that the cleverness of the anti-Christ would be such as to deceive the very elect should their faith be grounded in objective evidence. Rather, the believer's assurance that Scripture is the word of God comes directly and immediately from God himself. Yet it comes in such a way as to confirm, not to circumvent, the previous inspiration of the prophets, which we have already discussed.

For as God alone is a suitable witness for his own word, so also the word will never gain credit in the hearts of men until it is sealed by the internal testimony of the Spirit. It is necessary that the same Spirit who spoke by the mouth of the prophets should penetrate our hearts in order to convince us that they delivered faithfully the message which was divinely given.[288]

What witness has the believer that the prophets spoke what God commanded? Not a theory of inspiration, but the present witness of God himself given by the same Spirit which inspired the prophets.

If someone objects, "how can this be known?" [that Law and Prophets were "dictated" by God], I reply that God is made known to be the author, both to teachers and pupils, by the revelation (*revelatione*) of the same Spirit . . . The same Spirit, therefore, who made Moses and the prophets certain of their own calling now also testifies to our hearts that he has used them as his servants to instruct us. Thus, it is not surprising that so many have doubts as to the author of Scripture. For although the majesty of God is displayed in it, yet only those who have been illuminated by the Holy Spirit have eyes to discern what ought to have been seen by all, for it is visible to the elect alone.[289]

[288] I.vii.4 (OS III,70.2–8).

[289] Com. II Tim. 3:16 (CO LII.383b).

The Spirit "convinces us that they delivered faithfully the message," and "testifies to our hearts that God had used them as his servants to instruct us." This is not the recognition of truth through an inconsequential medium. It is an accrediting of the medium itself, it is a sanction for the prophets' own claim that they spoke for God. It is a doctrine of the internal witness of the Spirit that has as its necessary corollary, not a general doctrine of truth,[290] but the inspiration of certain individuals by whom God chose to bring into the world a truth that is available nowhere else. By thus confirming the outer through the inner witness and identifying both as the "same Spirit" Calvin binds together a high objective evaluation of the Bible with the principle that "God alone is a suitable witness for his own word."[291] For this Dorner praises Calvin in contrast to Zwingli, who in his zeal to avoid bibliolatry reduces the external word to a "spur" or "incentive" or "signal," "whose purpose is to incite us to seek the truth inwardly."[292] "The doubleness of the *Verbum Dei externum* and *internum* of Zwingli is softened by Calvin by virtue of a more inward union of both sides. Scripture is to him not the mere sign of something absent, but has the divine content, the divine breath, within itself, which makes itself felt."[293]

Reinhold Seeberg describes the relation between the inspiration of the Scripture and the testimony of the Holy Spirit as if they were for Calvin twin supports for revelation.

Calvin therefore founded the authority of the Holy Scripture on the one hand on the idea that it is divine dictation, on the other upon the witness of the Holy Spirit which goes out from or falls upon the Scrip-

[290] Calvin has a doctrine of universal truth, in which all truth found among the pagans is the work of the Spirit and is to be recognized as such, II.ii.13–15; cf. Com. Titus 1:12 (CO LII.415a); Com. Jn. 4:36 (CO XLVII.96b). In *Psychopannychia,* he buttresses a quotation from Job with one from Ecclesiasticus 37:28, then adds "But as the authority of that writer is doubtful, let us leave him, and listen to a prophet admirably teaching the same thing in his own words." (CO V.230c). Thus, not only objective truth but also where it is found recorded is important to Calvin.

[291] V. *supra,* n. 288.

[292] Dorner, *Geschichte der protestantischen Theologie,* p. 290.

[293] *Ibid.,* p. 380.

ture. Viewed historically, he combined the idea of inspiration of the late Middle Ages with Luther's conception.[294]

This is a neat analysis, but not quite true to Calvin's doctrine as we have already presented it. Because Seeberg has arranged the outer and the inner word side by side, he is offended when Calvin at times implies that the Scripture carries its own authority, and again that the authority is from the inner testimony.[295] This "dissonance"[296] however, does not really occur, because it is a misreading of Calvin to construct, as Seeberg has done, an independent support for the authority of the Bible out of the "dictation" passages.[297] True enough, the Bible has intrinsic validity. But this does not constitute its authority or even one source of its authority. The authority derives solely from the inner witness of God himself through which the intrinsic validity or inherent truth of the sacred oracles is recognized and confirmed. The "dictated" word and the subjective witness are not, as Seeberg implies, two ways of knowing God before which man stands and between which Calvin "fluctuates" in deriving Scriptural authority. Clearly the internal testimony is witness to the truth of the external word, and "dictation" (whether taken figuratively or literally) is an answer to the subsequent question of how the writings came to be. "Faith in the divine truth is the condition of, not the result of, true belief in the inspiration of the Scriptures."[298]

The objective revelation is there, or "out there" in Scripture, which is *ἀυτόπιστον*, self-authenticating. But it is "self" authenticating only to those who have been empowered by the Spirit to perceive this authentication.

Let it therefore remain fixed that those who have been taught inwardly by the Holy Spirit assent fully to Scripture; which being, indeed, self-authenticating and not subject to demonstrations and reasonings, yet rather obtains among us the credit it deserves by the testi-

[294] *Lehrbuch der Dogmengeschichte,* p. 569.

[295] "Sometimes the Bible receives its authority through its contents; again, it is by virtue of its authority that recognition is conferred upon the contents." *Ibid.,* p. 591.

[296] *Ibid.,* p. 568.

[297] *Ibid.,* p. 566 f.

[298] Dorner, *Geschichte der protestantischen Theologie,* p. 380.

mony of the Spirit. For although of itself it commands our reverence by its own majesty, nevertheless it seriously affects us only when it has been impressed on our hearts by the Spirit. Therefore, illuminated by him, we now believe that the Scriptures are from God, not from our own judgment or that of any others, but above human judgment we establish a certainty more firm, as much as if we beheld the divinity of God himself (*ipsius Dei numen*) in it, that it came to us by the ministry of men from the very mouth of God (*ipsissimo Dei ore*).[299]

The question of certainty supplies the dominant motif in Calvin's doctrine of Biblical authority, as well as his doctrine of faith in general. No hearsay about God can be the foundation of Christian assurance. The whole doctrine of Scripture is introduced to "remove all doubt,"[300] to give an "indubitable persuasion,"[301] "the assurance which piety requires,"[302] founded on "certain and solid truth,"[303] which will support "wretched consciences, seeking solid assurance of eternal life,"[304] and give a foundation for the "certainty of the pious."[305] Within the doctrine of Scripture it is the *testimonium internum Spiritus Sancti* which is meant to take the weight of the authority of Scripture off of unstable supports and rest it solely upon the "author," God.[306] In the search for a firm foundation Calvin rejects the authority of the church on two grounds: first, at best church authority is only the uncertain "judgment of men,"[307] and secondly, such legitimate authority as the church has is derived from Scripture, not vice versa.[308]

The divine origin of Scripture, the fact that it has come "from heaven,"[309] is that to which the Spirit gives witness, and this transfers authority from men to God. The "highest proof" of the Scripture is the "character of God," who has spoken in it.[310] The prophets and apostles furnish the pattern in that they do not "insist upon reasons, but bring forth the sacred name of God, by which the whole world may be compelled to submission."[311]

[299] I.vii.5 (OS III.70.16–26).
[300] I.vii.1 (OS III.65.7).
[301] I.vii.4 (OS III.68.29).
[302] *Ibid.* (p. 69.33).
[303] I.vii.3 (OS III.68.26).
[304] I.vii.1 (OS III.66.9).
[305] I.vii.3 (OS III.68.11), cf. (p. 70.14).
[306] I.vii.4 (OS III.68.29).
[307] I.vii.1 (OS III.66.10).
[308] I.vii.2 (OS III.66.16 ff.).
[309] I.viii.1 (OS III.65.15).
[310] I.vii.4 (OS III.68.30).
[311] *Ibid.* (p. 69.3–4).

Now if we wish to consult the best interest of our consciences, that they may not be unstable, carried round about in perpetual doubts, or wavering, or hesitating at the slightest scruples—this persuasion must be sought for higher than human reasons, judgments, or conjectures, namely, from the secret testimony of the Spirit.[312]

We do not seek arguments or probabilities on which to rest our judgment, but we subject our judgment and intellect as to a thing elevated above the necessity of being judged.[313]

The "judgments of men," however certain, even if they include the consensus of the church, are not strong enough for the "solid assurance" of faith.[314] This, however, does not mean that the mind of man is untouched by the testimony of the Spirit any more than that the *testimonium Spiritus Sancti* belies the out-there-ness of God's word in the Bible. Accepting the authority of Scripture is not a hasty, ill-considered capitulation of the mind or abandonment of reason. The mind itself is caught up in a higher, transcendant kind of knowing. It is rationally convinced, yet the conviction rises far above what can be rationally grasped. Calvin puts it eloquently. We are

indeed not like those who are wont sometimes hurriedly to take hold of something unknown, which displeases as soon as it is examined, but we have rightly a conviction that we hold an invincible truth. Nor are we like those wretched men who surrender their minds captive to superstition, but we feel indubitably a divine energy (*vim numinis*) living and breathing in it [Scripture], by whch we are drawn and inflamed to yield, knowingly, indeed, and willingly—but it is more vivid and effectual than any human will or knowledge. . . . It is therefore such a persuasion (*persuasio*) as requires no reasons; such a knowledge (*notitia*) as that to which highest reason agrees, indeed, in which the mind rests more securely and steadily than in any reasons; it is finally such a perception (*sensus*) as could not be produced by anything but a revelation from heaven. I say nothing but what every believer experiences himself, except that my words fall short of a just explanation of the thing.[315]

312 I.vii.4 (OS III.69.7–11).

313 I.vii.5 (OS III.70.26–30); cf. (CO III.96d), "comme à une chose élevée par dessus la necessité d'estre iugée."

314 I.vii.1 (OS III.66.10).

315 I.vii.5 (OS III.70.30–71.14).

This is neither intellectualism nor anti-intellectualism. The "judgment of men," human reason, is not battered down, but is "inflamed," "ignited," and "drawn along." "Highest reason agrees."[316] Still, as the conviction is beyond all comprehension, we come finally beyond all mere reasonings to such a perception as if we beheld the divinity of God himself in it. "In a peculiar way a strong spiritualism and a lively Biblicism are here intertwined."[317] The believer's certainty, therefore, which thus far we have discussed only in terms of Biblical authority, is the certainty of a mind that concurs understandingly in that of which it is convinced and at the same time rises beyond what it can explicitly comprehend to participate in the mystery of revelation.

We see, then, that the Biblical revelation is intrinsically valid, but that it has authority with us only when the *testimonium internum Spiritus Sancti* accredits that validity.

Now we can look at (down at!) the so-called proofs by which the Bible is said to be demonstrably the word of God. This is exactly what Calvin does. These proofs do not constitute the rationality or reasonableness or convincingness of which we have just spoken, by which the mind willingly assents to Biblical authority. That quality is found in the overwhelming persuasiveness of the revelation itself by which the mind finds its true home in the truth of God. These, on the other hand, are *indicia* (Warfield), or evidences brought to court. They are not the truth of God, but statements about the Bible, based upon observed facts.

[316] Lobstein, "La Connaissance religieuse," does injustice to Calvin's doctrine of the testimony of the Spirit by equating its witness to Scripture too quickly with scholastic "belief" (*croyance*) as against another motif in Calvin's theology, which he calls evangelical "faith" (*foi*), e.g., pp. 82–85, 105 f. We shall criticize Calvin, below, for incongruity between his doctrines of Scripture and of faith in Christ, but not at the expense of a full evaluation of both.

[317] Seeberg, *Lehrbuch der Dogmengeschichte*, p. 594. These words are from Seeberg's evaluation of Calvin's doctrine of faith. They apply here for obvious reasons. The quotation continues: "These two elements both delimit and complete one another. In this union they call forth a piety in which a rigid Biblicism and a pious subjectivism demand one another and promote one another." Because Seeberg fails to pursue the theme of the revelatory work of the Spirit in faith as given in III.ii, much that he says, pp. 592–594, about faith and certainty is more applicable to the problem of the authority of Scripture than that of faith proper, where the theme of certainty culminates for Calvin in the doctrine of election and the concept of union with Christ, v., *infra*, pp. 185, 197.

By their very nature they cannot be regarded as essential because some of them, for example, the antiquity of the books and their survival intact could not possibly have been known by early believers. They have neither the immediacy nor the irrefragability of Calvin's doctrine of the testimony of the Spirit. They are the subjects of argument, observation, discussion—which is the function Calvin allows them to serve [318]—and never once are brought into the correlation of word and Spirit in which the believer's assurance is founded.

We must note well that in the *Institutes* Calvin has already completed his argument for the validity of Scripture in I.vii before he turns to these "secondary aids to our weakness." He introduces the *probationes* with a strong warning to this effect:

> without this [aforementioned] certainty, in every way better and stronger than human judgment, the Scripture will in vain be fortified by arguments, or established by the consent of the church, or confirmed by any other supports; since, unless this foundation be laid, it remain always in suspense. On the other hand, when recognizing it as exempt from the common rule, we once receive it religiously (*religiose*) and according to its dignity, then those things which were not strong enough to produce and fix the certainty of it in our minds, are most appropriate helps.[319]

Having given this precondition—"once religiously received"—Calvin enumerates some of the human arguments which assist our faith in Scripture "in so far as natural reason admits."

With reference to the Old Testament, Calvin points to the sublimity of the matter, related in both humble and eloquent style; the antiquity of the books; the honesty of the writers in reporting disgraces of the patriarchs; the miracles, publicly attested—this flagrantly begs the question, since the books under scrutiny contain also the attestation; predictive prophecies subsequently seen to have been fulfilled; and the fact of the preservation of the text through the often-precarious exigencies of history.[320] More sketchily for the New Testament, he cites the ability of unlettered men to expound heavenly mysteries; the

[318] I.vii.3, 4; I.viii, *passim.*, e.g., par. 13.

[319] I.viii. 1 (OS III.71.39–72.6).

[320] I.vii.1–10, *passim.*

survival of the books intact; the universal consent of the church; and the blood of the many martyrs who died in witness to the Biblical faith.[321] And

> there are other reasons, neither few nor weak, by which the dignity and majesty of the Scriptures not only are maintained in the hearts of the pious but also are completely vindicated against the subtleties of calumniators; but such as alone are not strong enough to produce firm faith in it until the heavenly Father frees the reverence due it from all controversy by manifesting his own divinity therein. Wherefore the Scripture will suffice to give a saving knowledge of God only when it is founded on the internal persuasion of the Holy Spirit. Indeed, those human testimonies which stand in confirmation of it will not be without effect if they follow that first and highest proof as secondary aids to our weakness (*secundaria nostrae imbecillitatis adminicula*). But those persons act foolishly who wish to prove to infidels that Scripture is the word of God, which cannot be known except by faith.[322]

There we have both the arguments and their evaluation.

These arguments are of uneven value, and some of them have become quite useless, at least in the form Calvin gave them, since modern historical method and the historical criticism of the Scripture. For example, in the argument from antiquity Calvin asserts that the Scripture is the oldest of all books and jokes about the Egyptians whose false chronicles extend their own antiquity to a point beyond the creation of the world.[323] Correspondingly, the mere survival of the books is not so impressive today as it was to Calvin. The arguments from predictive prophecy are mechanical and go rather too heavily on the traditional dating of the Penteteuch, Deutero-Isaiah, and Daniel, to serve us now without refurbishing,[324] and the chronicles of patriarchal disgrace might well be construed as examples of human honesty rather than proofs of divine inspiration. Others, such as the sublimity of the matter when contrasted with even the greatest non-Biblical writers, the consent of the church, and the price willingly paid by the martyrs cannot fail to impress a reader, although none of them

[321] I.viii.11 f., *passim*.

[322] I.viii.13 (OS III.81.17–29).

[323] I.viii.3, 4.

[324] I.viii.7, 8.

leads necessarily to conclusions about the divine origin of Scripture. Our main concern, however, is not with the details of these arguments and their individual validity, but their place in Calvin's theology as contributions to the knowledge of God. Here there is interesting divergence of opinion among Calvin scholars.

Doumergue and Pannier both take note of Calvin's expansion of the rational arguments across the years [325]—Pannier, almost with alarm. Both fully appreciate, however, the nonessential role of these proofs in Calvin's theology, although Doumergue characteristically appraises their descriptive value higher than Pannier. Of *la grande preuve* Doumergue exclaims, "The divinity of the Bible directly sensible to the heart of the faithful; certainty immediate and divine, the most certain of certainties and the only sufficient one; in a word, the testimony of the Holy Spirit!" [326] Concerning the miracles and other *preuves subsidiaires,* he asserts that Calvin "gives the great place to the great miracle, the testimony of the Holy Spirit," and carefully surrounds whatever he says of these proofs with the doctrine of the inner witness.[327] Pannier, without reservation, attributes the "divinity, integrity, unity, authenticity, and canonicity of Scripture" to the witness of the Spirit alone.[328] As for the rational arguments, "Theological controversies with the learned lead him to delineate at times, from an apologetic point of view, some rational arguments which he had discarded a priori. But these were always for him 'helps and secondary means to aid us in our imbecility.'" [329] Seeberg does not consider the rational proofs even worth mentioning. This is striking, since he makes much of the idea of dictation and the resultant infallible book. Nonetheless, he shows along with the two men just mentioned a very keen perception of the fact that the "self-authenticating" quality of Scripture is part of the terminology of faith for Calvin, one of the chief attributes of God's revelation, and that therefore it be-

[325] Doumergue, *Jean Calvin,* IV, 60–62, Pannier, *Le Témoignage du Saint-Esprit,* pp. 96–101. [326] *Jean Calvin,* IV, 59.

[327] *Ibid.,* p. 62.

[328] *Le Témoignage du Saint-Esprit,* p. 83, cf. p. 202.

[329] *Ibid.,* p. 104.

longs to the basic correlation of word and Spirit and does not depend upon these secondary human observations about Scripture. "For Calvin, this second way of looking at Scripture according to which the Scripture itself brings the Spirit—for which the property ἀυτόπιστον esse is the fitting designation—is only an abbreviation of the first—the witness of the Spirit." [330]

While Doumergue has highest praise for *les preuves subsidiaires*—higher than anyone else except Warfield—he keeps them, as we have seen, in the secondary role to which Calvin assigned them. Across the danger line in this regard are Köstlin, who does not personally value the "proofs" very highly, and Warfield, who admires them. Köstlin regards the *indicia,* of course, as secondary, but sees in them, particularly the miracle stories,[331] the objective excellencies of Scripture which impress us and *through which God works from without*—in contrast to the inner testimony.[332] He reproves Calvin for not having related the two after placing them "side by side." [333] Warfield agrees with Köstlin that "Calvin has not at this point developed this side of his subject with the fullness which might be wished," [334] then he explains what Calvin "thought" on the subject, over and above what he actually said. Since Calvin has said that the *indicia* are "aids" to the believer, Warfield sets out to describe the nature of that aid. He does it in such a way that he formulates for Calvin a doctrine contrary to Calvin's own.

> But what about the *indicia* in conjunction with the testimony of the Spirit? It would seem to be evident that on Calvin's ground they would have their full part to play here and that we must say that when the soul is renewed by the Holy Spirit to a sense for the divinity of Scripture it is through the *indicia* of that divinity of Scripture. In treating of the *indicia,* Calvin does not, however, declare this in so many words. . . . Of their part in forming faith under the operation of the testimony of the Spirit, he does not appear explicitly to speak . . .[335]

[330] Seeberg, *Lehrbuch der Dogmengeschichte,* p. 569.
[331] Which Calvin included among the evidences for the first time in ed. '50.
[332] "Calvins Institutio nach Form und Inhalt," pp. 412 f.
[333] *Ibid.,* p. 413.
[334] *Calvin and Calvinism,* p. 90.
[335] *Ibid.,* p. 87.

Nevertheless, there are not lacking convincing hints that there was lying in his mind all the time the implicit understanding that it is through these *indicia* of the divinity of Scripture that the soul, under the operation of the testimony of the Spirit, reaches its sound faith in Scripture, and that he has been withheld from more explicitly stating this only by the warmth of his zeal for the necessity of the testimony of the Spirit which has led him to a constant contrasting of this divine with these human "testimonies." Thus, we find him repeatedly affirming that these *indicia* will produce no fruit *until* they be confirmed by the internal testimony of the Spirit . . .[336] he thought of the *indicia* as *co-working with the testimony of the Spirit* to this result . . .[337] we must accredit Calvin as thinking of the newly implanted spiritual sense discerning the divinity of Scripture only *through the mediation of the indicia* [!] of divinity manifested in the Scripture.[338]

What Warfield does here is to elevate the *indicia,* or statements *about* Scripture, to a level of importance equal to that of the text of Scripture itself. The mysterious divinity of Scripture, which for Calvin is the divinity of God himself secretly perceived, becomes for Warfield assent to these rational arguments. "To taste and see that the Scriptures are divine is to recognize a divinity actually present in Scripture; and, of course, recognition implies perception of *indicia,* not attribution of a divinity not recognized as inherent."[339] With the first part of this sentence we agree heartily. In the second part, however, which identifies the divinity of Scripture "of course" with the "secondary aids," we see a serious departure from Calvin. It is, in fact, the very thing Calvin was trying to avoid in his doctrine of the internal testimony. Warfield's view would bind together one of the permanent contributions of Calvin to theology, the doctrine of the *testimonium internum Spiritus Sancti,* with one of the most impermanent elements of his system, the rational proofs of Scripture. It is precisely Calvin's refusal to do this, even in a century when his *indicia* were less dubious than they are today and though he considered them so cogent that with them an unskilled arguer could defeat all opposition—that marks his theological genius.

[336] *Calvin and Calvinism,* p. 89.
[337] *Ibid.,* p. 89, italics added.
[338] *Ibid.,* p. 90, italics added.
[339] *Ibid.*

We can best sum up our preceding argument by using the word-pair "word and Spirit." These terms express the heart of Calvin's doctrine of special revelation, as far as he treats of it with reference to the revelation of God the Creator.

The word itself has not much certainty with us unless confirmed by the testimony of the Spirit. For the Lord has joined together by a kind of mutual connection the certainty of his word and Spirit so that our minds are possessed of a genuine reverence for the word when the Spirit shines upon it, enabling us there to behold the face of God; and on the other hand, we embrace the Spirit without fear of illusion when we recognize him in his image, that is, in his word.[340]

"The word is the instrument (*organum*) by which the Lord dispenses to believers the illumination of his Spirit." [341] The word is the Scripture, the oracles of God objectified—previously inspired and recorded. The Spirit's testimony is the present subjective illumination by which alone the Scripture is recognized for what it is.[342] "God works in his elect in two ways: internally by the Spirit and externally by the word." [343] These two elements are not to be separated from one another. They are functionally one term. I.viii makes the most of the independent *indicia,* but begins and ends with a warning against abstracting Spirit from word or word from Spirit. Granting that the oracles were dictated letter perfect, Calvin is unwilling to make them an autonomous authority apart from the living witness of the Spirit, and granting the living witness of the Spirit, Calvin is unashamed to call the Spirit to an "examination" (*examen*) and hold him to the "letter" (*litera*) of what he formerly revealed.[344] "We are governed not less by the voice of God (*voce Dei*) than by the Spirit; hence we infer that those villains are guilty of detestable sacrilege who tear apart that which the prophet (Isaiah 49:21) has connected in an inviolable union.[345]

[340] I.ix.3 (OS III.84.13–20). [341] I.ix.3 (OS III.84.37).
[342] Köstlin, "Calvins Institutio nach Form und Inhalt," p. 417.
[343] II.v.5 (OS III.303.11) and throughout the paragraph.
[344] I.ix.1–2 (OS III.83.29 and 84.3, and *passim,* pp. 83 f.).
[345] I.ix.1 (OS III.82.19–21).

In one bold stroke, by the exact correlation of word and Spirit, Calvin answered in principle the question of the canon.[346] He devotes no separate dogmatic or historical treatment to it in the *Institutes* apart from the section on the witness of the Spirit in I.vii–ix. And here there is no indication that a separate canonical problem exists for Calvin. That is, he is under no compulsion to *construct* a canon, let us say on historico-critical grounds, nor even to defend the existing canon so far as its accepted composition was concerned. Evidently he was not greatly impressed with Castellio's humanistic objections to the Song of Songs. He mentions the number of books to be taken as Scripture, not as if it were his task to determine it, but only in contesting the authority of the Roman Church to add the Apocrypha to it. The latter, however, is no problem to Calvin's own theology, as he does not find the "majesty of the Spirit" in the Apocrypha. If there were some other criterion than the Spirit for the recognition of Scripture, Calvin would be inexcusable for not having devoted a section to it in his systematic masterpiece. In fact, it is not his conception of his theological task to construct a canon on historico-critical grounds, as Warfield would have it, and then see if the Spirit approves.[347]

346 The distinction between "canon" as an official list of books determining the extent of Scripture and "canon" meaning "divinely given" (Warfield, "Doctrine of the Knowledge," *Calvin and Calvinism*, pp. 97 ff.) is foreign to Calvin, except when he disowns an incorrect "canon," e.g.,IV.ix.14. I use the term solely in the second sense, which Lecerf calls "the purely religious sense," as the only one meaningful to Calvin.

347 "Far from discarding the *via rationalis* here, he determined the limits of the canon and established the integrity of the transmission of Scripture distinctly on scientific, that is to say, historico-critical grounds," *Calvin and Calvinism*, p. 92. "Calvin's own practice in dealing with the question of canonicity and text makes it sufficiently clear that he held their settlement to depend on scientific investigation, and appealed to the testimony of the Spirit only to accredit the divine origin of the concrete volume thus put into his hands," *ibid.*, p. 101. Warfield's elaborate case for this interpretation is made in an effort to defend Calvin from the criticism that he "conceived the mode of the delivery of the testimony of the Spirit to be the creation in the soul of a blind faith, unmotivated by reasons and without rooting in grounds," *ibid.*, p. 91. These "grounds" are, as in Warfield's interpretation of the *indicia*, so complete that had Calvin concurred, he would never have needed to have formulated the doctrine of the internal testimony. Against Warfield, and Cramer as cited by Warfield are the equally enthusiastic Calvinists: Pannier, *Le Témoignage du Saint-Esprit*, pp. 197–207; Reuss, *Die Geschichte der Heiligen Schriften*, II, 335, 549; and more recently, Auguste Lecerf, *Introduction to Re-*

Who can persuade us that this book ought to be received with reverence and that expunged from the list (*numero*) unless the church prescribes the rule of all these things with certainty? It depends, therefore, they say, upon the determination of the church what reverence is paid to Scipture and which books are to be inscribed (*conscendi sint*) in its canon (*catalogo*). . . .[348] But if this is so, what is to become of miserable consciences seeking a solid assurance of eternal life, if all the extant promises concerning it rest solely upon the judgments of men? [349]

As for the question, "How shall we be persuaded that it came from God without having recourse to the decree of the church?" This is just as if anyone should inquire, "How shall we learn to distinguish light from darkness, white from black, sweet from bitter?" For Scripture does not exhibit its own truth more obscurely than white or black things their color, and sweet or bitter things their taste.[350]

---

formed Dogmatics, as well as the Lutheran Köstlin, "Calvins Institutio nach Form und Inhalt," p. 419. Lecerf writes, "For Rome, the canon derives its authority *quoad nos* from the authority of the teaching church. The originality of the Reformers' view consisted in reversing these terms and basing the Church on canonical Scripture, whose authority is founded immediately on the testimony which God himself renders to it," p. 338. "The subject of the present chapter and the two following [on the determination of the canon] is the testimony of the Holy Spirit," p. 321. Cf. *ibid.,* pp. 319–347, for an interesting attempt to remain true to Calvin's doctrine of the immediate witness of the Spirit to the canon, while taking into consideration relativities in the historical development of the canon of which Calvin was not aware and which are fatal to Warfield's view. Warfield's interpretation, however, is of compelling interest, because it is an example as recent as 1911, implimented by vast learning, of that same powerful drive toward rationalistic orthodoxy that has marked Calvinism since Calvin himself. Even though there was much of this in Calvin, it did not conquer his essential genius. For the degree to which this went in Warfield see the unlikely process of establishing the canon that he attributes to the Reformer, *infra,* p. 123. Warfield, *Calvin and Calvinism,* p. 49, quotes Leipoldt as follows: "We obtain the impression that it is only for form's sake that Calvin undertakes to test whether the disputed books are canonical or not. In reality it is already a settled matter with him that they are. Calvin feels himself therefore in the matter of the New Testament canon bound to medieval tradition," *Geschichte des Neuen Testamentlichen Kanons,* II, 140.

348 Calvin's own French of ed. '60 adds "le congé de discerner entre les livres Apocriphes" (OS III.66, note a).

349 I.vii.1 (OS III.65.26–66.11). Warfield regards this passage as Calvin's rejection of the authority of the church over Scripture, but he says it does not imply Calvin's own way of arriving at the canon, *Calvin and Calvinism,* p. 94.

350 I.vii.2 (OS III.67.2–7).

Scripture is "not subject to demonstrations and reasonings, yet rather obtains among us the credit it deserves by the testimony of the Spirit."[351] Of a passage in II Maccabees he says, "How very alien this acknowledgment from the majesty of the Holy Spirit!"[352] Elsewhere, "It is true [the Apocrypha] are not to be despised, seeing that they contain good and useful doctrine. Nevertheless, it is only right that what we have been given by the Holy Spirit should have pre-eminence above all that has come from men."[353]

It is not inappropriate to recall here that it was the Spirit, not the unlikely objective evidence that differentiated Balaam's true prophecies from his false ones and caused the Israelites to accept the words of Moses rather than Pharaoh, although the latter's magicians were also empowered with miracles.[354]

Yet, although the doctrine of word and Spirit answers the question of the canon in principle and gives him concretely the sixty-six traditional books, Calvin's approach to criticism of the canon outside the *Institutes* is not a priori, but a posteriori. He does not reply to critics with a monolithic canon, but meets objections on the merits of individual books, and in one instance, of a single passage. That this is possible results from one of the master strokes of his doctrine, for the authority of special revelation is not an a priori proposition, but is sensed like a color or flavor in the actual experience of Scripture.[355] Faith does not entail the acceptance of a formal proposition concerning the ex-

[351] I.viii.5 (OS III.65.7).

[352] "Acts of the Council of Trent, with Antidote" (CO VII.413d).

[353] Preface to the Apocryphal Books (CO IX.827).

[354] *Supra,* p. 97.

[355] Calvin is not so flexible as to establish a subjective canon of revelatory passages as they appear to the individual. Clavier's catalogue of Calvin's practical canon consisting of the frequency of his illusions to various books, *Etudes sur le Calvinisme,* p. 87, shows what he considered central or peripheral with regard to the Gospel. But Calvin still does not distinguish degrees of inspiration. Whatever writing is accepted is taken *en bloc,* and the same faultless authority is ascribed to historical material as in central doctrinal passages. If we should dare the Barthian expression that the Bible "becomes" the word of God in faith, we must confess that it becomes it for Calvin by book-size units. To this degree we can approve Seeberg's criticism that "the founding on religious experience is weak because experience by no means attests every single word of Scripture," *op. cit.,* p. 569, n. 1.

tent of Scripture as catalogued in the Reformed confessions or by the Roman church, but faith results, a posteriori, in the acceptance of all the sacred books. The true canon is constant in all ages. Yet this uniformity does not come from the authority of tradition or a council, nor any other source outside the experience of the individual Christian. It exists because of the constancy of the Holy Spirit who does not vary his witness from individual to individual. As the church is composed of the individually "called," but has a constant character, so the internal witness of the same Spirit produces throughout the years a constant canon. Thus, Castellio can be admonished not to scorn the consensus of the church concerning the Song of Songs, while at the same time the real reason for his dismissal was that the consistory did not wish to introduce the precedent of "discussing whether or not a book is worthy of the Holy Spirit." [356] Thus, also, Calvin can deal a posteriori with the specific problems of certain books when they are questioned, at the same time ending with the traditional canon judged by the Spirit's witness, as we shall now see.

John 8:1–11 was "unknown formerly to the Greek churches. . . . But because it has always been received by the Latin churches, and is found in many old Greek manuscripts, and contains nothing unworthy of an apostolic spirit, we will not refuse to apply it to our own advantage." [357] Only the "cunning of Satan" could have caused the reluctant acceptance of the Epistle to the Hebrews, since it "speaks so clearly of the priesthood of Christ . . . so fully explains that Christ is the end of the law," and so forth, although its author is unknown.[358] The Epistle of James "contains nothing unworthy of an apostle of Christ," and "though it seems more sparing in proclaiming the grace of Christ than it behoved an apostle to be," the difference is no wider than that elsewhere observable between the Psalms and the Wisdom literature or John the Evangelist as against the "other three." [359] II Peter, although in a style not Peter's, contains "nothing unworthy of Peter,

[356] Cited by Warfield, *Calvin and Calvinism*, p. 53.
[357] Com. Jn. 8:3 (CO XLVII.188c).
[358] Com. Heb. "Argument" (CO LV.5b).
[359] Com. James, "Argument" (CO LV.381).

so that it shows everywhere the power and grace of an apostolic spirit."[360] Since "in every part of the Epistle the majesty of the Spirit of Christ appears,"[361] Calvin will not repudiate it.

The situation throughout is the same: the author unknown and the writing questioned by or unknown to some part of the early church, yet Calvin accepts it upon recognition of "apostolic doctrine" or "the majesty of the Spirit," which are two ways of stating the same thing. True, the appeal is not to the Spirit with that immediacy which we might expect on the basis of the teaching of the *Institutes*—citing the "apostolic doctrine" implies testing the antilegomena by the homologoumena as the process by which the "bitter" and "sweet" are tasted—and Calvin does not rail at those who reject James and II Peter as he usually does against those he regards as corrupters of the word. Castellio was not allowed to minister because of rejecting the Song of Songs, but Calvin wrote, "If he was not admitted, it is not some impious doctrine or a chief point of the faith which stands in the way."[362] Further, Calvin's words as remembered by Jean Bodin would not seem to imply great zeal in the defense of the Apocalypse, although he does quote it as Scripture. Bodin said,

> I thoroughly approve of the reply of Calvin, not less polished than sagacious, when he was asked his opinion about the book of the Apocalypse. He candidly answered that he was totally at a loss regarding the meaning of this obscure writer, whose identity was not yet agreed upon among the erudite.[363]

While the latter examples of Calvin's practice, as compared with his doctrine in the *Institutes,* forbid the flat proposition that for Calvin the testimony of the Spirit marks out the canon in the sense of proposing mechanically to the believer the sixty-six books in a lump, they do not alter our contention that it is in the correlation of word and Spirit that the Biblical canon has its existence.

Warfield contends that Calvin makes a complete historico-

[360] Com. II Peter, "Argument" (CO LV.441c).
[361] *Ibid.* (p. 441d).
[362] Cited in Pannier, *Le Témoignage du Saint-Esprit,* p. 119.
[363] John Bodin, *Method for the Easy Comprehension of History,* p. 291.

critical case for a book before considering the testimony of the Spirit.

The movement of his thought was therefore along this course: first, the ascertainment, on scientific grounds, of the body of books handed down from the Apostles as the rule of faith and practice; secondly, the vindication, on the same class of grounds, of the integrity of their transmission; thirdly, the accrediting of them as divine on the testimony of the Spirit.[364]

Cramer regards this alleged critical process as inconsistent with the doctrine of the Spirit's witness.[365] Neither of these interpretations, however, can cope with such a rude dismissal of critical opinion, albeit only in defending one of the *indicia,* as where Calvin suggests corporal punishment for those who doubt that Moses ever lived.[366] And elsewhere, in the "Argument" to II Peter, Calvin writes,

If it be received as canonical (*pro canonica*) [and it is, on the strength of its "apostolic doctrine"], it is necessary to acknowledge that Peter is the author, not only because it has his name inscribed but also because it testifies that the writer had lived with Christ. . . . So then I conclude, that if the Epistle be deemed worthy of credit, it must have proceeded from Peter.[367]

However, recognizing a style not Peter's, Calvin satisfies himself with the critical makeshift that someone else recorded what was genuinely Peter's teaching.[368] The important thing to note is that the "historico-critical" data is in this instance arranged after the book is accepted on other grounds.

Although for Calvin the authorship of II Peter was dubious and that of James and Hebrews unknown, he in no concrete instance found the historical evidence damaging to the authenticity of any of the received books. This, however, is not so impressive as the fact that, as with the *probationes* (I.viii), he was finally independent of such evidence. His doctrine of the testimony of the Spirit points to a miraculous, supernaturally induced, suprarational conviction that is essentially inaccessible to criticism that remains

364 "Doctrine of the Knowledge," *Calvin and Calvinism*, p. 102.
365 Cited by Warfield, *ibid.*, p. 101.
366 I.viii.9 (OS III.77.30).
367 (CO LV.441c).
368 *Ibid.* (p. 441d).

on the level of the historical and rational. He believed that in critical matters he had in nearly all instances indubitable historico-critical corroboration of revealed truth, and of course he never envisioned having to do without such material. But he did not allow himself to lean upon this evidence, like a Mohammedan *isnad,* for such an important matter of faith as the delimitation of the boundaries of the canon of Scripture.[369]

Calvin offers finally no other standard by which believers can recognize Scripture than the *testimonium internum Spiritus Sancti,* a concept he introduces specifically for the purpose of accrediting Scripture. What is "accredited" (Warfield's term) is not a historico-critical pedigree, but the word of God in the form of Scripture.[370] His whole doctrine of revelation rests confidently upon the correlation of word and Spirit, whereby the previously inspired oracles are identified as such by the subjective illumination of the mind of the believer. It cannot be denied that this tends to exalt a book rather than a Person as the object of faith. At the same time, such a verdict as this cannot be pronounced until we have investigated Calvin's entire doctrine of faith in the Redeemer. For the present, we have simply observed Calvin supporting his contention that God has given in Scripture a valid special revelation of himself as Creator. We shall now analyze the contents of this revelation and its relation to the general revelation.

THE KNOWLEDGE CONTENT OF SCRIPTURE WITH REFERENCE TO GOD THE CREATOR.—As a result of two special acts of God, inspiration and revelation, which in concrete, personal experience are the giving of the objective word and the subjective testimony of the Spirit, mankind has a special revelation in addition to the general revelation of God the Creator. The content of the special revela-

[369] Lehmann points out that both Luther and Calvin accepted naïve, sixteenth-century views of the scientific corroboration of Biblical material, "but that holding them, they made the case for the Bible on quite other terms." "The Reformers' Use of the Bible," p. 342.

[370] If the evidence is scanty on this problem of the canon as compared with some others, it may be because apart from the apocryphal books Calvin was neither attacking nor fearful of attacks upon the traditional canon. Normally, the areas of his theology where he broke with tradition or fought innovation are those of expanded and polemic treatment.

tion can be easily and briefly summarized if we keep to the problem of theological epistemology and do not discuss these doctrines in detail. This knowledge of the Creator in Scripture is of two classes: (1) that still obtainable in creation with the aid of the "spectacles" of Scripture [371] and (2) that available solely in Scripture.

What are the "marks and tokens" [372] of God the Creator "committed, as it were, to public records," [373] which he gave to his church in addition to the "mute teachers"? [374] "Moses seems to have wished to comprehend briefly whatever it is possible for men to know concerning him," in the words of Exodus 34:6 f.[375]

Here we may observe that his eternity and self-existence (ἀυτοσίαν) are proclaimed by that magnificent name twice repeated and, secondly, that in the recalling of his attributes (*virtutes*) is described what he is, not in himself, but in relation to us, in order that our knowledge (*agnitio*) of him may consist rather in a lively perception (*sensu*) than in empty and vain speculation. Moreover, the attributes here enumerated are those which we saw, as we have already remarked, to shine forth in the heavens and the earth: clemency, goodness, mercy, justice, judgment, truth. Also, power and energy are comprised under the name Elohim.[376]

Calvin continues by showing that the prophets distinguished God by these same epithets [377] and that in Psalm 145 such a complete catalogue is given that nothing seems to be omitted.[378] So also for Jeremiah 9:24.[379]

[371] *Infra,* p. 143.

[372] I.vi.2 (OS III.62.19) "notis et insignibus."

[373] *Ibid.* (line 10) ". . . quasi publicis tabulis consignata esse."

[374] *Ibid.* (p. 60.42).

[375] The verse reads, "The Lord, the Lord God, merciful and gracious, long suffering, and abundant in goodness and truth, keeping mercy for thousands, forgiving iniquity, and transgression, and sin, and that will by no means clear the guilty; visiting the iniquity of the fathers upon the children, and upon the children's children."

[376] I.x.2 (OS III.86.14–23).

[377] Cf. Com. Isa. 40:26 ff. (CO XXXVII.24 ff.).

[378] I.x.2 (OS III.86.24 ff.). Compare also Com. Ps. 147 and 148 (CO XXXII.425–436, *passim.*), and Com. Ps. 19:7 ff. (CO XXXI.199 ff.).

[379] The verse reads: "Let him that glorieth glory in this, that he understandeth and knoweth me, that I am the Lord, which exercise mercy, judgments, and righteousness on the earth."

Certainly these three things are highly necessary for us to know: mercy, in which alone consists all our salvation; judgment, which is daily exercised on the wicked and awaits them more severely in eternal death; righteousness, by which the faithful are preserved and most benignly cherished. . . . Nor is there thus any omission of his truth, power, holiness, or goodness. For how could the knowledge (*scientia*) exist which is here required of his justice, mercy, and judgment, unless it rested upon his unchanging truth (*veritate eius inflexibili*)? And how could his judgment and justice in governing the world be believed, apart from a comprehension (*intellecta*) of his power? Or whence his mercy, except from his goodness? If, finally, all his ways are mercy, judgment, and righteousness, then also his holiness is conspicuous in them.[380]

Thus, in very unscholastic form, Calvin gives us God's attributes, holding that we are taught in Scripture (apart from Christ) [381] the eternity and self-existence, clemency, goodness, mercy, justice, judgment, truth, power, and energy of God. Or, stated in other words, his mercy, justice, and judgment, which imply his holiness, goodness, power, and unchanging truth. The whole of I.x.2, which contains these two lists of attributes, was carried unchanged from the edition of 1539 through all succeeding editions into the 1559 edition.[382] Throughout, until 1559, it was a concluding summary, a kind of final doxology at the end of Chapter I, *De cognitione Dei*. Only the last sentence was dropped in 1559,[383] which says that "nevertheless," in spite of all this, God is known truly only in the face of Christ and that this latter subject will be studied in another place.

The summary of the foregoing attributes of God the Creator seen in Scripture, or rather in nature with the aid of the "spectacles" of Scripture, is followed in the edition of 1559, Book I, by the doctrines of the Trinity, Creation, and Providence. These three doctrines are known only in Scripture, not from nature. They are therefore the peculiar property of the church in principle, as well as in fact, while the attributes listed above are only in fact limited

380 I.x.2 (OS III.87.1–14).

381 I.x.1, *loc cit.*, *supra*, p. 45*n*.

382 Except for minor stylistic improvements and the dropping of the final sentence in the last edition, cf. OS III.86 f., and Pannier ed., I, 77–79.

383 *Supra*, p. 47*n*.

to the faithful. Yet they concern solely the Creator and have essentially nothing to do with the work of the Redeemer, which is a special gratuitous activity within the frame established by the conception of the Triune God and his world. These teachings apparently belong to what man would have known of "God and ourselves" from creation, had not sin intervened. This does not mean that the elaborate and mostly negative doctrine of the Trinity would have been known, but God himself in his eternal Tri-unity.

For his final edition Calvin collected these three doctrines together as follows: The doctrine of the Trinity [384] was brought forward from its place as prologue to the Apostle's Creed analysis [385] where it had been classified under the general category of "faith." The doctrine of the general creation [386] was taken from the analysis of the first article of the Creed,[387] and that of the creation of man in a state of perfection [388] was separated from the material on the fallen state with which it had stood in the chapter *De cognitione hominis, et libero arbitrio. . . .*[389] The doctrine of providence [390] was detached from the chapter *De praedestinatione et providentia Dei,*[391] which had stood in the series of chapters on justification.

Calvin's doctrine of the Trinity, the first of the exclusively Biblical teachings about God in the *Institutes* of 1559 is derived from assembled Scripture references from both Old and New Testaments. These are clarified, and their meaning is defended in the classical Trinitarian terminology. The doctrine does not include Calvin's Christology. Nor is it meant to establish the divinity of Christ, but rather of the Eternal Son or Wisdom of God who became incarnate in Christ and of the Spirit. Father, Son, and Spirit are of one simple undifferentiated divine essence in which they all participate equally, so that when referred to alone, each can be said to be God, eternal and self-existent. Yet the distinc-

[384] I.xiii.
[385] Eds. '36–'54.
[386] I.xiv.
[387] Eds. '36–'54.
[388] I.xv.
[389] Eds. '39–'54. In ed. '36 this subject was scarcely treated.
[390] I.xvi–xviii.
[391] Eds. '39–'54, also briefly treated in ed. '36.

tion of persons is such that each has a peculiar mark and relation with the other two, making the Son and Spirit subordinate in respect to order (*ratione ordinis*) while of equal divinity with regard to essence. The distinctions found in Scripture are: "to the Father is attributed the principle of action (*principium agendi*), the fountain and source of all things; to the Son, wisdom, counsel and management in the operation of things (*in rebus agendis dispensatio*); and to the Spirit is assigned the power and efficacy of action." [392] These are intimately related, because the Son is the Wisdom of the Father and the Spirit, and the Spirit is the Spirit of the Father and the Son.[393]

It was the Triune God who created the world. Hence, Calvin's doctrine of creation follows the doctrine of the Trinity. From Moses we learn that

> God created heaven and earth out of nothing by the power of his word and Spirit; and thence produced things animate and inanimate of every kind, distinguished an innumerable variety of things by an admirable order, giving each kind its proper nature, assigning its office, and appointing its place and station; and, since all things are subject to corruption, he has, moreover, provided that each species be preserved sound until the last day.[394]

God decorated heaven and earth like a magnificent mansion, and, "lastly, by making man and adorning him with so many and so great abilities and such splendid beauty he has exhibited in him the most excellent specimen of all his works." [395] The general revelation teaches that the world was not its own maker, but Scripture alone "explains the time and manner" of creation,[396] points out how God made all things for the sake of men, and even arranged the days of creation for our instruction.[397]

The bulk of Calvin's doctrine of creation in I.xiv concerns angels, devils, and Satan, which Calvin includes here on his own

[392] I.xiii.18 (OS III.132.9–11). In I.xvi.3 (OS III.190.26 ff.), Calvin disowns the idea of a mere prime mover.

[393] I.xiii.14 (OS III.127.16); III.i.4 (OS IV.6.10).

[394] I.xiv.20 (OS III.170.33–171.4). That the trinitarian God is meant by "Moses" in Genesis 1 is emphasized in I.xiv.2 (OS III.154.22–26) and in Com. Gen. 1:26 (CO XXIII.25d).

[395] I.xiv.20 (OS III.171.11–13).

[396] Com. Ps. 19:1 (CO XXXI.195b).

[397] I.xiv.2 and 22, cf. *supra*, p. 9.

authority,[398] Moses having "omitted" it from Genesis in "accommodation" to the capacities of his readers. He also includes here his anthropology of the time before the Fall, which is largely his own construction from the New Testament and the philosophers.[399] The doctrine of creation proper, based on Genesis 1, is extremely brief throughout all editions. The central idea, namely, that all things were created by God out of nothing, was easily expressed, but once expressed, it did not admit of much elaboration without recourse to speculation, which Calvin always rejected. Calvin regarded further discussion of Genesis 1 as adequately done long before by Basil, Ambrose, and others.[400]

Calvin's doctrine of providence, or more properly of "particular providence" [401] (since even the heathen can perceive in a general way the divine power in the world) [402] is the continuation of the doctrine of creation, "because unless we proceed to his providence we cannot rightly comprehend what this [article of the Creed] means, that God is the Creator." [403] Providence is God's preservation of creation—not, however, by a mere "universal motion" or by "fixed laws," but by the active, special volition of God in every event, from the fall of a drop of rain [404] to the conscious will and even thought of man.[405] This omniactivity of God is based on such texts as Psalms 104:27–30 and 115:3, Proverbs 20:24, Jeremiah 10:3, Matthew 10:29, and Acts 17:28, and is the practical expression of what is meant by the attribute of "omnipotence." [406]

And, indeed, God claims omnipotence to himself and would have us acknowledge it, not such as the sophists imagine, vain, idle, and almost asleep, but vigilant, efficacious, operative, and engaged in continual action; nor, indeed, that [omnipotence] which is a general principle of confused motion, as if he should command a river to flow through the channel once made for it, but applied in every single and particular

[398] Added to the *Institutes* in ed. '43.

[399] I.xv.

[400] I.xiv.20 (OS III.170.31 f.).

[401] I.xvi.1 (OS III.188.5).

[402] I.xvi.1, *passim*.

[403] *Ibid.* (p. 187.19–21).

[404] I.xvi.5 (OS III.195.25).

[405] I.xviii.2 (OS III.221.24 ff.).

[406] I.xvi.1. It is likely that the attribute of omnipotence is not expressly mentioned in I.x among the list of attributes to avoid its misinterpretation as *potestas absoluta*. Here, in the doctrine of providence, it is seen not as power which may be conceived of as potential or unexercised, but as active power that, as it were, "inflates" the world.

movement. For he is accounted omnipotent, not because he can act, but he may cease or be idle, and not in that he continues the order of nature by a general instinct appointed by him, but because governing heaven and earth by his providence. he so regulates all things that nothing happens without his counsel.[407]

This all-encompassing activity of God may be either directly or indirectly applied, for the providence of God "regulates all things so that it works at one time through the interposition of means, at another time without means, and again in opposition to all means."[408]

Beyond this, Calvin's exposition of the doctrine is largely devoted to excluding from his view the pagan concepts of blind fate on the one hand and chance on the other,[409] assuring a place within his doctrine for contingency, chiefly in terms of responsible human volitions,[410] and finally, in one of his most paradoxical chapters, asserting that while God in his "omnipotence" does everything, yet the evil done by men and Satan opposes God's "will."[411]

This concludes, in summary form, the content of knowledge of God the Creator learned from Scripture. It remains only to point out another element of this knowledge that by the standards of the *duplex cognitio Domini* belongs in Book I, but is not found there: the moral law. As we have already hinted, the moral law given to Moses and also the ethical utterances of Jesus and the apostles have no other content than the *lex* or *ius naturae*. This ranges them with God's eternal orderly will for creation under the general category of law, rather than the special activity of redemption. Because of the peculiarity of Calvin's having located the exposition of the Law (except for the commentary on the second Commandment)[412] in Book II (*De cognitione Dei redemptoris in Christo*), we have chosen the law as the element of Calvin's theology which best illustrates the relation of the two parts of the "twofold knowledge." Since this is studied in our

407 I.xvi.3 (OS III.190.14–24).
408 I.xvii.1 (OS III.202.9–11).
409 I.xvi.
410 I.xvii.
411 I.xviii, *passim*, for example, I.xviii.3 (OS III.225.11–22).
412 I.xi–xii.

Chapter V, we conclude the present analysis simply by noting the curious absence in the edition of 1559 of the Mosaic law from the knowledge of the Creator seen in Scripture, although it plays a large role in Calvin's conception of the knowledge of the Creator in general.

The Relation of the Knowledge of God the Creator Learned from Creation to That Learned from Scripture

Before considering the relation which is our topic we must summarize, comparing briefly the means of presentation, the content, the purpose, and the actual functions of the general and special revelations of the Creator. These are, respectively, as follows: Both revelations are presented to the mind objectively in creation and Scripture, and subjectively in the *sensus divinitatis,* conscience, and the internal testimony of the Holy Spirit. The content is identical up to a point: both teach the eternity and self-existence, power, wisdom, truth, goodness, righteousness, justice, mercy, and holiness of God, and both reveal identically God's orderly will for his creation, the former in conscience and the latter in the Mosaic moral law. The revelation in Scripture, however, goes beyond what can be learned from creation since the Fall (1) in teaching of the Trinity, (2) in giving the time and manner of creation, plus an angelology, a demonology, and a picture of man's original state, and (3) in revealing the full scope of God's particular providence. The purpose of both revelations is the eternal felicity of men in glorifying the Creator, while the actual function of the revelation in creation is solely to leave man inexcusable before God. In short, Scripture repeats by objective source and subjective witness everything that creation teaches about the Creator, and then adds to it. Further, it contributes to the true purpose of this revelation rather than the accidental function of condemning.

Then has Scripture, according to Calvin, entirely supplanted the revelation in creation for the believer? Has the revelation in creation no continuing constructive function or constitutive theological value for the man of faith?

These two questions, in spite of the possibility of an affirmative answer implied in the foregoing summary, embody an idea strange to Calvin: the idea that the Creator's revelation in creation ceases to be relevant to the believer who has Scripture.[413] We must consider these two questions, not because they arise from a study of Calvin, but because they have arisen as a problem of Calvin interpretation under the influence of Karl Barth. The motive has been to clear Calvin of all suspicions of natural theology, that is of constructing an independent avenue to God that stands outside special revelation. This can be done legitimately. But the zeal with which it has been pursued—partly in an effort to set the theology of Calvin in clearer opposition to Thomism, to neo-Protestantism, and to the "German Christian" movement of the last decade—resulted in a statement of the case which falsifies Calvin by not admitting, or by minimizing, the degree to which Calvin as a reader of Scripture finds himself referred by Scripture and under the guidance of Scripture to God's revelation in creation.[414] As we shall now see, Calvin, calmly and without

[413] "But Calvin has not the least intention of setting up a kind of opposition between the Biblical and natural revelation. Rather, God's word elucidates his revelation in nature." Wernle, *Der evangelische Glaube*, p. 175.

[414] Wilhelm Niesel's *Die Theologie Calvins* is a good example. Niesel's chapters follow the order of discussion of ed. '59 throughout, with one exception: Chapter II, "The Knowledge of God," reverses the order that Calvin followed without exception from ed. '39 through '59, by placing the doctrine of Scripture (pp. 19–36) before "The Question of the Natural Knowledge of God" (pp. 36–49). His justification for doing this is the primacy of Scripture in Calvin's theology as stated in his preface to the *Institutes* and to the French Bible and even in the opening words of ed. '36. The fact that Calvin changed these words, "the sum of sacred doctrine" ('36) to "the sum of almost all our wisdom" ('39 ff.) at the same time he added his material on the revelation in creation does not prove the two issues related, but it certainly does destroy Niesel's and Peter Barth's (*Das Problem*, p. 7) appeal to them. Calvin never used these words that Niesel quotes after the first edition. But even if he had, the question remains as to why Calvin, from whom Niesel gets the references, did not arrange his book like Niesel's. Further, Niesel's exposition of Calvin's doctrine of Scripture and the testimony of the Holy Spirit ignores much of the actual content of these doctrines as they appear in Calvin in all editions after '39, while Niesel urges upon us enthusiastically that for Calvin the substance, goal, *scopus* of the Bible, testified to by the Spirit, is Christ. Granting, of course, both that Calvin's theology is derived exclusively from Scripture and that the chief aim of it is to point through Scripture to the encounter with God in Christ—we still cannot use these central ideas like swords to slash away problems. We must still explain why Calvin, in spite of this, persisted for twenty years in beginning his systematic work with the general revelation. Why did he in edition after edition develop his doctrine of the word and Spirit

polemic, considered the revelation in creation as part of the believer's knowledge of God.

Calvin calls seeing God in nature a "way of seeking God" that is "common to aliens and to those of his family."[415] And the fact that the Jews had the moral law in addition to the general revelation meant that they were bound by a "double tie" to honor God.[416] Were the God of nature known to the Christian exclusively in Scripture, Calvin's I.x comparing the two revelations and maintaining the identity of their content would be frivolous. He begins,

But since we have shown that the knowledge of God, which is otherwise exhibited without obscurity in the machine of the world and in all creatures, is yet more familiarly and more clearly explained in the word, it is now useful to examine whether the Lord exhibits himself to us in Scripture in the same character in which we have already seen that he is delineated in his works.[417]

Twice he concludes in the affirmative: "Moreover, we find here enumerated the same attributes which we have already seen shining brilliantly both in heaven and on earth."[418] And when Psalm 145 summarizes "all His attributes," "yet it contains nothing but what may be contemplated in creation. Thus, by the teaching

---

with little mention of Christ? Why did Calvin continue, from ed. '39 on, to *compare* the revelation in creation with that in Scripture, as in I.x.1–2? Why, finally, was the knowledge of the Creator always kept separate from that of the Redeemer? We may wish that he had not done these things, but we may not pretend that he did not do them. Niesel's aim is to answer the problem of the general revelation in Calvin before it can be asked, by showing the exclusively Christological character of the theology as a whole. He is so interested in denying the possibility of natural theology as an auxiliary to revealed theology in Calvin—which Calvin himself does well enough in I.i–v—that he suppresses Calvin's believing view of nature. Thus, we must take the time here to show that after renouncing the general revelation from the point of view of unregenerate man, Calvin points the believer to it again, as directed by Scripture.

415 *Supra,* p. 74.

416 Com. Ps. 19:7 (CO XXXI.199b) ". . . unde sequitur Iudaeos duplici vinculo ad Deum colendum obstrictos esse."

417 I.x.1 (OS III.85.7–12).

418 I.x.2 (OS III.86.19–21). "We" in this instance is clearly the man of faith. Calvin is certainly not referring to Plato's or Cicero's readings from nature about God.

of experience (*experientia magistra*) we perceive God to be just what he declares himself in his word."[419]

This is a recurrent theme of the Commentary on First Corinthians, where Calvin joins Paul in setting the "wisdom of this world" and the "foolishness of God" in sharp opposition. But Calvin never fails to make the further allowance that once faith has done its work, this formerly rejected wisdom is not to be scorned.[420]

There is also a solution furnished at the same time to the question, how does it happen that Paul in this way throws down upon the ground every kind of knowledge that is apart from Christ and tramples, as it were, on what is manifestly one of the chief gifts of God in this world? For what is more noble than man's reason, in which man excells the other animals? How richly deserving in honor are the liberal sciences. . . . [But] Paul does not expressly condemn either man's natural perspicacity or his wisdom acquired from practice and experience or his cultivation of mind attained by learning; but declares that all this is of no avail *for acquiring spiritual wisdom.*[421]

The Apostle does not require that we should altogether renounce the wisdom that is implanted in us by nature or acquired by long practice, but simply that we subject it to the service of God, so as to have no wisdom but through his word.[422]

"*Without Christ,* sciences in every department are vain and the man who knows not God is vain, though he should be conversant with every branch of learning."[423]

A section of the "Argument" to the Commentary on Genesis is directed specifically to our problem. First Calvin describes the

[419] I.x.2 (OS III.86.27–30).

[420] From this commentary Karl Barth, *No!,* and also Niesel, *Die Theologie Calvins,* cite only places which demonstrate man's inabilities where the saving mysteries of God are concerned. But Calvin makes perfectly clear that man's abilities as such are not to be scorned. Cf. Com. I Cor. 1:17 (CO XLIX.321b); 1:20 (pp. 324 f.); 1:21 (pp. 326 f.) is the strongest condemnation of human intellectual pretense; 3:19 (p. 359d–360a), the world's wisdom is a "handmaid," subject to Christ; 8:1–2 (pp. 427d–430).

[421] Com. I Cor. 1:20 (CO XLIX.325b, italics added).

[422] *Ibid.,* 3:18 (CO XLIX.359b).

[423] *Ibid.,* 1:20, (CO XLIX.325c, italics added).

magnificence of the works of God in which alone men should seek him rather than in idle speculation. Next he shows that because of dulled sight man gains nothing but his inexcusability from surveying God's works and must therefore turn from them to the special revelation and to faith. Thirdly Calvin points out that although Paul belittles the "wisdom of the world" and teaches that we must be carried on high above the world to behold those things which eye has never seen nor ear heard,—where natural nourishment and the light of the sun and stars are replaced by Christ, and the air by his Spirit,—that nevertheless, we are not to conclude that God's revelation in nature no longer concerns us.

There [with Christ in faith], in short, the invisible kingdom of Christ fills all things and his spiritual grace is diffused through all. Yet this does not prevent us from applying our senses to the consideration of heaven and earth that we may thence seek confirmation in the true knowledge of God. For Christ is that image in which God presents to our view not only his heart but also his hands and his feet. I give the name of his heart to that secret love with which he embraces us in Christ: by his hands and feet I understand those works of his which are displayed before our eyes. As soon as we depart from Christ there is nothing, be it ever so gross or insignificant in itself, respecting which we are not necessarily deceived.[424]

This is, of course, a denial of any "natural theology," for only in Christ do we see even the "hands and feet" of God. Yet we see these "hands and feet" actually before our eyes in the works of creation.

The minds of men, therefore are blind to this light of nature (*naturae lucem*) which shines forth in all creatures until being irradiated by the Spirit of God they begin to understand what otherwise they cannot

[424](CO XXIII.10d–11a), and *passim.* Since Wilhelm Niesel calls it "unpardonable" that Gloede should cite this passage after Peter Barth in *Das Problem,* p. 25, had proved it unusable, one feels called upon to remark that Peter Barth's comment consisted solely of italicizing the sentence in which Christ is mentioned and leaving in small type the preceding and following sentences that make the point. See Niesel's review of Gloede's work in *Theol. Literaturbeilage der Reform. Kirchenztg.,* pp. 15 f.

comprehend. . . . We have in this world a conspicuous image of God . . . a theater of divine glory. . . . Discriminately is this world called a mirror of divinity, not because there is sufficient clearness for a man to know God by looking at the world, but he has thus revealed himself to us by works, in these, too, we ought to seek him. . . . The faithful, however, to whom he has given eyes, see, as it were, sparks of his glory shining in every created thing.[425]

Man must not, however, venture to dispense with Scripture, for "it is better to limp in the way, than run with greatest swiftness out of it."[426]

Again, in the Geneva Catechism questions on the Apostle's Creed, after God is said to be our "Father" solely in Christ, we read,

Why do you say "Creator of heaven and earth?" As he has manifested himself so that the ignorance of the impious is without excuse. The world itself is, therefore, a kind of mirror in which we may view him in so far as it concerns us to know.[427]

All these passages relate to the believer and encourage continued attention to the works of God, not as in idle curiosity or as something apart from Scripture, but in obedience to Scripture. Further,

Let us not disdain to receive a pious delight from the works of God, which everywhere present themselves to view in this very beautiful theater of the world. For this, as I have elsewhere observed, though not the principal, is yet in the order of nature, the first lesson of faith, to remember that wherever we turn our eyes all the things which we behold are the works of God; and at the same time to consider with pious meditation for what end God created them.[428]

And again, he sums up a passage on the same subject with:

to be brief, therefore, let the readers know that they have then truly apprehended by faith what is meant by God being the Creator of heaven and earth, if in the first place they follow this universal rule, not to pass over with ungrateful inattention and oblivion those glorious attributes which God manifests in his creatures and, secondly,

[425] Com. Heb. 11:3 (CO LV.145b–d, 146a).
[426] I.vi.3 (OS III.64.2 f.).
[427] (CO VI.16c).
[428] I.xiv.20 (OS III.170.23–29).

learn to make such an application to themselves as thoroughly to affect their hearts.[429]

Then follows an enthusiastic hymn to nature. Similarly, David wrote Psalm 19:1–7, "wishing to encourage the faithful to consider the glory of God, [thus] he sets before them first a mirror of it in the machine of the heavens and the exquisite order of their workmanship."[430]

To account for these positive evaluations of the revelation in creation to the man of faith as an indication of Calvin's insufficient fear of Thomas Aquinas[431] is to overlook the degree to which they are characteristic of his whole theological mentality. These evaluations, together with very rash statements in which Calvin condemns the world's wisdom,[432] are comparable to those by which he condemns good works as a ground of merit or a basis of salvation, then reintroduces them in equally vigorous criticism of the antinomians, once the utter graciousness of salvation has been observed and good works can be put in their proper place.[433] The same way of thinking was seen above in this chapter, where Calvin rejected completely all the rational proofs of the divinity of Scripture as helpful in the formation of faith, then reasserted these objectively adequate *indicia* as of positive value to the believer once faith has been established. So the law is rescinded as an ethical imperative (in which light, while objectively true, nonetheless it functions as the contradiction of the Gospel), only to reappear in the *usus tertius* as the Christian's guide to love.[434] Barth chides Brunner for making statements about the wholly

[429] I.xiv.21 (OS III.171.34–172.4).

[430] Com. Ps. 19, "Argument" (CO XXXI.194b). Barth writes, "The fact that God is revealed in all his works is God's scriptural testimony to us against the ignorance of man." Calvin did not conclude "that this knowledge has to be put to a positive use in theology either antecedently or subsequently ('in faith')." *No!*, p. 108.

[431] Barth, *No!*, pp. 100–105, refers to the *Institutes* I.i–v. Calvin is actually on more dangerous ground in Com. Acts 17:16 ff. (CO XLVIII.403 f.).

[432] ". . . man with all his acuteness is as stupid for obtaining of himself a knowledge of the mysteries of God as an ass is unqualified for understanding musical harmonies." Com. I Cor. 1:20 (CO XLIX.325a); cf. II.vi.1 (OS III.320.29–321.5).

[433] II.xiv–xvii, *passim*.

[434] II.vii, *passim*.

gratuitous character of grace followed by observations upon nature or creation that would seem to have been excluded by the former.[435] And yet here Brunner is both dialectic and Calvinistic, for there is to this extent a dialectic in Calvin between *Natur und Gnade,* or more nicely put in terms of our present problem, between the general and special revelations of God as Creator. It is as distorting to rearrange Calvin's theology making the rational elements[436] preliminary and preparatory to God's miracle, a tendency we have already observed in Warfield, as it is to deny altogether their subsequent and subsidiary, but nevertheless essential, place. When Calvin condemns absolutely all men's efforts to know God outside Christ, but subsequently urges them in faith to look upon the wisdom, power, and goodness of the Creator in creation, he seems equally aware of the possibility of an "intellectual work-righteousness,"[437] and of work-righteousness proper. At the same time he is unwilling to go to the extreme of denying the positive value of either "terrestrial" human learning or knowledge of the "image" of God in creation, when both are put under the "leading and teaching" of the Biblical message. It

[435] *No!,* p. 78; cf. Brunner, *Nature and Grace,* p. 18. Barth's criticizing of Brunner's anthropology follows the same pattern, *Dogmatik,* III/2, 153–157. Cf. *supra,* p. 84, Calvin's comments on Com. Acts 17:16 ff.

[436] By "rational elements" I mean to indicate, for example, that the wisdom of God in creation, as pointed out by one of the Psalms, is more compatible with human reason than the suffering of the eternal Son. Still, the fact of creation itself is for Calvin as gratuitous as the grace by which men are saved.

[437] Barth's point is that Luther and Calvin "saw and attacked the possibility of an intellectual work-righteousness in the basis of theological thought. But they did not do so as widely, as clearly and as fundamentally as they did with respect to the possibility of a moral work-righteousness in the basis of Christian life. . . . It is not possible . . . to find in those introductory chapters [of the *Institutes*] any direct and explicit delimitation of Calvin's method against that of Thomism," *No!,* p. 102. Barth continues farther on, "what Calvin wrote in those first chapters of the *Institutes* has to be written again and this time in such a way that no Przywara and no Althaus can find in it material for their fatal ends," p. 104. But it is not I.i–v upon which the case for the Christian's positive evaluation of the revelation in creation rests. This would be a false natural theology. It rests upon I.x and I.xiii–xviii, the exegesis of the "nature" Psalms, and of Romans and I Corinthians, and so forth, that is to say, upon the Biblical teaching that the Triune God makes himself known to believers in creation and providence, when God's world is seen under the guidance of Scripture. See Appendix III.

is only the immediate reading of God from nature in which the sinful mind of man perverts and prejudges God's revelation to which Calvin objects. He does not thereby fall into a "naïve intellectualistic Biblicism," but he understands the Scripture in this connection as pointing necessarily to that of which it is witness.[438] "Through Scripture is a second and, so to speak, buried source of the knowledge of God opened up and made useful."[439] Hence, Calvin writes:

> For to observe the stars, what is it but to contemplate the wonderful workmanship in which the power as well as the wisdom and goodness of God shines forth? And, indeed, astrology may justly be called the alphabet of theology; for no one can with a right mind come to the contemplation of the celestial framework without being enraptured with admiration at the display of God's wisdom, as well as of his power and goodness.[440]

"And certainly we profit little in the spectacle of universal nature, if we do not behold with the eyes of faith that spiritual glory of which an image is presented to us in the world."[441]

The "applying of our senses to the consideration of heaven and earth" includes all those studies for which the best general term today is "natural science," or, for Calvin's time, "philosophy" as well as some of the "liberal arts and sciences." As we have already shown under the principle of correlation in Chapter II above, Calvin sees even very modest facts of nature in their theological implications as well as in the realm of their merely practical use. Everything we learn of the world, every true thing, redounds both to God's glory and the increase of our piety. Calvin is a supporter of the pious contemplation of nature and of pious research into the processes of nature, which to him are "secrets of divine wisdom."[442] He was moderately well informed in the natural sci-

[438] P. Barth, *Das Problem,* p. 11. "God's word opens to us the view toward God's self-witness in his work of creation. God takes us, as it were, by the hand and shows us the miracle of his works," p. 17.

[439] Emil Brunner, *Natur und Gnade,* 2d ed., p. 54.

[440] Com. Jer. 10:1–2. (CO XXXVIII. 58d–59a).

[441] Com. Ps. 104:3 (CO XXXII.86b, italics added).

[442] I.v.2 (OS III.46.14).

ences of his time, although he did not accept the Copernican cosmology.[443] His commendations of the work of pagan science are frequent, although his Genevan academy, like most schools of the time, contained no special place for such studies.[444] He was constantly in the hands of a doctor during his adult life, therefore had reason to be thankful to medical science. When Calvin derided scientific discovery in the realm of nature, it was only in criticism of a naturalistic positivism which would explain the entire nature of man, the world, and God in terms of phenomena observable only by man's sinful reason and believed to the exclusion of special revelation.[445] True, he rejected arbitrarily Egyptian chronicles which would have modified the Biblical picture of the age of the earth, but for the most part so far as there was a problem for him of science and the Bible he tended to understand the latter in terms of the former, as a few examples from his exegesis will show.

Calvin decided the question of what is meant by the "waters above" in Genesis 1:7 in terms of the accepted cosmology of his day, as against the assertion of the radical Biblicists that there must be water beyond the arc of sky because "it is written." [446] And in 1:9 it was necessary that God should as it were supernaturally clear the waters from the dry land, because water "being an element must be circular, and being the element heavier than air but lighter than earth, it ought to cover the latter in its entire circumfer-

[443] "We are indeed not ignorant that the circuit of the heavens is finite and the earth, like a little ball, is located in the middle." Com. Gen. "Argument" (CO XXIII.10a); Com. Ps. 104:5 (CO XXXII.86c–87) and 148:3 (CO XXXII.433). These commentaries were issued thirteen and sixteen years, respectively, after the publishing of Copernicus' works in 1543.

[444] Kampschulte, *Johann Calvin,* II, 335. Kuyper, *Calvinism,* traces an interest in science in Calvinistic countries to Calvin's attitude toward nature, particularly his doctrine of preserving grace.

[445] Kampschulte's statement "Calvin had an outspoken antipathy to natural sciences and especially natural philosophy" is unfounded. Calvin criticized natural science only when it exercised theological pretensions. This is true even in Kampschulte's citation from Com. Ps. 29:5 (CO XXXI.288/9); cf. I.ii. 15–16. Cf. Choisy, *Calvin et la science,* pp. 16 f.

[446] The "waters above" mean clouds and rain, Com. Gen. 1:6–7 (CO XXIII.18–19); also, Com. Ps. 148:3 (CO XXXII.433d), since Moses and the prophets *ut se accommodent,* "ordinarily speak in popular style. . . . It would be absurd, then, to seek to reduce what they say to the rules of philosophy."

ence."[447] He understood that the perpetual miracles (according to the Old Testament) of rain and the seasons have "natural causes,"[448] as does the rainbow, although the latter took on additional meaning under God's special revelation to Noah.[449] A beginning of serious criticism of Genesis 1 is implied where Calvin cites that Saturn is larger than the moon, although Moses stated the contrary. "As was proper to a theologian, [Moses] had regard to men rather than the stars," and accommodated himself to the uninstructed rather than writing learned astronomy.[450] Much recent harmonizing of the creation story with science, for example, interpreting the "days" as geological ages, follows this pattern.[451] Calvin enlarges upon the praise of creation in Scripture by citing facts not given in the Bible, such as the marvel of fixed stars high above the orbits of the planets,[452] which he had learned from pagan astronomy. He frankly confessed the superiority of the ancients of the East in this most impressive discipline, in which Moses and Daniel had been instructed by Egyptians and Chaldeans as youths.[453] In this realm he sharply distinguished between superstitious astrology[454]—birth stars, alleged planetary influence on business transactions, and so forth—and what he regarded as within the reign of natural causation, for example, that the stars affect seasons, crops, the coming of pestilence, and the weather.[455] The latter he judges to fall within the Biblical prescription that the sun and the stars are "signs." Thus, he at once accepts the Biblical critique of astrology and supplements the Biblical praise of the

[447] Com. Gen. 1:9 (CO XXIII.19c).

[448] Com. Gen. 1:6 (CO XXIII.19a). Com. Ps. 147:7 (CO XXXII.428b–c).

[449] Com. Gen. 9:13 (CO XXIII.149b–d). "Hence it is not for us to contend with the philosophers concerning the rainbow, for although its colors proceed from natural causes," cf. IV.xiv.18, *passim.*

[450] Com. Gen. 1:15 (CO XXIII.22a) and *passim,* 1:15–16.

[451] *Ibid.* (p. 22a–b). Note Calvin carefully deciding whether the moon is opaque, fiery, or dark and whether its light is its own or reflected, etc., so as to do credit to science yet preserve Moses from either ignorance or error.

[452] Com. Ps. 148:3 (CO XXXII.433c).

[453] It is on the basis of Moses' Egyptian education that Calvin could picture him as sophisticated in science, but writing simply for the unlearned reader, Com. Acts 7:20 (CO XLVIII.140a–d). Cf. Com. Dan. 1:4 (CO XL.538c, f.) *passim.*

[454] Cf. *Advertissement contre l'astrologie judiciaire* (CO VII.513 ff.).

[455] Com. Isa. 19:12 (CO XXXVI.336b).

heavens by additional information gained from what he regarded as legitimate astronomy[456] gained from the science of his time.

While Calvin knew and used some science for deepening his appreciation of the Creator's work in conjunction with and even in explanation of Scripture, and deplored the scorning of scientific learning in his own day,[457] it is really the naïve rather than the scientific view of nature that was constitutive and essential in his theology. Knowledge of the intricacies of natural process are for him "interesting," but the mere beauty of the stars or the sun's heat or the wonder of the succession of days and seasons, which are universal and unavoidable human experiences of the Creator's goodness, are integral to his theology. It is on this level, therefore, that the most unlearned pagan is inexcusable for rejecting the universal revelation, and the most unlearned Christian is directed by his Biblical faith to see that the God of his salvation is the Maker and Sustainer of heaven, earth, and man, and the Lord of human history. "But since the meanest and most illiterate of mankind, who are furnished with no other assistance than their own eyes, cannot be ignorant of the excellence of the divine skill . . . it is evident that the Lord abundantly manifests his wisdom to everyone."[458] The most erudite student of "secondary causes" learns nothing really important if by faith he does not perceive with the most unlearned believer that the secret decree of God governs everything. "It is thus that Aristotle, in his 'Treatise on Meteors,' has shown such ingenuity that he discusses their natural causes most exactly, but omitting the main point, upon which the most ignorant layman, at least instructed in true piety, has superiority over him."[459]

Granting, then, that the spectacle of creation is not superfluous to the Christian, but that in Calvin's understanding the Scriptures urge the believer to see the world as a revelation of God, and that Calvin goes so far as to use the older science of his day, derived largely from non-Christians, as an aid in the exegesis of Scripture, we still face the question of the exact relationship be-

456 Calvin used one word for both, *astrologia*.

457 Com. Dan. 1:4 (CO XL.538c).

458 I.v.2 (OS III.46.21–26).

459 Com. Ps. 147:15 (CO XXXII.430d).

tween the general and the Biblical revelations of God as Creator. Several visual metaphors of Calvin give an indication of the answer. Calvin refers to creation as a mirror[460] or theater[461] in which is reflected or displayed or written the revelation of the Creator. Man, however, because of sin, has weak sight and must use the "spectacles" of Scripture to see what is before him:

For as the aged or those with sore eyes or those whose sight has by any means become darkened, if you show them the most beautiful book, though they perceive something written, they can scarcely read two words together; however, by the assistance of spectacles, they will begin to read distinctly—so Scripture, collecting the otherwise confused knowledge of God in our minds, dispells the dimness and shows us clearly the true God.[462]

This metaphor would imply neither the substitution of a new object of vision for an old one nor a complete cure of the eyes, but the use, because of a permanent defect in sight, of an aid in perceiving the original object, the revelation in creation. Another statement, embodying two of these figures, gives an almost complete analysis of the two revelations and their relation: the objective clarity of the mirror or theater of the world as a revelation, man's subjective inability or blindness, man's inexcusability, the inadequacy of the revelation in creation for salvation, the Scriptures as eyeglasses, and the Biblical incitement to behold, not to neglect, God's glory in creation.

However, in describing the world as a kind of mirror in which we ought to behold God, I do not wish to be understood to assert either that our eyes are clear-sighted enough to discern what the fabric of heaven and earth represents or that the knowledge to be obtained from this is sufficient for salvation. And whereas the Lord invites us to himself by means of created things, with no other effect than that of thereby rendering us inexcusable, he has added a new remedy (as was necessary), or at least by another aid he has assisted the ignorance of our minds. For by the Scripture as our guide and teacher (*scriptura duce et magistra*), he not only makes plain what otherwise would escape us, but almost compels us to behold them, as if he assisted our

[460] I.v.1 (OS III.45.26). [461] I.xiv.20 (OS III.170.23).
[462] I.vi.1 (OS III.60.25–30); also I.xiv.1 (OS III.153.13–16).

dull sight with spectacles. On this point . . . Moses insists. For if the mute instruction of heaven and earth were sufficient, the teaching of Moses would have been superfluous. This herald therefore approaches, who excites our attention, in order that we may perceive ourselves to be placed in this theater for the purpose of beholding the glory of God.[463]

The relation, thus, is one of clarification, in which Scripture is a pair of eyeglasses or a guide and teacher. The special revelation of the Creator in Scripture is not a substitute revelation, a completely new picture placed before the eyes. It does not make irrelevant God's other works which Christians have objectively in common with all men, but it is an aid in understanding these works—an indispensable aid. In another figure: God repeats in a loud voice in Scripture what we can no longer hear when spoken in the ordinary tones of creation itself.[464] Scripture points to the beauties of the stars or the restraining of the sea or the political order, at the same time naming the wisdom or power or goodness of God[465] which these are meant to convey. Thus, the wisdom of God or the mercy and justice of God are not mysterious names for God's unknowable essence, but qualities of his actual relation to the believer in creation. The general revelation thus becomes knowledge of God. With Scripture as our "guide and teacher," we actually see God at work in creation. In Calvin's geocentric world this meant living on a dry patch of earth from which God held back the sea and elevated the clouds in a daily miracle, around which he revolved the sun, moon, and stars in a way most advantageous for man, and upon which he provided not only nourishing food and drink, but even the luxuries of wine and oil, marble and gold,[466] all so that the believer would give the Creator the praise due him for building and furnishing the "beautiful mansion" of the world.

This clarification has to do with an aid or a new means of

[463] Com. Gen. "Argument" (CO XXIII.10b).

[464] Sermon on Job (CO XXXIII.604).

[465] These three attributes and often "justice" are those most commonly used to summarize what is known of God in nature, for example, Com. Ps. 145 and 147 "Argument" (CO XXXII.412d, 425c); I.xiv.21 (OS III.171.27); Geneva catechism (CO VI.18a).

[466] III.x.2.

communicating the general revelation only in so far as its content is in principle, even since the Fall, available to all men in creation: strictly speaking, that part of its content contained in the material Calvin compressed into I.x, plus the moral law, which we shall discuss later. Scripture is a lens magnifying the evidence in creation of God's holiness, wisdom, mercy, power, self-existence, and so forth, and his orderly good will. Therefore, in this specific area of revelation, Scripture is a special revelation in regard to the *means* God uses to reach men, but with regard to the *content* it is nothing else but the general revelation. Scripture is, so far, a special means by which a select group can see the general revelation. It is a finger pointing to God's work in the world; it is not yet a new "source" of the knowledge of God.

But over and above this, Scripture also presents a new knowledge content about the Creator in the doctrines of the Trinity, creation, and particular providence. Here the metaphor of the spectacles is no longer useful, because since the Fall these teachings are no longer communicated by creation, but only by Scripture. Scripture here is the sole source, not a lens held up to nature. It goes without saying that Calvin's doctrine of the Trinity is exclusively Biblical in origin. As for creation, man sinfully forgot, except for the patriarchal tradition which God kept alive, the details of the six-day creation which had been especially intended for his instruction. This creation process is not to be deduced from or observed in creation today by the "aid" of Scripture, as is, for example the wisdom of God. Scripture teaches it *de novo*. The same is true of particular providence. While a Plato [467] can see that the world and the life of men is upheld by the will of God, only the man of faith, instructed by Scripture, can penetrate to the knowledge of God's particular providence, the "special care" of God by which alone his "paternal favor" is known.[468]

The carnal sense (*carnis sensus*), when once it has perceived the power of God in creation, stops there; and when it proceeds farthest, examines and considers nothing other than the wisdom, power, and goodness of the Author in producing such a work (which spontaneously offer themselves to view, even obtruding upon the unwilling), or in some

[467] Com. Ps. 104:29 (CO XXXII.95c). [468] I.xvi.1 (OS III.188.29).

general agency of action in conserving and governing, on which the power of motion depends. In short, it thinks that all things are sustained by a divine energy infused at the beginning. But faith must penetrate further. For when it has learned who is the Creator of all things, it must immediately infer that he is also their perpetual governor and preserver and that, not by some sort of universal motion activating the whole machine of the world as well as its individual parts, but by a particular providence (*sed singulari quadam providentia*) sustaining, nourishing, and providing for everything which he has made.[469]

Thus, the special revelation of God the Creator in Scripture not only clarifies but also complements, by the addition of new content, what can be known of God the Creator in creation. The doctrines of the Trinity, creation, and particular providence, are a special revelation of God with regard to both the means of communication and the content, and yet neither surpasses the bounds of the knowledge of God the Creator. We have not yet come to the specific knowledge of the Redeemer, although we are in an area of Calvin's thought where faith in Christ is presupposed. Faith must be discussed thoroughly before the larger problem can be considered.

Conclusion

In summary: The awesome reality of the Holy God is presented to all men subjectively as the *sensus divinitatis*. His power, eternity, self-existence, wisdom, goodness, mercy, justice, righteousness, and truth are laid before all men in the structure of the world and the course of history; and God's orderly will for creation is known in all consciences. But because of the willful ignorance of sin all this revelation issues only in a mass of both crude and refined idolatries, in which men alternately cower in fright or rise in self-justified revolt against the true God. God had pity on men in this predicament, and to save them, gave them the revelation recorded in the Scripture. He continues to witness through Scripture and the Spirit's testimony. The Scripture pronounces the just condemnation of idolaters and functions for believers as a

[469] I.xvi.1 (OS III.187.22–188.7).

magnifying glass which clarifies their perception of God in creation, both in his attributes and in his will for men. In addition, Scripture, as a second source of knowledge of God, complements the specially revealed general revelation by the manifestation of the Trinity, the account of the original perfection of creation, and the doctrine of particular providence. All these elements together and in this relationship comprise the knowledge of God the Creator in Calvin's theology, as assembled in Book I of the *Institutes* of 1559. They constitute what men would have known of God the Father, Son, and Spirit in his creating and preserving work, and all they would have needed to know to glorify him, but for the Fall. Had man not fallen, no special work of the Son would have been necessary. The actual situation, however, is that men have fallen beyond even such self-help as might be afforded by God's renewal of the revelation of the Creator, and for them to have it "again," they must first become recipients of a special work of God, redemption. The strata of special revelation called the knowledge of the Creator is available only as part of the historical revelation, of which the center and substance is Christ. Even now we do not, within the realm of special revelation, ascend to or infer or deduce the work of the Redeemer from what we know of the Creator. Instead, we take a whole new orientation. We jump to another starting point theologically, as we do in the disposition of the *Institutes,* and will now look at the whole from the point of view of the unaccountable mystery of redemption, taking as our base Calvin's description of the miracle of faith in III.ii. For the first time in our study, we shall be in the realm of the second element of the *duplex cognitio Domini,* the *cognitio Dei redemptoris.* Then we shall return to the question of relating the two elements.

·IV·

THE KNOWLEDGE OF GOD THE REDEEMER

CHRISTIAN THEOLOGY is always predominantly soteriology. It is so with Calvin. The knowledge of God in his theology as we studied it in the last chapter had no saving function, although we have seen it to be relevant to the believer and gained through a means that has significance only for the believer, special revelation. We now turn to Calvin's soteriology, to the knowledge of God the Redeemer. For the most part, however, we shall delay pointing out the relationship between the two until our final chapter.

Calvin has already described the need for Redemption,[1] the successive forms of revelation in which Redemption was promised,[2] and the actual redemptive work of Christ [3] in the *Institutes*—which altogether are placed in Book II under the title "Of the Knowledge of God the Redeemer in Christ, which was first manifested to the fathers under the law, and thereafter to us in the gospel"—before he addresses himself again squarely to the problem of knowledge in Book III. All of Book II, although under the title "knowledge," deals rather with man's need and God's objective provision to meet that need than with man's knowledge or subjective awareness of the work of redemption. It presents the "knowledge of God and ourselves" [4] only in so far as its objective source is concerned. But the objective revelation and Christ's work of salvation are not enough and do not comprise either salvation or knowledge of the means of salvation. Since the work of salvation was not undertaken for the sake of God's "private use, but to enrich the poor and needy," [5] it is "useless and of no importance so long as there is a separation between Christ and us." [6] It must be applied. "Whatever he [Christ] possesses is . . . nothing to us until we are united with him." [7] This application is the

[1] II.i–v.

[2] II.vi–xi.

[3] II.xii–xvii.

[4] Cf. I.i.1. and II.i.1–3, vi.1.

[5] III.i.1 (OS IV.1.9).

[6] *Ibid.* (lines 10–13).

[7] *Ibid.* (line 18).

work of the Holy Spirit, who is the "bond which efficaciously unites us to Christ."[8]

Faith, from man's side, is the "instrument" by which we "receive" Christ,[9] by which the righteousness of Christ is "attained"[10] or "possessed"[11] by us, by which we "perceive"[12] our salvation. Again, "through faith Christ is communicated to us; by it we come to God and enjoy the benefits of adoption."[13] Faith is a "channel"[14] through which Christ can flow to us and a "vessel" by which we draw upon or drink him.[15] The noetic aspect of this faith relationship which the Spirit works in man is now our concern.

It is chiefly in four places in the *Institutes* that Calvin treats of the work of the Spirit for the salvation of man. The first we have already considered as the *testimonium internum Spiritus Sancti,* which appeared in the role of accrediting the authority of the Scriptures, supporting the claim that in them God the Creator revealed himself. The second specific treatment occurs in II.ii.18–25. Here, after praising the abilities granted by God even to sinfully corrupt human reason, Calvin shows that nevertheless man's mind is totally incapable of grasping the truths of redemption until illuminated by a special work of the Holy Spirit. The third treatment is the general exposition of the illumination of the understanding and cleansing of the will with reference to the "gratuitous promise in Christ," or Calvin's doctrines of faith and repentance, III.i–iii. This is the parent discussion of the work of the Spirit in the *Institutes* and is presupposed by all the others. Again in III.xxiv we read of the illumination of the understanding in terms

[8] III.i.1 (OS IV.2.5).

[9] Com. Rm. 3:21 (CO XLIX.60b); Com. Jn. 1:12 (CO XLVII.13a).

[10] Com. Rm. "Argument" (CO XLIX.3a); 5:10 (p. 94b).

[11] Com. Gen. 15:6 (CO XXIII.213a); Com. Rm. 3:25 (CO XLIX.62d); 4:3 (p. 70b).

[12] Com. Isa. 12:2 (CO XXXVI.252a).

[13] Com. Eph. 1:18 (CO LI.150b).

[14] Com. Jn. 1:15 (CO XLVII.16d).

[15] *Ibid.,* 1:18 (p. 19b). The instrumental function of faith is sometimes expressed by Calvin in connection with the whole work of salvation in Aristotelian terms; for example, Rm. 3:24–25, "shows that God's mercy is the efficient cause, that Christ with his blood is the material cause, that the formal or instrumental cause is faith derived from the word, and that, moreover, the final cause is the glory of the divine justice and goodness." Com. Rm. 3:24 (CO XLIX.61c); III.xiv.17 (OS IV.235.20–28).

of the "effectual" or "internal" call in connection with the doctrine of election. In this instance Calvin is describing how the eternal decree is implimented by the preaching of the word and why only part of those who hear preaching are redeemed. Probably a fifth place should be cited, IV.xiv.8–10, where the illumination of the Spirit is seen to make the sacraments effective.

In perusal of these four or five discussions, the reader of Calvin can scarcely fail to note, although it would seem that many have failed, that in the first the whole concern is for the authority of the sacred book [16] and the resulting correlation is word and Spirit, or the Scripture and the *testimonium internum Spiritus Sancti.* But in all the others, and particularly in III.ii, the whole concern is for the appropriation of the work of Christ in redemption and the resulting correlation is Christ and faith. The relation between these two sets of concepts, "word and Spirit" and "Christ and faith," needs to be clarified in terms of the problem of knowledge, particularly in their objective aspects, because the terms "word" (Scripture, or special revelation) and "Christ" (saving revelation) are not exactly congruent. The treatment which keeps these two elements separate in Calvin's theology is not a vagary of method of a single edition of the *Institutes,* but Calvin's consistent practice from 1539 on, as well as in the revised Geneva catechism of 1542. It may satisfy Warfield to say that the latter word-pair is nearly enough identical with the former to need no separate discussion so far as the problem of knowledge is concerned,[17] or, vice versa, Wilhelm Niesel may explain the former in terms of the latter, denying any discrepancy by denying that Calvin was concerned with the inerrancy of the Bible as a formal

[16] I.vii.1 (OS III.65.6) "de Scripturae authoritate"; I.viii.1 (OS III.71.40). This is finally, as we have shown, the inerrancy of the documents of the sacred canon.

[17] Warfield never cites once from III.ii in his essay on "Calvin's Doctrine of the *Knowledge* of God" (my italics). He may have planned essays on subsequent parts of the *Institutes* and purposely delayed discussion of faith until another time, but the whole direction of the present article leads one to believe that he would still have been vulnerable to this criticism. For him the Bible was the object of faith for Calvin, *Calvin and Calvinism,* pp. 264 ff. On p. 300, he remarks that Christ is the "substance" of Scripture, but adds, "Calvin would certainly have said that our faith in Christ presupposes faith in the Scriptures, rather than that we believe in the Scriptures for Christ's sake."

authority.[18] But Calvin was aware that he dealt with two different magnitudes, as an analysis of the place of knowledge in his doctrine of faith will now show, although his own statement of the relation of the two elements is not adequate.

Before analyzing the doctrine of faith itself, a few general observations will be useful on its place in Calvin's systematic thought as seen in the development of the *Institutes,* not in the development of the doctrine itself, for it was essentially complete already in 1539, but in the way it took its place along with other doctrines.

From the first edition to that of 1554, the material that makes up III.ii, "Of Faith, where its definition is proposed and its properties explained," stood at the beginning of the section called "Of Faith, where the symbol which is called Apostolic is explained." It was followed in the same chapter by the doctrine of the Trinity, then the full analysis of the Creed. In the edition of 1539 the material on repentance was separated from that on the false sacraments and placed after the Creed analysis. It was followed by justification by faith, to make up as early as 1539 the core of the later Book III. Three more major movements occurred, which were, broadly speaking, as follows:

1) With subsequent additions and changes, the chapters on "Of faith, where the . . . creed is explained" (edition of 1554, chapters v–viii) contained a tremendously large part of the whole *Institutes.* They included both the main teachings on the person and work of Christ (which were removed forward in 1559 to form Book II), and on the church and sacraments (which were moved back in 1559 to make up Book IV). This shows the real scope of the doctrine in Calvin's theology, embracing the whole of the *cognitio Dei redemptoris* in its three main branches: its object in Christ (Book II), its subjective appropriation, which is faith proper (Book III), and the external means for this appropriation, or the church and the sacraments (Book IV). Until his last edition Calvin placed faith first in order in his soteriology as a kind of epistemological introduction, parallel to presenting his doctrines

[18] *Die Theologie Calvins,* p. 27. Throughout "The Knowledge of God," pp. 19–36, the doctrine of Scripture is merged with Calvin's teaching that Christ is the object of faith in a polemic against both verbal inerrancy and natural theology, with little positive reference to III.ii, where Calvin chose to discuss it.

of the revelation in creation and Scripture as an epistemological introduction to the "knowledge of God the Creator." In using the doctrine of faith (III.ii) as a point of departure, therefore, I am simply following Calvin's own earlier practice, one which the final disposition of the 1559 edition in no way invalidates.

The final arrangement of the *Institutes* proceeds in a more or less historical and logical order: from God, to creation, to the Fall of man and the need for Christ, to Christ himself, and then to the appropriation of Christ. But we are following the *ordo cognoscendi,* and from this point of view the center of and introduction to the *Institutes* is the doctrine of faith, because the believer actually in his own experience progresses from his own present knowledge and experience of Christ to see with new eyes his needy condition as well as to recognize God's work in creation which had formerly been mostly hidden from him in its religious significance, although continuing to exist.

2) The section called "Of the life of the Christian man" was moved from the very end of the *Institutes,* where it had stood next to the teachings about the state, and became an integral part of Book III. Thus sanctification comes to its rightful place along with repentance and justification, in close connection with the doctrine of faith.

3) In 1559 Calvin not only moved both the doctrines of Christ and of the church and sacraments away from that of faith, but he developed and added to that doctrine in the following way: The tiny section on "I believe in the Holy Spirit," which had been almost buried in the Creed analysis and was untouched after 1539, was greatly enlarged for the final edition and placed at the head of Book III. It retains its original character, stressing the application of Christ's work by the Spirit in illumination, regeneration, justification, and sanctification,[19] but comes into its own systematically as a prologue to faith, repentance, and the entire Book III. The prologue is made adequate to its new place by the

[19] This existed as early as ed. '36, but with extreme brevity. At that time 44 lines (CO I.71–72) were devoted to the Spirit's work, more than half of which repeated the Spirit's place in the Trinity, but in what remained, the expressions of the larger and later treatment were already present (p. 72b).

extremely important addition of the theme of union with Christ,[20] which is comprehensive enough to include all aspects of faith and regeneration. This theme will be treated toward the end of the present chapter as best expressing the character of faith according to Calvin.

Faith as Knowledge

THE OBJECT OF FAITH'S KNOWLEDGE.—Calvin defines faith by proceeding to the center of a series of concentric circles corresponding loosely to that which we referred to under the principle of accommodation: the existence of God, his power, his "veracity," God's will "toward us" as revealed in Scripture; then his benevolent will rather than his threats, and finally Christ, the only pledge of this beneficence. All of these circles are implied in faith, but only the last is properly speaking the object of faith. The aim of the progression is to arrive at a core of "explicit knowledge,"[21] clearly perceived and understood, without which there can be no saving faith. We shall consider first the object of this knowledge, then the illumination of the Spirit by which the mind of the elect perceives it.

We have already pointed to Calvin's disavowal of the possibility of man's knowing God's essence and of the irrelevance of the bare proposition "God exists," under the concepts of accommodation and the existentiality of all our knowledge of God. Accordingly, he calls it an error that the schoolmen make God the "object" of faith, thus releasing the mind to speculations.[22] He does, however, place special emphasis upon the power and, indeed, omnipotence[23] of God, together with his "veracity," in connection with faith. Only on the basis of these are his will and his work *erga nos* capable of supporting our confidence. These

[20] "Here is the place to note that all these declarations [of union with Christ, mostly from III.ii], except for a few words, were added in 1559." Doumergue, *Jean Calvin,* IV, 241.

[21] III.ii.2 (OS IV.11.1) "explicitam agnitionem."

[22] III.ii.1 (OS IV.7.19) "obiectum," cf. (pp. 8.10 ff. and 9.3 ff.); II.vi.4 (OS III.325.22 ff.); Com. Jn. 14:1 (CO XLVII.321–322a). "God *in himself* cannot be the connecting point of faith, but only God *toward us,*" Peter Brunner, *Vom Glauben,* p. 67.

[23] III.ii.31 (OS IV.40.26 ff.), par. 35 (p. 46.9).

are presuppositions of faith, without which we would be unable to believe that God can and invariably will do what he promises.[24] Thus, the veracity of God—which means both truth and trustworthiness, or truth with the connotation of unchangeability [25]—is styled the "general object" [26] of faith, the "foundation" and "presupposition" of trust in the divine will even as revealed in Scripture.[27]

God is true (*veracem*) not only because he is prepared to stand faithful to his promises, but because he really fulfills whatever he declares. . . . On the other hand, man is false. . . . The first clause contains the primary axiom of all Christian philosophy (*primarium axioma totius christianae philosophiae*).[28]

"Our faith cannot rest on anything other than his eternal truth (*aeterna eius veritate*)." [29] Mere knowledge, even the knowledge of faith, cannot stand alone without a "persuasion of the divine truth," [30] upon which we rightly presume when we renounce all self-dependence, and upon which all our hope is based.[31]

Linking together the motifs of all-powerful will, "toward us," as revealed in Scripture, Calvin makes a preliminary definition of faith based upon the veracity of God:

Faith is a knowledge of the divine will toward us received from his word. And the foundation of it is a previous persuasion of the truth

[24] Com. Mt. 9:27 (CO XLV.260 f.).

[25] Calvin links the two aspects by the frequent use of the words *verax* and *veritas* together, for example, III.ii.6, (OS IV.15.15 ff.), par. 12 (p. 22.3–9); III.xxii.43 (OS IV.54.24, 30). When used alone *veritas* often has the connotation of trustworthiness or constancy. Cf. Com. Ps. 40:11 (CO XXXI.414c) "truth (*veritas*) by which we are taught that God remains the same." Com. Jn. 1:17 (CO XLVII.18b). "Truth (*veritas*) denotes in my opinion a fixed and permanent state of things"; also Com. Rm. 3:4 (CO XLIX.48a–c). The central meaning is the correspondence of knowledge with its object. "In a word, truth (*veritas*) is a right and sincere knowledge of God (*Dei cognitio*) which frees us from all error and falsehood." Com. Titus 1:1 (CO LII.405a).

[26] III.ii.30 (OS IV.39.37). "Fateor, ut iam dixi, generale fidei obiectum (ut loquuntur) esse Dei veritatem."

[27] III.ii.6 (OS IV.15.10–13).

[28] Com. Rm. 3:4 (CO XLIX.48a–b), and *passim*.

[29] Com. Gen. 17:4 (CO XXIII.236a).

[30] III.ii.14 (OS IV.25.16) "divinae veritatis persuasione."

[31] III.ii.42 (OS IV.53.2).

of God (*veritate Dei*); concerning which if any doubt is entertained in the mind, the authority of the word will be dubious and weak, or will be no authority at all.[32]

But this is only preliminary, because it does not define closely enough. Scripture is not the exact object of faith. Even Satan knows that God is God and will do what he promises in his word. Unbelievers, as well as believers, can accept the "evangelical history"[33] and may even go so far as "to regard the word of God as an infallible oracle (*Dei sermonem pro certissimo habent oraculo*), and they do not wholly disregard its precepts and are moved in a measure by its threatenings and promises"[34]—but these do not have faith. This definition must still be narrowed.

Note that Calvin has here introduced Scripture before he has arrived at the differentia of faith. The reason is that only a part of Scripture is, strictly speaking, the object of faith. In the citations now to follow we find Calvin excluding elements of Scripture from his definition of the object of faith and at the same time stoutly defending the proposition that the whole of Scripture must be believed by the faithful man. Thus, it will emerge that for Calvin the Scripture is the formal authority of special revelation, but Christ alone is the material of saving faith and the proper object of faith's knowledge.

But since the heart of man is not aroused to faith by every utterance (*vocem*) of God, *we must further inquire what it is that faith properly has respect to in the word*. The declaration of God to Adam was "Thou shalt surely die," and the declaration to Cain, "The voice of thy brother's blood crieth unto me from the ground." But these of themselves, far from being fitted to establish faith, tend only to shake it. We do not deny, however, that it is the office of faith to subscribe to the truth of God (*veritati Dei*) whenever, whatever, and in whatever manner he speaks, but just now we are inquiring what faith finds in the word to lean upon and rest upon.[35]

[32] III.ii.6 (OS IV.15.10–15).
[33] III.ii.1 (OS IV.7.18), and par. 9 (p. 19.18 ff.).
[34] III.ii.9 (OS IV.19.21–24).
[35] III.ii.7 (OS IV.15.19–28, italics added).

Not the truth, validity, authority of *whatever* God says—although that, too, is to be accepted—but the specific object of faith. He continues,

When our conscience beholds nothing but indignation and vengeance, how can it but tremble and be afraid? And how can it but flee from God whom it fears? But faith ought to seek God, not fly from him. It appears, then, that we have not yet a full definition of faith, since knowing the will of God in any way whatever cannot be counted faith. What if instead of will—which is often the messenger of sorrow and the herald of terror—we substitute benevolence or mercy? Thus, we shall certainly approach nearer to the nature of faith. . . . The *promise of grace* is needful which testifies to us that he is a propitious father, since we cannot approach him without it, and it is upon this alone that the human heart can securely depend. For this reason the two things, mercy and truth (*misericordia et veritas*) are generally united in the Psalms, as they really belong together, because it would be of no avail to us to know that God is true (*Deum esse veracem*) did he not allure us to himself by his mercy, nor could we embrace his mercy, did he not offer it with his own mouth.[36]

Then follow citations from the Psalms linking mercy and truth, illustrating, incidentally, that the Old Testament references are as valid a support for his contention as what he finds in the New.

Elsewhere appears the same distinction, that faith, although it believes every word of God, has for its specific object the promise of God's mercy.

We make the foundation of faith the gratuitous promise, because in it faith properly consists. For although it holds that God is always true (*veracem*), whether he command or forbid, whether he promise or threaten; although it obediently receives his commands, observes his prohibitions, and attends to his threatenings; yet properly it begins with the promise, stands upon it, and ends in it. For it seeks life in God, which is not found in the commands nor in the edicts of punishment but in the promise of mercy, and that only which is gratuitous, for a conditional promise, which sends us back to our works, promises life only insofar as we find it in ourselves. . . . Wherefore the Apostle bears this testimony to the gospel, that it is the word of faith (*verbum*

[36] III.ii.7 (OS IV.15.28–16.9, italics added); cf. Com. Rm. 4:22 (CO XLIX.85c).

fidei), which he denies to both the precepts and promises of the Law, since there is nothing which can establish faith except that free embassy by which God reconciles the world to himself. Hence repeatedly the same apostle uses faith and gospel as correlatives (*correlatio*).[37]

Here in the process of defining accurately the object of faith, Calvin produces the correlative formulae "faith and the gospel," which is the same as faith and Christ. This excludes several elements of sacred Scripture, because Scripture for him contains words of God that are not words of salvation, namely, various oracles of condemnation, the precepts, promises, and threats, or altogether, the conditional salvation of the law.

The "law," taken in its broadest sense, meant for Calvin the whole Old Testament religion, including the moral law, with its legal promises and threats, the ceremonial law, and the covenant of grace.[38] But faith never did embrace the whole of this. The faith, for example, of Abraham, which is in substance the same as ours, was attached to the promise of the covenant rather than the precepts of the law.[39] True, "the law contains here and there promises of mercy, but as they are borrowed from elsewhere, they are not considered as belonging truly to the law when its real nature is being discussed."[40] The law cannot be the object of saving faith, because it throws responsibility back upon man. Even the reprobate know the revelation of the moral law either as written or in conscience, as well as God's faithfulness in maintaining it, but they do not thereby have faith, which springs from God's mercy.

. . . faith is reduced to nothing if supported by works . . . faith perishes except the soul rest secure in the goodness of God. Therefore faith is not a bare knowledge either of God or his truth, or a simple persuasion that God is or that his word is true, but a sure knowledge received from the gospel, which obtains peace and repose of conscience with regard to God. The sum of the matter therefore is this—that if salvation rests upon the keeping of the law, the soul can have no con-

[37] III.ii.29 (OS IV.39.1–21, italics added); the same occurs in Com. Heb. 11:7 (CO LV.150d–151a).

[38] II.vii.1, *passim*.

[39] Com. Rm. 4:13 (CO XLIX.76c–d).

[40] II.xi.7 (OS III.429.30–34).

fidence concerning it. . . . Therefore we are wretched and lost if we are sent back to works to seek the cause or certainty of salvation.[41]

This is not exclusively an Old Testament problem, for much of the teaching of Jesus also belongs to the moral law, and to the curse upon the reprobate.[42] Not the law, but "the *gratuita promissio,* the *promissio misericordia,* the *liberalis legatio qua sibi Deus mundum reconciliat*—these constitute the essence of the Gospel and the firm foundation of faith." [43]

The formula Christ and faith, sometimes alone, sometimes with the explicit exclusion of the law, occurs throughout the commentaries. "Faith looks at nothing but the mercy of God and a dead and risen Christ." [44] This reference continues by rejecting the law, both moral and ceremonial.

Everything which faith ought to contemplate is exhibited to us in Christ, hence it follows that a bare and confused knowledge of God is not taken for faith, but that which is directed to Christ in order to seek God in him, and this cannot be except where the power and offices of Christ are understood.[45]

For faith ought to look to him [the Son of God] alone; on him it relies, in him it rests and terminates.[46]

It is Christ alone on whom, strictly speaking (*proprie*) faith ought to look. . . . This is the proper look of faith, to be fixed on Christ.[47]

Therefore Christ proposes himself as the object (*scopum*) to which our faith ought to be directed. . . . It is one of the chief articles of our faith, that our faith ought to be directed to Christ alone.[48]

The Spirit is said to testify of Christ, because he retains and fixes our faith in him alone, that we may not seek elsewhere any part of our salvation.[49]

[41] Com. Rm. 3:14, 15 (CO XLIX.78b–c).

[42] Com. Mt. 23, int. to vv.13 ff. (CO XLV.626d). Like the moral law, the woes pronounced upon the Pharisees both contribute to the Pharisees' inexcusability and serve as admonition for the elect.

[43] Bavinck, in *Calvin and the Reformation,* p. 115.

[44] Com. Gal. 3:6 (CO L.205d).

[45] Com. Eph. 3:12 (CO LI.183d).

[46] *Ibid.,* 4:13 (p. 200c).

[47] Com. Jn. 3:16 (CO XLVII.64d).

[48] *Ibid.,* 14:1 (p. 321d, 322a).

[49] *Ibid.,* 15:26 (p. 354b).

Because of this bold distinction within the realm of special revelation, Calvin had to defend himself against the claim that he rejected parts of Scripture.

Therefore, when we say that faith must rest upon the gratuitous promise, we do not deny that the believers embrace and accept the word of God in all its parts, but we designate the promise of mercy as its special object (*in proprium scopum destinamus*). Believers, indeed, ought to recognize God as judge and avenger of wickedness, and yet they behold specially his clemency.[50]

The two magnitudes are differentiated clearly: (1) the whole of Scripture, which must be believed and is accredited by the Spirit and (2) the gratuitous promise in Christ, the substance of Scripture, which alone is *proprie* the object of saving faith. Calvin distinguishes between them, not to chose one rather than the other, but to affirm both.

These calumniators [Pighius, chiefly] unjustly charge us as if we denied that faith has respect to the word of God in all its parts (*ad omnes verbi Dei partes*). We mean only to maintain these two points: first, that it [faith] never stands firmly until it comes to the gratuitous promise; secondly, that it reconciles us to God only because it joins us to Christ.[51]

The man of faith accepts all of Scripture, but faith cannot be identified with the acceptance of Scripture, for then unbelievers could not be distinguished from believers. "Shall everyone who believes that God is just in what he commands and true in what he threatens be on that account classed among the believers?"[52] At the same time Calvin fights every enthusiastic effort to separate faith from Scripture, which cannot be divided any more than rays of light from the sun[53] or the roots from the fruit of a tree.[54] "Take away the word, and no faith will remain."[55] "And this

[50] III.ii.29 (OS IV.39.25–31). This reference continues with a quotation of Rm.1:15–17.

[51] III.ii.30 (OS IV.40.2–7).

[52] *Ibid.* (lines 9–11).

[53] III.ii.6 (OS IV.14.9).

[54] III.ii.31 (OS IV.40.22).

[55] III.ii.6 (OS IV.14.27); Com. Isa. 25:9 (CO XXXVI.421c).

connection of faith with the word ought to be well understood and carefully remembered, for faith can bring us nothing more than what it receives from the word."[56]

Calvin calls this progression from the word at large to the gratuitous promise a descent from "genus to species,"[57] or reversing the movement; he says "the gospel is called the word of faith by synecdoche for the principle part [of God's whole word including threats]."[58] In the latter instance he goes on to state the precedence of the gratuitous promise in the order of knowing. But he shows no further relation of the two elements. Both of these characterizations can express the fact that as an object of knowledge the gospel alone is "smaller" than the total utterance of God, but it cannot account for the qualitative difference between the acceptance of Scripture as such and the acceptance of Christ in faith. Although our analysis of faith is not yet complete, we have come far enough to see the inadequacy of this method of relating two elements of knowledge in faith and to consider briefly what it may mean.

Calvin had in his hand, as it were, the very instrument by which Luther had already freed himself of slavish adherence to the Bible and tortuous exegesis: the principle of "Christ, the Lord of Scripture"[59]—but he did not wield it. He developed, as we shall see, a lofty, psychologically subtle, and exclusively Christo-

[56] Com. Rm. 4:22 (CO XLIX.85c).

[57] III.ii.6 (OS IV.14.6) "Quanquam facilior erit et aptior methodus, si gradatim a genere ad speciem descendimus."

[58] Com. Heb. 11:7 (CO LV.151a).

[59] *Christus dominus scripturae,* cited by Emil Brunner, *Dogmatik,* I, 116, cf. pp. 113–118 on the history of the doctrine of scriptural authority. A passage in Calvin that seems near this Lutheran principle is the comment on I Jn. 4:1–2, "Try the spirits," and "hereby ye know": "I grant that doctrines are to be tested by the word of God, but to have God's word in our hands will avail little or nothing, for its meaning will not appear to us unless the spirit of discretion (*spiritus prudentiae*) be present." And finally, having discussed private and church opinion and the place of counsels, Calvin adds, "He lays down a special mark by which true prophets might be better discerned from false. Yet he only repeats here what we have met with before, namely, Christ, for as he is the goal (*scopus*) at which a right faith aims, so is he the stone (*scopulum*) on which all heretics stumble" (CO LV.347d, 348d). The *spiritus prudentiae* is the *lapis Lydius* (p. 348a) of true doctrine. The *scopus* of faith, Christ, is the *scopulus* of stumbling for heretical interpretations.

centric doctrine of faith that could have come only from a living faith unencumbered by heteronomous formal authority, yet, as far as his theology in general was concerned, he never was willing to deny authority to a single casual expression in Scripture, except minor and theologically unaccounted for blunders of copyists and translators. That he developed such a living doctrine of faith[60] without the freedom surreptitiously allowed by the elasticity of the allegorical exegesis and without Luther's real freedom from the letter and canon of Scripture is a credit to both his personal faith and his exegetical skills. But still he must be judged to have two not entirely reconcilable theological explanations of the faithful man's knowledge of God's special revelation. This flaw can be described, although he never used the terms, as a discrepancy between the so-called formal and material principles of the Reformation: the authority of Scripture and justification by faith in Christ.[61]

Paul Lehmann, in "The Reformers' Use of the Bible," says that Calvin's "interpretation" of the place of Scripture in faith is, like Luther's, christocentric,[62] but that his "apperception," his deep-lying, inherited recognition of their authority derived from the Middle Ages, follows the old pattern of inspired words.[63] This is a helpful description, but I believe the incongruity in Calvin can be made still more explicit. Even his "interpretation," his consciously stated theological analysis of the object of faith, contains this dissonance. We must conclude, in fact, that two "interpretations" exist side by side in Calvin's theology concerning the object of the knowledge of faith, because he never fully integrated and related systematically the faithful man's acceptance of the authority of the Bible *en bloc* with faith as directed exclusively toward

[60] For the similarity of Luther's and Calvin's doctrines of faith and Calvin's dependence on Luther, see Brunner, *Vom Glauben,* p. 139, n. 3.

[61] For the history of this terminology see Ritschl, *Dogmengeschichte,* I, 42 ff. Ritschl rejects the terms in his own analysis, p. 46.

[62] Pages 330, 336–338.

[63] "Apperception has to do with all those ways in which in their use of the Bible the Reformers were children of their time. . . . What has unhappily occurred is that the ways in which the Reformers were children of their time have triumphed over the ways in which they were pioneers in the use of the Bible." *Ibid.,* pp. 342, 344.

Christ. And in addition his "apperception" remained on the level of verbal inerrancy.[64]

Why Calvin failed to be more specific here is a problem difficult to solve. The ordering of his systematic writings is of little assistance, because he separated the problem of accrediting Scripture from the problem of faith in Christ and gave few methodological statements relating the two. Probably the issue did not stand out to him as it does today, because of Calvin's preoccupation with the special problems of the Reformation and its opponents, particularly with organizing the Reformation into an enduring theology and church institution. I offer the following suggestions: Calvin did not face or did not realize that he was facing serious historical criticism of the Bible, which has driven theology since the nineteenth century to discard the doctrine of verbal inerrancy. Instead, he was challenged by Rome and the Anabaptists—not on the question of whether or not Scripture had authority—but upon the issue of extending a religious authority that had already included and accepted Scripture, on the one hand, to the traditions of the church, and on the other, to private revelations. Since some of the papal and Anabaptist doctrines did not differ materially from many of the peripheral teachings of Scripture, particularly as found in the apocryphal books, only a rigidly held formal authority could combat them, and this Calvin presented in the sole authority of Scripture and the authority of the whole of Scripture, which he restated in such a way as to preclude the two then-current errors.[65] Further, under the duress of polemic he was driven, as was Luther, to take recourse to proof-texts as a countermeasure against the centuries of scholastic philosophical and allegorical isogesis. The "simple" [66] meaning of a text became in his

[64] The distinction of Lehmann is better than that of Lobstein, who sees Calvin combining "the evangelical and Protestant notion of faith (*foi*) with the scholastic and intellectualistic conception of belief (*croyance*)." "La Connaissance religieuse," p. 83. He discusses the latter without showing how it differed from the scholastic view, for example, in reference to church authority, pp. 82 ff.

[65] Lehmann, "The Reformers' Use of the Bible," p. 343; Heim, *Das Gewissheitsproblem*, pp. 269–271; Lobstein, *Die Ethik Calvins*, pp. 83 f.

[66] "Let us know, therefore, that the true meaning of Scripture is that which is natural and simple (*qui germanus est ac simplex*)." Com. Gal. 4:22 (CO L.237a); the same occurs in Com. Ps. 42:4 (CO XXXI.427d).

hands such an effective weapon for the criticism of the papal church that it is small wonder that he took it unconditionally for God's own authority. The wonder is that he did not stop there. The strength of Calvin's theology and his genius in this area of it shows through in spite of the elements that remain of the older view, in that reflection upon the deeper issues of faith—not retreat from historical criticism—led him to a strongly Christocentric, not merely Bibliocentric, view of faith. While this makes it all the more remarkable that his doctrine of faith depended upon the material rather than the formal principle, it may account for the fact that he never felt urged to give up the doctrine of verbal inerrancy and that there remain in his theology all too ample grounds for the turn that Calvinistic orthodoxy took.[67] What was adequate for him on this score cannot but be judged inadequate by a theologian today. The newness of the so-called "new" Reformation theology [68] is more than anything else an affirmation that living faith in Christ as conceived by the Reformers has survived the nineteenth century's successful attack upon the formal authority of the sacred canon. That both Luther and Calvin found Christ and not a book the real center and object of faith long before criticism became powerful shows that the rediscovery of the Gospel in this century by those who no longer can consider the Bible's inerrancy an axiom of faith is not a retreat, but a rediscovery of one of the deepest insights of the Reformation.

Let us now continue with Calvin's doctrine of faith, and particularly the problem of knowledge as it appears in this new orientation, not in terms of a book accredited by the Spirit, but with

[67] That the unresolved problem to which we have referred actually exists in Calvin and therefore that Calvin points in two different ways at once is illustrated by the two following modern judgments. A. M. Hunter writes, "Though Calvin might have disclaimed responsibility for the mode of expression, the article in the Formula Consensus Helvetica pertaining to the Scripture only carries his views to their conclusion." *The Teaching of Calvin,* p. 69. This may be cautiously said with an eye on Calvin's doctrine of Scripture. But Paul Lehmann writes, "This confession . . . was as remote as could be from the mind of the Reformers." "The Reformers' Use of the Bible," p. 342, n. 32. This may be said with an eye on Calvin's doctrine of faith.

[68] This name is loosely applicable to Barth, Brunner, Niebuhr, and their fellow opponents of rationalistic liberalism.

Christ as object and the Spirit's work described by the less restricted word "illumination."

We shall discuss this problem on two levels: the knowledge of God's mercy possessed before the coming of Christ, as limited in the economy of revelation; and the incomplete state of the knowledge of faith as limited by individual and subjective factors.[69]

THE CHANGING FORMS OF THE HISTORICAL REVELATION.—Calvin maintains stoutly the identity of the object of the knowledge of faith throughout the changing forms in the history of revelation.[70] The object has always been Christ. "Christ was always exhibited to the holy fathers under the law as the object (*objectum*) toward which they should direct their faith."[71] "The fathers, when they wished to behold God, always turned their eyes to Christ. I mean not only that they beheld God in his eternal Logos (*sermone*), but also they attended with their whole mind and the whole affection of their heart to the promised manifestation in Christ."[72] He is the "substance" and "foundation" of both the old and the new covenants,[73] which have the "same inheritance" and the "same Mediator" of a "common salvation."[74] "It is the identical faith that is held by us today and by our fathers, for both acknowledge the same God and father of our Lord Jesus Christ."[75] The variations as far as the object of faith is concerned are only in the "mode of administration,"[76] or "instruction,"[77] which, as we have pointed out elsewhere, represent successive accommodations of God's mysteries to human capacity. They represent a

[69] Calvin makes exactly this distinction, Com. Gal. 4:1 (CO L.225–226). Thus, in the first sense Abraham and the prophets are our inferiors, but in the second, we compare to them as mere children.

[70] It is odd that Peter Brunner does not touch upon this problem in his book *Vom Glauben,* particularly in his section on knowledge, pp. 116–137.

[71] II.vi.2 (OS III.323.30); cf. II.vi, vii, ix–xi, *passim.*

[72] Com. Jn. 1:18 (CO XLVII.20a); cf. 9:58 (p. 215d).

[73] II.xi.1 (OS III.423.11–15); Com. Isa. 42:6 (CO XXXVII.64d).

[74] II.x.1 (OS III.403.10).

[75] Com. Isa. 40:21 (CO XXXVII.21c), and 43:10 (p. 89a); II.x.2 (OS III.404.20–22).

[76] III.xi.1 (OS III.423.12, 22); II.x.2 (OS III.404.7).

[77] II.xi.6, 13 (OS III.428.22, 435.10).

change, not in the object of faith, but in the degree of clarity with which God makes it known. Christ appeared in the ceremonies of the Old Testament in "the same image in which he now appears in full brightness to us." [78] Calvin speaks of the "clearness of the Gospel, and the more obscure dispensation of the word which preceded it," [79] the latter consisting of "prophecies," [80] "shadows and figures," [81] or "types." [82] The relation is not that of simple promise and fulfillment, but promises of different degrees of clarity. Even the Gospel is a promise. Faith believes what it does not yet possess, thus must be supported by hope.[83] We must consider the "nature or quality of the promises, because the Gospel points with the finger to what the law shadowed under types." [84] The ceremonies of the Old Testament Law were "symbols of confirmation" [85] of the one eternal covenant of grace, they were "shadowy, inefficacious," and therefore "temporary." [86] The Old Testament consisted in "figures," exhibiting only the "image and shadow in the absence of the reality, but the latter [New Testament] exhibits the present truth and the solid body." [87]

The development in forms of revelation was a regular progression, not haphazard, having as its only explanation that it was God's will so to reveal himself. But in spite of Calvin's sense of the historic development of revelation he insists throughout that Christ was pointed to, and he can therefore call the Old Testament people the "faithful," or the "church" in the same manner as those of the New Testament and speak of their relation to Christ. "The difference between us and the ancient fathers lies in accidents, not in substance." [88] "The faithful [Old Testament] were plainly and publicly taught by the sacrifices of the law that salvation was to be sought solely in that expiation which Christ alone completed. . . . The prosperous and happy state of the church

[78] II.ix.1 (OS III.398.14).
[79] II.xi.10 (OS III.432.35).
[80] II.vi.4 (OS III.325.3).
[81] II.vii.1 (OS III.327.1); II.ix.1 (OS III.399.21).
[82] II.xi.6 (OS III. 428.25).
[83] III.ii.41, *passim*.
[84] II.ix.3 (OS III.401.19–21).
[85] II.xi.4 (OS III.427.11).
[86] *Ibid.* (lines 24–26).
[87] *Ibid.* (p. 426. 10–13); Com. Gal. 3:23 (CO L.220d).
[88] Com. Gal. 4:1 (CO L.224d); cf. III.xxii.6 (OS IV.385.22–24): "it ought not to be doubted that Jacob was ingrafted with angels into the body of Christ, that he might be a partaker of the same life."

was always founded on the person of Christ."[89] David was a "lively image of Christ (*vivam Christi imaginem*)."[90] The Jews has a "taste" of Christ under the law.[91] The patriarchs had Christ as the "pledge (*pignus*) of their covenant."[92] The Old Testament sacraments served the Jews in every respect equal to ours as "a seal of the righteousness of faith." "Therefore, whatever is presented to us today in our sacraments was anciently received by the Jews in theirs, namely, Christ with his spiritual riches."[93] "The hope of all the pious had never been placed anywhere but in Christ."[94] The people of the old covenant "both possessed and knew Christ the Mediator (*habuisse ipsos et cognovisse mediatorem Christum*), by whom they were joined to God and were made partakers of his promises."[95]

Throughout the Old Testament commentaries Calvin discusses faith in exactly the same language as in the New Testament and in the *Institutes*. The definition toward which our present discussion is moving is just as applicable to Adam or Able as to the Apostles or any subsequent Christian. The only distinguishing mark of faith in the old covenant is the lesser degree of knowledge caused by the more obscure manner in which Christ is presented. The existence or nonexistence of this knowledge, which is knowledge of God through the promise in Christ, is designated as the difference between the heathen and the chosen people, and the degree of it as the difference between the Old Testament and the New Testament, as in the following from the comments on Isaiah.

It is proper to observe the contrast between that dark and feeble kind of knowledge (*obscurum et tenuem notitiae modum*) with which the fathers were endowed under the law and the fullness which shines forth to us in the Gospel. Though God deigned to bestow upon his ancient people the light of heavenly doctrine, he became more familiarly known through Christ. . . . There is no other way in which God can be known but through Christ, who is the image and pattern of his

[89] II.vi.2 (OS III.321.33–37).

[90] II.vi.2 (OS III.322.22); II.vii.2 (OS III.328.3 ff.); Com. Habak. 3:13 (CO XLIII. 581d).

[91] II.vii.1 (OS III.327.36).

[92] II.x.23 (OS III.421.31).

[93] IV.xiv.23 (OS V.281.13–15) and *passim*.

[94] II.vi.3 (OS III.324.24).

[95] II.x.2 (OS III.404.20–22).

substance. . . . Although Jews, Turks, and other infidels boast that they worship God the Creator of heaven and earth, yet they worship an imaginary God; however obstinate they may be, they follow vague and uncertain opinions instead of truth; they grope in the dark and worship their own imagination instead of God. In short, outside of Christ, all religion is deceitful and transitory and every kind of worship ought to be abhorred and condemned.[96]

INDIVIDUAL LIMITATIONS OF FAITH'S KNOWLEDGE.—Next to this limitation of knowledge caused by the limitations of revelation in the period in which it occurs there are the more subjective and individual limitations on the knowledge of individual believers. Here Calvin comes to a conception of "implicit faith."

Moreover, I do not deny that in some sense there may be a kind of implicit faith (*fides implicita*) which is not accompanied by a full and distinct knowledge of sound doctrine, provided that we hold this, that faith always springs from the word of God and takes its origin from true principles, and therefore is always connected with some light of knowledge (*aliquam scientiae lucem*).[97]

Faith is called implicit with reference to its degree of knowledge, that is, the depth to which the mind has penetrated in understanding the mystery of Christ, which it has for its object. This appears on two levels: (1) the implicitness of a "preparatory" state of faith and (2) the necessary implicitness of all faith in that no one ever understands completely the saving mysteries while in this life.

First, the "preparatory" implicit faith. The origins of this theme are Biblical accounts of persons whom Calvin regards as faithful, although obviously uninstructed or but little instructed. The theme is frequent in the commentaries, and incidentally an evidence for his conviction of the inerrancy of the Scripture, for each use of the words "believe," "know," and "faith" is investigated closely upon the assumption that writings as different and as far separated as II Kings and Paul's epistles should be consistent in verbal details. The sacrifices of Namaan the Syrian were approved by the prophet of Israel, and the prayers of Cornelius the

96 Com. Isa. 25:9 (CO XXXVI.420c–d).
97 Com. Mt. 15:22 (CO XLV.456d, 457a).

Roman were acceptable to God, "which neither could have obtained without faith." So also for the Ethiopian eunuch, who would scarcely have made such a long and difficult journey "without some endowment of faith." Yet none of these had received instruction concerning the Mediator or the Person of Christ or his high office and power with the Father, so their faith was in some measure "implicit."[98] "Still, it is certain that they were imbued with principles which might give some foretaste of Christ (*gustum aliquem Christi*), however slight."[99] "Therefore, although their knowledge [!] of Christ (*Christi cognitio*) may have been obscure, it is not reasonable to suppose they had none at all, because they practiced the sacrifices of the law which they must have discerned by their end, which is Christ, from the illegitimate sacrifices of the heathen."[100]

In the same vein in the commentaries we find Calvin guarding against the impression that anyone can be said truly to have faith without knowledge. He shows that the "doctrine of Christ" preceded Zaccheus' conversion.[101] In the case of the Syrophoenician woman, Matthew 15:22 ff., he insists that the woman must have had some familiarity with the law and prophets in order to call Christ "son of David," and he assumes that Christ also spoke to her by a "secret inspiration," although the text specifically states that Christ "made no reply." She, therefore, "continually hears the sound of that doctrine which she had already learned, that Christ came as redeemer."[102] This tiny "seed of doctrine," not some false knowledge, finally yielded abundant fruit in faith.[103] The "faith" that saved blind Bartimaeus was no mere "confused knowledge," but faith in the Messiah based on the law and the prophets. This Calvin maintains because he, too, called Jesus the "son of David."[104]

In these foregoing instances Calvin is seen to defend by a

[98] II.ii.32 (OS. IV.43.15–30). [99] *Ibid.* (line 31).

[100] *Ibid.* (pp. 43.38–44.3). [101] Com. Lk. 19:9 (CO XLV. 565b).

[102] (CO XLV.457b). Note in the place cited how Calvin harmonizes this story with Rm. 10:14, where it is said that one must already believe in order to call on Christ.

[103] *Ibid.* (p.457c), also "spark of doctrine" (p. 459d).

[104] Com. Mk. 10:52 (CO XLV.562a, cf. p. 561a).

sometimes strained exegesis his contention that "faith consists, not in ignorance, but in knowledge (*cognitione*)" [105] and that "there is no faith without knowledge (*notitia*)." [106] "A bare and confused knowledge (*notitiam*) of God must not be taken for faith, but rather that which is directed to Christ, in order in him to seek God, and this cannot be unless the power and offices of Christ are understood." [107] It is the same when he insists that faith and "doctrine" are inseparable and shows that the words "believer" and "disciple" refer synonymously to the faithful.[108]

Even this preparatory state of knowledge, however, must have the right object, Christ, for it to be considered faith.[109] The friends of the woman of Samaria are said improperly (*improprie*) to "believe" in John 4:39, because they had simply taken the woman's word that Jesus was a prophet.[110] In verse 40, when two days had elapsed in which Jesus taught, "the word *credendi* is used in another sense, because it signifies not only that they were prepared for faith, but that they were instructed in correct faith." [111] The same is true of the nobleman whose son was healed, who at first merely believed that Jesus could work a miracle—a "particular faith." [112] But this is not even a knowledge that can be said to

[105] III.ii.2 (OS IV.10.12). [106] Com. Titus 1:1 (CO LII.404d).

[107] Com. Eph. 3:12 (CO LI.183d).

[108] II.ii.6 (OS IV.13.20); Com. Isa. 19:21 (CO XXXVI. 344d–345a); cf. Com. Jn. 1:12 (CO XLVII.12a–b).

[109] "The twelve did not all at once comprehend what Christ had taught, yet it is enough that according to the capacity of their faith they confessed him the author of salvation and submitted themselves to him in all things." Com. Jn. 6:69 (CO XLVII.163b), cf. 9:37 (p. 232d). The state of mind of the disciples who returned to the sepulcher on resurrection morning and whose knowledge certainly exceeded that of blind Bartimaeus, Calvin calls "faith, although inaccurately (*improprie*), because it was produced only by the doctrine of the gospel, and it tended to no other but Christ. . . . When the Scripture speaks of the feeble beginnings of faith, it says that Christ is born in us, and we in turn in him. But the disciples must be placed almost below infancy, because they are ignorant of the resurrection of Christ." Com. Jn. 20:3 (CO XLVII.428b).

[110] Com. Jn. 4:39 (CO XLVII.97c). [111] *Ibid.*, 4:40 (p. 98a).

[112] Calvin detects more than one use of the word "faith" in Scripture. "Particular" faith relates to trust in some special promise such as that a miracle will be performed or the power to work miracles itself as in I Cor. 13:2. Cf. Com. I Cor. 12:8 (CO XLIX.500a) where Judas' power to work miracles is called by Calvin a "particular" faith. Again it may refer to purity of doctrine. Sometimes Scripture by catachresis applies the term to a false profession. Cf. III.ii.13, *passim*.

grow into faith. "For now [after the completion of the miracle] he began to believe in a different manner, namely, embracing the doctrine of Christ, he professed himself to be one of his disciples."[113] No general trust in Christ as a prophet is accepted as a beginning of faith. Such, however great, is entirely superseded by knowledge, however slight, of Christ as God's salvation. The latter knowledge may be enveloped in all kinds of misunderstanding and may even be a spur to a sinful effort to force God's hand, but of whatever degree and however incomplete, it is real knowledge and has the proper object.[114]

Secondly, Calvin maintains that in a sense all faith is implicit.

> We grant, indeed, that as long as we wander about the world our faith is implicit, not only because as yet many things are hidden, but because surrounded by many clouds of error we do not attain to all. The highest wisdom of even those who are most perfect is to advance and to strive forward in a calm and docile manner.[115]

This aspect has already been treated under the subjects of accommodation and of the comprehensibility of what is revealed. Connected with it is Calvin's frequently reiterated idea that the believer progresses constantly in the knowledge of faith. There must be "a continual growth, both in knowledge and in conformity to the image of God."[116]

> In proportion to the progress we afterwards make (and we ought continually to improve) we arrive at a nearer and more certain view of him, and the very continuance of it renders it more familiar to us.

[113] Com. Jn. 4:53 (CO XLVII. 103b); cf. 2:23 (pp. 49–50).

[114] Calvin says Rebecca acted in admirable faith in recognizing that Jacob rather than Esau was the chosen one, yet she is to be blamed for her lies, since she sinfully refused to wait for God's carrying out of his promise. "Thus we see her faith mixed with an unjust and immoderate zeal. This is to be noted carefully, so that we may understand that a pure and clear knowledge does not always light the souls of the pious so that they are governed in all their actions by the Holy Spirit, but that the scanty light which shows them the way is enveloped (*implicitam*) in various clouds of ignorance and error, so that while they hold a right course and strive to the goal, yet they continually err." Com. Gen. 27:5 (CO XXIII.374c). Cf. Com. Mt. 9:20 (CO XLV.256d–257a).

[115] III.ii.4 (OS IV.11.28–30, and throughout).

[116] Com. II Cor. 3:18 (CO L.47a); Com. Jn. 2:11 (CO XLVII.42c) and 8:32 (p. 202c).

Thus, we see that the mind illuminated by the knowledge of God is at first involved in much ignorance, which is gradually removed.[117]

Calvin rejects the scholastic notion of *fides implicita* on two grounds. First, such a faith has a wrong object, the church.

For we do not obtain salvation by our promptitude to embrace as truth whatever the church may have prescribed or by transferring to her the province of inquiry and of knowledge. But when we know God to be a propitious father to us through the reconciliation effected by Christ and that Christ is given to us for righteousness, sanctification, and life—by this knowledge, I say, not by renouncing our understanding, we obtain an entrance into the kingdom of heaven.[118]

We have already seen Calvin's rejection of church authority in matters central to faith, as the "judgments of men."[119] Secondly, such a faith precludes the increasing progress in knowledge that is one of the marks of a true, although implicit, faith. The above-mentioned characters from the New Testament were all pressing toward fuller knowledge, and "this docility with a desire for improvement is far from the gross ignorance in which those are stupefied who are content with the implicit faith which the papists have invented."[120] The faith of the "papists," then, according to Calvin, instead of being an (1) increasing (2) knowledge (3) of Christ, consists in a static assent to the authority of an idolatrous substitute, the church.[121]

In summary: One can see the importance of knowledge of Christ in Calvin's conception of faith by the forced effort he makes to include it in the case of Naaman, as well as his rejection of mere ecclesiastical authority. Yet the very use of the term "implicit," in spite of his hatred for what it signified among the scholastics, shows that he is unwilling to say that the minimum limit of knowledge is more than theoretically conceivable. It is

[117] III.ii.19 (OS IV.29.31–36), cf. par. 20 (p. 30.15 ff.); also Com. I Cor. 13:9 ff. (CO XLIX.513c, 514); Com. Heb. 5:13 (CO XLV.66c).

[118] III.ii.2 (OS IV.10.13–20). [119] *Supra*, p. 109.

[120] II.ii.5 (OS IV.13.9–11).

[121] The argument between Calvin and the schoolmen on *fides implicita* occurs in modern form, Calvin's point taken by Lecerf, with a disclaimer by Gilson, in *Christianity and Philosophy*, pp. 53 ff., *passim*.

further noteworthy for the place of knowledge in faith that Calvin drives his discussion of faith's knowledge to the degree of trying to distinguish between the faithful and the unfaithful in terms of knowledge rather than simply abandoning the problem to the mystery of election. Even in his doctrine of election he makes it the advent of knowledge via the external (preaching) and the internal (illumination of the Spirit) calls, not some enduring quality or growing "seed" planted at birth in the elect, by which salvation is obtained.[122] Even here faith retains its instrumental function, and knowledge is one of the essential elements of it.[123]

Thus far we have been able to see the indispensable place of knowledge in faith as Calvin conceived it. "Some foretaste of Christ" (*gustus aliquis Christi*) is "knowledge of Christ" (*cognitio Christi*), although it may be extremely "obscure" (*obscura*). This knowledge involves a conscious turning away from false gods and an awareness of the promise of mercy of the true God as revealed in Christ. Although the knowledge may be limited "accidentally" on the one hand by God's economy of revelation, or, on the other, it may be so incomplete as to be more accurately termed preparatory rather than a part of faith itself, still Calvin insists that it is somehow present. Man at no point turns to God by a blind instinct. God addresses him, "calls" him, appeals to him in terms of the highest part of his nature, his intelligence. God speaks a word, which man must comprehend and answer. God's revelation must become man's *knowledge*. There is no faith, so far as Calvin is concerned, without knowledge.

The Illumination of the Mind by the Holy Spirit

A description of the object of faith's knowledge and the indispensability of knowledge to faith does not fully describe Calvin's

[122] III.xxiv.3, 4, 10, etc.

[123] Knowledge never becomes a criterion by which the faithful can be distinguished from the unfaithful, because God has enlightened some of the reprobate with true knowledge of the gospel to deepen their inexcusability. The favorite examples are Saul, Judas, and Simon Magus. But these never have the full enjoyment and confidence which true faith brings, and they lack the quality of perseverance. Knowledge, then, while it belongs to the definition of faith, is not an external criterion of it. III.ii.10–12; III.xxiv.6, 7.

doctrine of faith or even the place of knowledge in it. Even less does it tell what Calvin means by "knowledge" in this connection. For this is not a simple, natural perception of what God sets clearly before the mind of man. Just as its object is the supernaturally given promise of grace in Christ, so subjectively a special activity of the Holy Spirit is necessary to enable the sin-darkened mind of man to comprehend what God clearly sets before him. The true object of faith's knowledge on its hither side lies hidden in historical data, so that even nonbelievers may accept the revelatory narratives without seeing Christ in them. And on its nether side it is beyond the comprehension of the human mind, so that a special inner work of the Spirit is necessary before man can know. It is knowledge of God's historical revelation and at the same time hidden wisdom. This follows the same pattern as Calvin's doctrine of Scripture, in which objective revelation and inner testimony to the authority of the revelation are both supernatural acts of God. More accurately put, that doctrine follows the pattern of this one, for certainly the doctrine of faith is proving to be the more basic and central of the two in its religious significance as it was prior in Calvin's own development.

ILLUMINATION.—In the last section we learned that the object of saving faith is a different and narrower category than the total word of God. Now we find a new subjective category, or at least a new term, describing the inner "secret" work of the Spirit. Instead of the *testimonium internum Spiritus Sancti,* we meet the concept of "illumination." [124] "Illumination" seems to be a more basic and comprehensive category of the Spirit's work than the "testimony." The latter, if a quantitative comparison is meaningful, is the "smaller" term. When seen in the context of Calvin's more general doctrine, the "internal testimony" appears to be used as a technical term which is particularly concerned with the accrediting of Scripture. "Illumination" occurs a few times in the

[124] II.i.2 (OS IV.2.20) "illustratione Spiritus"; par. 4 (p. 6.7) "eiusque illuminationem mentis nostrae aciem ad videndum"; (line 14) "illuminans nos in Evangelii sui fidem." Cf. III.ii.33 (OS IV.44.9, 11) and par. 34 (p. 45.23), etc. Cf. Heim, *Das Gewissheitsproblem,* p. 279, on the relation of the medieval concept of illumination to Calvin's.

doctrine of Scripture,[125] but is greatly outnumbered and outweighed by the other. In the three major discussions of the Spirit's work, apart from I.vi–ix, which we have mentioned above, "illumination" is constantly used instead of "testimony." No great importance can be attached to the terms themselves, since the function signified is largely the same, the use is not entirely consistent,[126] and Calvin does not give any description of the relation (not even that of genus to species) that would indicate that he conceived them differently. Yet we are simply following his own practice in the *Institutes* when we speak now, not of the "internal testimony of the Holy Spirit," but of the "illumination of the Holy Spirit."

Doumergue, who mentions just in passing that the proper object of faith is less than the total word of God,[127] perceives a whole-part relationship with reference to Calvin's designations of the inner work of the Spirit. He says we should remember "that the doctrine of the witness of the Holy Spirit is not for Calvin a special doctrine relating exclusively to the authority of Scripture. Far from it! There is for Calvin a general doctrine, that of the Teaching of the Holy Spirit (*Maîtrise du Saint-Esprit*), according to which the Spirit is the sole teacher capable of instructing us in all that concerns the Christian faith, true religious knowledge. And the doctrine of the Witness of the Holy Spirit (*Témoignage du Saint-Esprit*) is only a particular application of the general doctrine of the Teaching of the Holy Spirit." [128] Doumergue realizes that "illumination" is the term Calvin uses in his doctrine of faith, but he gives it very short treatment—simply as a part of the "Teaching of the Holy Spirit." [129] I have chosen to use "illumination" to

[125] I.vii.3 (OS III.68.7). Calvin here uses Augustine's word quoted a few lines before; cf. par. 5 (p. 70.23). I.ix.1 (OS III.82.9) and par. 3 (p. 84.38).

[126] Cf. Com. Rm. 8:31 (CO XLIX.163a); Com. I Cor. 1:6 (CO XLIX.310d), and 1:20 (p. 324b).

[127] *Jean Calvin*, IV, 247.

[128] *Ibid.*, p. 68.

[129] *Ibid.*, p. 247; also Pannier in *Le Témoignage du Saint-Esprit* speaks of a "general work of the Holy Spirit," pp. 102 ff., in terms of faith and illumination, but even though all his references to Calvin at this point belong to what we have called the correlation of Christ and faith and not one refers directly to scriptural authority, Pannier goes on to conclude that they have to do with the origin and results of faith "almost exclusively with reference to the certainty of Scriptural authority." P. 104. Cf. Warfield, *Calvin and Calvinism*, pp. 72 ff.

describe in general the inner work of the Spirit as the term closest to Calvin's own usage. The "teaching" is a term applicable to both objective and subjective or external and internal sides of revelation.

"The simple and external demonstration of the word of God ought, indeed, to suffice fully for the production of faith, did not our blindness and perversity interfere. But such is the propensity of our minds to vanity that they can never adhere to the truth of God, and such is their dullness that they are always blind even to his light. Hence, without the illumination of the Holy Spirit (*Spiritus sancti illuminatione*) the word has no effect."[130] "Let no one hesitate to acknowledge that he can understand the mysteries of God only in so far as he is illuminated by his grace. He who ascribes to himself more understanding than this is the blinder for not acknowledging his blindness."[131] The enlightenment is a "special illumination, not a common gift of nature," because man, unaided, lacks the "eyes" for it.[132] Note in the following instance that objective clarity is claimed, not for Scripture as such, but for the work of Christ. Then, in addition, the Spirit must illumine.

> What? Did he not descend to earth in order to manifest the will of the Father? And did he not faithfully fulfill that mission? He did. But his preaching accomplishes nothing unless the Spirit, the inner teacher, open up the way to the mind. Therefore, none come to him but those who have heard and learned from the Father. And what is the nature of this hearing and learning? It is when the Spirit by a wonderful and special power forms the ears to hear and the mind to understand. . . . We must understand therefore that no one can enter the kingdom of God except he whose mind has been renewed by the illumination of the Holy Spirit.[133]

In the context of the doctrine of election Calvin points out that the "nature and dispensation of calling" is not solely the preaching of the word but consists in the "illumination of the Spirit."[134] We must recognize "two kinds of calling. For there is the universal

[130] III.ii.33 (OS IV.44.4–10). [131] II.ii.21 (OS III.264.17–20).
[132] II.ii.20 (OS III.262.11, 32); Com. I Cor. 2:15 (CO XLIX.344c).
[133] III.ii.20 (OS III.262.32–263.9); cf. Com. Jn. 14:17 (CO XLVII.329d–330a).
[134] III.xxiv.2 (OS IV.412.15–18) and the paragraphs following.

call, by which, through the external preaching of the word, God incites all men indiscriminately to himself, even those for whom he designs it as the savor of death and the ground of heavier condemnation. There is also a special call which, for the most part, is bestowed on believers only, when by the internal illumination of his Spirit he causes the word preached to sink into their hearts."[135] The latter is called also the "interior"[136] and "effectual"[137] call, and it is nothing else but the noetic aspect of faith. "We know the promises to be effectual to us when we receive them by faith."[138]

Calvin always keeps both the objective and the subjective aspects of knowledge in sight. Knowledge is not inserted internally in faith,[139] but consistently through preaching and the Scripture an external manifestation of revelation is given, clear enough to increase the guilt of those who reject, yet able to be accepted only by the elect to whom God has given inwardly the grace of illumination. Thus, as in the instance of Scripture, what is offered outwardly is confirmed within. The characteristic phrase is the Pauline metaphor of the "seal" or "sealing" of the Holy Spirit.

This elegant comparison is taken from seals which among men take away all obscurity. Seals give validity to letters and testaments. . . . In short, a seal distinguishes what is genuine and certain from what is false and spurious. This office Paul ascribes to the Holy Spirit. Our minds never become so firmly established in the truth of God as to resist all the temptations of Satan until we have been confirmed in it by the Holy Spirit.[140]

Then, continuing, he rejects all human arguments as a basis of faith, all rational *indicia*.

The true persuasion therefore that the faithful have of the word of God, of their own salvation, and of the whole of religion, is not from carnal reason (*ex sensu carnis*), or from human or philosophical arguments, but from the sealing of the Spirit, which renders their con-

[135] III.xxiv.8 (OS IV.419.15–22); cf. Com. Jn. 1:43 (CO XLVII.32d).

[136] III.xxiv.2 (OS IV.412.31). [137] *Ibid.*, par. 1 (p. 410.27).

[138] *Ibid.*, par. 17 (p. 429.36–430.1).

[139] This "ordinary economy and dispensation of the Lord" may have one exception in the instance of infant baptism. IV.xvi.19 (OS V.323.9, cf. 5–31).

[140] Com. Eph. 1:13 (CO LI.153b).

sciences more certain so as to remove all doubt. For the foundation of faith would be frail and unsteady if it rested on human wisdom.[141]

Calvin thinks highly enough of this term to use it in his formal definition of faith, "and sealed to our hearts by the Holy Spirit."[142]

The whole of faith takes its start from the time when Christ is known by the illumination of the Spirit. To say this is to say at the same time that human reason, the "natural" reason of the "flesh," contributes nothing to what faith knows. The preparatory stage of faith of which we have spoken is not man preparing himself, but the first stage of God's work in him. "For if it be only when the Father has drawn us that we begin to come to Christ, there is in us neither any beginning nor any preparation of faith."[143] The fact that the terminology of knowledge is used at all shows that the mind is not wholly left out of the process, but the sinful mind gets no credit for itself, for "to know God and his paternal favor toward us, in which our salvation consists . . . the wisest of men are blinder than moles."[144] "Human reason neither approaches nor tends nor aims toward this truth, to understand who is the true God or in what character he wills to be manifest toward us."[145] "In divine things [our discernment] is wholly blind and stupid,"[146] it is "mere darkness," for "we are despoiled of all faculty for spiritual understanding."[147] The animal or natural man cannot understand the things of God.[148] "Human perspicacity is here [in reference to faith] so confused and defective that the first step to advancement in the school of God is to abandon it."[149] Human reason is so despoiled that it weaves out of the very works in which God reveals himself, veils that hide him from us.[150] All this together is the meaning of the thrice repeated *humilitas* which is the "foundation of our philosophy,"[151] because "men are not capable of believing."[152] "There is

[141] *Ibid.* (p. 153c); cf. Com. II Cor. 1:21 (CO L.24c–d).

[142] III.ii.7 (OS IV.16.35).

[143] Com. Jn. 6:45 (CO XLVII.150b).

[144] II.ii.18 (OS III.260.29–33); Com. Jn. 1:5 (CO XLVII.5d, ff.).

[145] II.ii.18 (OS III.261.13–15).

[146] *Ibid.*, par. 19 (p. 261.17).

[147] Ibid. (lines 27, 29).

[148] Com. I Cor. 2:14 (CO XLIX.343d).

[149] II.ii.34 (OS IV.45.4–6); cf. I.vi.3, 1, *supra*, p. 82, where Calvin expresses exactly the same thought concerning the knowledge of the Creator in his works.

[150] Com. I Cor. 2:4 (CO XLIX.335c).

[151] II.ii.11 (OS III.253.29 ff.).

[152] III.ii.35 (OS IV.46.1).

no other way in which men can be prepared for receiving the doctrine of the gospel . . . than by withdrawing all their senses from the world and turning to God alone and seriously considering that it is with God that they have to do."[153]

The need for forsaking human reason and depending alone on divine illumination arises from two grounds. Primarily it is, as in the case of the general revelation, the subjective inability (combined with unwillingness) to see what God has clearly expressed in the person and work of Christ. "Let us remember that the light of reason which God has implanted in men has been so obscured by sin that amidst the thick darkness, shocking ignorance, and abyss of errors there are hardly a few shining sparks that are not at once extinguished."[154] "Our reason is wholly blind."[155] "No man can come to faith by his own sagacity."[156] On this ground the reason for forsaking all human approaches to the Gospel is quite clear, because the sinfulness of man's reason stands in opposition to God. But there is a second ground that is subtler and cannot be stated so flatly, it is the mysterious character of the revelation itself. I think Peter Brunner overemphasizes this hiddenness of the object of faith's knowledge when he writes, "The first step to overcoming the abyss (*Kluft*) between subject and object in faith's knowledge is, not a straight-line progression toward the object, but an apparent regress: a refusal to overcome this distance with the help of human thought, which refusal comes from an examination of the absolute distance between the finite thinking of men and the in-every-respect infinite object of faith's knowledge."[157] What faith grasps is not "in-every-respect" infinite, or revelation would have no significance. God reduced or

[153] Com. Jn. 6:44 (CO XLVII.128b). Still we must not disregard the legitimate *negative* contribution of "natural arguments," *supra*, p. 85.

[154] *Ibid.*, 1:9 (p. 9c).

[155] *Ibid.*, 3:21 (p. 68c).

[156] *Ibid.*, 6:65 (p. 161b).

[157] *Vom Glauben bei Calvin*, p. 131. Peter Brunner repeats the phrase "in every respect infinite" on pp. 129, 131, and 132 as a means of stressing the unknowability of the object of faith. It is his translation of a phrase from III.ii.14, *infra*, p. 183. He strengthens it with Calvin's comparison of man's incapacities to an ass's inability to appreciate music (CO XLIX.325). The latter is entirely irrelevant here because it refers to the non-believer. The former does not take sufficiently into account that Calvin uses this phrase with reference to Ephesians 3:18, which emphasizes the knowability in faith of what is otherwise unknowable.

accommodated his infiniteness to human understanding in revelation, not, of course, so that the mind of any man can ever exhaust its mystery—in its full "length, breadth, depth, and height," it always lies beyond comprehension—but so that when illuminated by the Spirit, the mind can grasp that revelation. Peter Brunner agrees with the latter statement, too, but in his book illumination appears much more as a means of overcoming man's finiteness than as it really appears in Calvin, overcoming his sinfulness.

Calvin ordinarily reads the most esoteric and mystical utterances of the Fourth Gospel and of Paul in terms of sinful blindness rather than finiteness. The "hidden wisdom" is hidden to all who depend upon their own faculties. It is not touched by the "weakness" of the human mind, which weakness is sin.[158] "The knowledge of divine calling exceeds the capacity of our minds, *until* the Spirit of God has made it known to us by a secret revelation."[159] Paul "denies that it [the doctrine of the Gospel] is hidden or obscure, except to the reprobate, whose minds the god of this world has blinded."[160] Elsewhere: "For 'to ascend to heaven' means to have a pure knowledge of the mysteries of God and the light of spiritual understanding," from which all "acuteness of the human intellect" is excluded. But since Christ the Son of God is also the Son of man, and is God's "counselor," "he admits us into those secrets which otherwise would have remained in concealment."[161] Of the "hard saying" in John 6:60, Calvin comments that "hardness was in their hearts, not in the saying. . . . For whoever will submit himself to Christ in true humility will find nothing in it harsh or disagreeable." This quality of what is certainly one of the most hidden and mysterious passages of Scripture, Calvin says, belongs to wickedness rather than the mystery itself. "However, since the same hardness is natural to all of us, if we judge the doctrine of Christ by our own feelings, it will contain as many paradoxes as words." Therefore we turn to the "guidance of the Spirit."[162]

[158] Com. I Cor. 2:11 (CO XLIX.342a). Note *imbecillitas* is explained by quoting Jn. 1:5, and "darkness" is not finiteness, but sin.

[159] Com. Eph. 1:16 (CO LI.156b, italics added).

[160] Com. Jn. 9:18 (CO XLVII.226c).

[161] *Ibid.*, 3:13 (CO XLVII.62a–c).

[162] Com. Jn. 6:60 (CO XLVII.157d–158a).

If we grant, then, that the element of sinfulness plays a greater role than mere finiteness in man's inability to receive the gospel, we must, however, go on to note that human creatureliness does act as a limit also to what faith knows. Calvin is justly called "the prophet of silence before God." [163] His zeal in exhausting every syllable of what God has made known and in constantly advancing his knowledge is exceeded only by his firmness in calling an abrupt halt before God's "secrets." Salvation, while the fact of it and some qualities of it are knowable to the mind enlightened in faith, is finally mysterious in that it rests in God's secret, eternal decrees. One word in Calvin's definition of faith points to this all-important aspect of it: the word "gratuitous." [164] The "gratuitous promise in Christ," is the promise rooted in the secret will of God and therefore unaccounted for by human reason. We know God's mercy—it is not "in every respect" beyond finite grasp, for we experience and are certain of it. But the cause of God's mercy is hidden from us as men. We know that our salvation is in Christ, although why it is so we cannot even ask, and we must not formulate speculative Christologies as Osiander did. That all men are guilty of sin and the guilt rests on them and that at the same time God, who decreed this lot, is just and guiltless—these things, according to Calvin, we know. But how this can be so, man must not even ask. "For it is not right that man should pry with impunity into those things which the Lord determines to be hidden in himself and to investigate, even from eternity, that sublimity of wisdom which God would have us to adore, not comprehend, and through which he promotes our wonderment." [165] Man can only stand amazed at the gratuitousness of God's merciful election:

> Let this be our conclusion to stand in awe with Paul before this great deep, and if petulant tongues will still clamor, let us not be shamed to exclaim with him, "O man who art thou that replyest against God?" For as Augustine justly contends, it is perverse to measure divine justice by the standard of human justice.[166]

[163] Engelland, *Gott und Mensch bei Calvin*, p. 5.
[164] III.ii.7 (OS IV.16.33).
[165] III.xxi.1 (OS IV.370.24–28).
[166] III.xxiv.17 (OS IV.432.2–8).

THE CERTAINTY OF FAITH'S KNOWLEDGE.—The illumination of the Spirit, like the *testimonium internum Spiritus Sancti,* is presented by Calvin in connection with the certainty of faith. "There are two operations of the Spirit in faith, just as faith consists of two principle parts: it both illuminates and establishes (*confirmat*) the mind."[167] Faith without certainty is no faith at all. "He is no believer, I say, who does not, relying on the security of his salvation, triumph over death and the Devil."[168] The certainty comes from God: "This is the character of faith, that it rests solely in God, without depending on men."[169] "The commencement of faith is knowledge (*notitia*); the completion of it is a firm and fixed persuasion (*persuasio*) which admits no opposing doubts. Both, as I have said, are the works of the Spirit."[170] Although this certainty has God's veracity and the authority of the word behind it, its real nature is seen in man's personal individual appropriation of God's promise. It is not an abstract or syllogistic certainty, but personal, existential assurance. It is always applied to the one whose faith is in question.

"The goodness of God cannot be placed beyond all doubt unless we really feel and experience its sweetness within ourselves."[171] "The chief axis on which faith turns is this: we must not think that the promises of mercy which God offers are true apart from us and not all in us, but rather we should make them ours by inwardly embracing them."[172] "In a word, none is truly a believer unless he is firmly persuaded that God is a propitious and benevolent father to him and promises him all things from his goodness, unless, relying upon the promise of divine benevolence toward himself he anticipates salvation with undoubting expectation."[173] Paul, according to Romans 8:33, was certain of his salvation,

> not by a special [that is, private] revelation (as some sophists feign), but by a perception (*sensu*) common to all the pious. Therefore, what is here said of the elect, every one of the godly may, according to the

[167] Com. Eph. 1:13 (CO LI.153d); Com. Rm. 8:38 (CO XLIX.168c).
[168] III.ii.16 (OS IV.27.7–9).
[169] Com. I Cor. 2:5 (CO XLIX.336a).
[170] Com. Eph. 1:13 (CO LI.153d).
[171] III.ii.15 (OS IV.26.20).
[172] *Ibid.*, par. 16 (p. 26.29–33).
[173] *Ibid.* (p. 26.39–27.4).

example of Paul, apply to himself. . . . But when we know that there is designedly set before us what everyone of the pious ought to appropriate to himself, there is no doubt but that we are all encouraged to examine our calling, so that we may become assured that we are children of God.[174]

The *erga nos,* of which we have spoken before, is now seen in its true perspective. "Toward us" is not merely toward men, or even toward the elect in general, but "toward me" as one among the elect. It is an unshakable conviction of one's own personal salvation, procured in Christ. "Faith is nothing unless we are certainly persuaded that Christ is ours and that the Father is propitious to us in him."[175] The believer looks exclusively at the mercy of God in Christ and at his own personal election to salvation through Christ, and thus the problem of formal authority vanishes by coalescing as it should with the "material" of salvation, Christ. It is almost superfluous to remark that here the assurance of a personal relationship has completely transcended the problem of the authority of the sacred book. This is the true center of Calvin's doctrine of faith. It is a highly personal encounter with and experience of God's mercy, whereby the individual knows his ultimate destiny.

We cannot overlook the fact that for Calvin this central, personal, existential conviction carries along with it doctrines that are formal and abstract because they have only a limited grounding in personal experience, for example, the doctrine of the inerrant authority of the entire Bible and the doctrine of double predestination. But all too often Calvin is dismissed in terms particularly of the latter as the theologian of an intellectualized and logically severe faith, without appreciation of this inner core of deep Christian experience. As we have shown, one of these two formal doctrines, that of Scripture, has competition within Calvin's own theology from a deeper doctrine of the knowledge of faith. We shall shortly look at predestination and see that there, too, the personal christocentric element actually has pre-eminence.

The illumination which brings the certainty of faith is super-

174 (CO XLIX.164c).

175 Com. Rm. 8:34 (CO XLIX.165a); Com. Heb. 11:6 (CO LV.149b).

natural. Although subjective in so far as it is an internal illumination, it comes from outside and is in no sense an accomplishment of man.[176] At the same time a closer inspection of what Calvin means by the term will show that the miracle of faith does not take place without the full participation of the mind. Remembering how firmly the concept of knowledge is fixed as a necessary element of faith, we now observe a tension in Calvin's analysis as he tries to state the supra-rational certainty of faith in terms of knowledge.

Therefore, as we can never come to Christ unless the Spirit of God draw us, so when we are drawn, we are raised both in mind and spirit above our own understanding. For illuminated by him, the mind receives as it were new keenness for the contemplation of heavenly mysteries by the splendor of which it had been formerly blunted. Thus, the human intellect, irradiated by the light of the Holy Spirit, begins to have a taste for those things which pertain to the kingdom of God, only when irradiated by the light of the Holy Spirit; previously, it was too stupid and senseless to have any relish for them.[177]

The mind receives new keenness and a new taste for things it formerly did not relish. Yet it is the mind, not some new and wholly strange faculty, that the Spirit prepares to receive its own message. Calvin goes farther.

When we call it knowledge (*cognitionem*), we do not mean a comprehension (*comprehensionem*) such as we have of those things which usually fall under human perception (*humanum sensum*). For it is so far superior that it is necessary for the mind of man to exceed and go beyond itself in order to reach it. Nor even when it has reached it, does it comprehend (*assequitur*) what it perceives (*sentit*), but having a persuasion (*persuasum*) of what it does not comprehend (*capit*), it understands (*intelligit*) more by the certainty of this persuasion than it could discern (*perspiceret*) of any human matter by its own capacity . . . [here he quotes Ephesians 3:18] What our mind grasps (*complectitur*) by faith is in all dimensions infinite (*modis omnibus infinitum esse*), and this kind of knowledge (*cognitio*) far surpasses all understanding (*intelligentia*).[178]

176 See Warfield, *Calvin and Calvinism,* pp. 109 ff., who points out that here Calvin differed from Castellio, for whom the Spirit was man's own "spirit."

177 III.ii.34 (OS IV.45.20–28).

178 III.ii.14 (OS IV.24.34–25.10).

This is knowledge, but not sense perception. It is such a superior knowledge that the mind must rise above itself, and even then it does not comprehend, but has a persuasion beyond its comprehension. But one thing more: it still understands more of the latter certain persuasion than it does of ordinary perceptions! Calvin will neither abandon the terminology of knowledge, nor will he be limited to it. He continues,

> Because, however, God has made known (*patefecit*) to the saints the secrets of his will, which had been hidden for ages and from generations (Colossians 1:26; 2:2), faith is therefore frequently for the best reason called *agnitio* and by John *scientia,* when he asserts that believers know (*scire*) themselves to be sons of God. And certainly they do know (*sciunt*) [and here Calvin returns to a former theme] but they are rather confirmed by a persuasion of the divine veracity than taught by any demonstration of reason.[179]

When Paul says "we walk by faith, not by sight," he shows that "that which we understand (*intelligimus*) by faith is yet distant and escapes our view. Whence we conclude that *the knowledge of faith consists more in certainty than in comprehension* (*fidei notitiam certitudine magis quam apprehensione contineri*)."[180]

The long passage quoted is Calvin's most complete on the subject. We have already seen the main ideas of it in the culminating words of his doctrine of the testimony of the Spirit,[181] where he finally promises to return to the subject again,[182] undoubtedly referring to this passage. Both were added to the *Institutes* in 1539, and were scarcely changed thereafter. Here, as there, "the words fall far short," yet this is the common experience of every believer. As in the former case, the certainty cannot be called a-rational or irrational, but is rather supra-rational. It is a supernatural gift, but it does not short-circuit the rational processes. It works through them and rises above them. To be sure this is not the "natural" reason, but it is nonetheless the human mind as purified and enlightened by the

[179] III.ii.14 (OS IV.25.11–17).

[180] *Ibid.* (lines 18–23, italics added).

[181] *Supra,* p. 110.

[182] I.vii.5 (OS III.71.15).

Spirit. We must be "emptied of our own understanding" in order to have a "saving knowledge of God." [183] But it is the forsaking of depraved, worldly or fleshly wisdom, not of all semblance of mental activity, because faith itself is knowledge, a new and spiritual wisdom, not only in its minimum definition but also in its supernatural certainty. "Let us remember therefore that the certainty of faith is knowledge (*scientiam*), but it is learned by the teaching of the Holy Spirit, not by the acuteness of our own intellect." [184] Again, "The word knowledge (*scientiae*) is used to express more fully the security of our trust. Let us observe, however, that it is not conceived in a natural manner, but depends entirely upon the revelation of the Spirit." [185] The "hidden wisdom" of God is not so hidden that "one should reckon he has nothing to do with it or that he should think it wicked to raise his eyes to it because it is not accessible to human capacity. He [Paul] teaches that the eternal counsel of God is communicated to us . . . [and] if God has appointed nothing in vain, it follows that the hearing of the Gospel will not be lost for us, because it is designed for us, for he accommodates himself to our measure (*se modulo nostro attemperat*) in addressing us." [186]

To sum up: the certainty of faith is knowledge, but a suprarational knowledge in which the mind, being raised above itself, achieves a supernatural certainty of personal salvation.

We must now examine the certainty of faith with reference to two further problems: election and eternal life. These two discussions will treat, respectively, two previously noted elements of faith, the gratuitousness of it and its promissory character, united in the term "gratuitous promise."

1) *Faith and election.* As faith is "gratuitous," it rests finally upon election. "Faith and election are related to each other like two opposite sides of a medalion. The idea of election is the reverse side of the idea of faith, standing silently behind it and

[183] Com. I Cor. 1:21 (CO XLIX.326b).
[184] Com. Eph. 3:19 (CO LI.188c) and *passim*.
[185] Com. I Cor. 2:12 (CO XLIX.342d).
[186] Com. I Cor. 2:7 (CO XLIX.337d).

determining its uniqueness, often with such weight that it comes out of its hiddenness and breaks into the idea of faith itself."[187] Election is about to "break through" again, as it did at the end of the preceding section. One of the key ideas of Calvin's doctrine of election is its gratuitousness, that is, its absolute graciousness unconditioned by any considerations of which men can conceive.

Calvin teaches that election "precedes" faith, is its "mother,"[188] and that "faith may, indeed, be connected with election, provided it occupy the second place."[189] On this basis, some interpreters subsume faith under election in Calvin's theology and indeed subordinate the whole soteriology in the same way.[190] It was characteristic of Reformed orthodoxy to place the decrees of God in theological systems before the doctrine of creation.[191] Although Calvin's view of God's predestination is supralapsarian, it always appears in his systematic work as a part of soteriology.[192] This is not arbitrary, but essential to his conception. Conceived in any other way, we no longer have Calvin's doctrine of election.[193] Calvin never sees the believer—even the believer!—as in direct connection with the precreation decrees. Instead, as he repeats often and especially in III.xxiv, the internal call or illumination or the beginning of faith, or a saving relation to God through Christ—this one thing, variously described, is the only opening in the impenetrable veil before God's hidden, secret will through which election may be seen. With the concept of illu-

[187] Brunner, *Vom Glauben*, p. iv.

[188] III.xxiii.10 (OS IV.392.5). [189] *Ibid.* (line 31).

[190] Otto Ritschl, *Dogmengeschichte des Protestantismus*, III, 156–199, and Hunter, *The Teaching of Calvin*, pp. 88–129.

[191] Heppe, *Dogmatik*, pp. 98 ff. Otto Ritschl, *Dogmengeschichte des Protestantismus*, pp. 162 f., sees Calvin's own doctrine in this light and regards its place in Calvin's theology as inadequately expressed by its formal attachment to his soteriology.

[192] For Jacobs, "the meaning and the goal of the four relocations of the doctrine [in succeeding editions of the *Institutes*] is the strongest possible christocentric tie," *Prädestination*, p. 71, cf. pp. 64, 66.

[193] This is a main theme of Jacobs' book. "Calvin does not build the ordo salutis on predestination as a thing in itself, but on the stable *fundamentum Christi*," *ibid.*, p. 54. "Christ and election belong inseparably together as much as water and fountain . . . rightly understood, Christ is election itself," p. 77. Cf. Köstlin, "Calvins Institutio nach Form und Inhalt," pp. 468–474.

mination, or the call, the two doctrines of faith and election meet, Christ is the point of contact, and neither can be discussed apart from him. It is extremely important to note that III.xxiv, in which the doctrine of election culminates, is a return to the same problems and even the same terminology that are characteristic of III.ii, the doctrine of faith proper—namely, "faith," "illumination," "confidence," "certainty," and the centrality of the knowledge of Christ.[194] The whole gist of this chapter is that divine election is to be viewed exclusively in terms of our own salvation, which exists solely "in Christ."[195] Regardless of the fact that the decrees "precede" creation, *sub specie aeternitatis,* the only saving relation with God is through Christ in faith. No one but the believer can even speak of God's decrees, and then only because he knows himself elect through his faith in Christ. A single passage from the commentary on John sums up the christocentric concept of election and its inseparable relation to faith, which is given in more detail in III.xxiv.

Whoever is not content with Christ, but indulges in curious inquiries about eternal election . . . desires to be saved contrary to the purpose of God. The election of God is in itself hidden and secret, and the Lord manifests it when he bestows it upon us by calling. They are madmen who seek their own salvation or that of others in the labyrinth of predestination not keeping the way of faith which is exhibited to them. Nay more, by this ridiculous (*praepostera:* inverted, backwards) speculation they endeavor to overturn the force and effect of predestination—for if God elected us to this end, that we may believe, take away faith, and election will be mutilated. For we have no right to break through the succession from beginning to end ordered and continued by the counsel of God. Besides, as the election of God, by an indissoluble bond, draws calling along with it, so when God has effectually called us to faith in Christ let this have as much influence with us as if he had engraven his seal to attest his decree concerning our salvation. For the testimony of the Spirit is nothing other than the sealing of our adoption. To every man, therefore, his faith is a trustworthy attestation of the eternal predestination of God, so that it is

[194] For example, in III.xxiv.1–7 (OS IV.410.24, 27; 412.17; 413.21, 26, 29; 415.9; 416.19, 24, 25, 38, 40; 418.14, 20, 21, etc.) See also par. 17.
[195] *Ibid.* (415.37).

sacrilege to inquire further; for that man offers an aggravated insult to the Holy Spirit who refuses to assent to his simple testimony.[196]

"The predestination of God is hidden, but it is manifested to us in Christ alone."[197] He is the "mirror" of our election,[198] apart from which it is completely hidden in God's secret will.

As we observed formerly in relation to the revelation in creation, the believer can never, despite the "internal testimony," see God in nature without the guidance of Scripture, so here he can never see God's redemption apart from Christ. The doctrine of election is not a gnosis, but the reverse: it is knowledge of God gained from a revelation accommodated to our capacities, and it is to be meditated upon in this Revelation, which is Christ, and not speculated upon apart from him. The decree of God "precedes" the call in God's activities, but our view of it remains limited by the kind of knowledge we have of it, namely, the knowledge of faith in Christ. If predestination is viewed other than in Christ, that is to say, if the double decree itself, aside from Christ, is viewed directly as the mode of God's relation to men, then the effect is exactly the opposite of certainty. Without Christ, predestination would simply be a foreordained fate in which a man would know his destiny to be fixed, but would not know what it is. This would bring the utter anomaly, again *praeposterus,* of the prayer "O Lord, if I am elect, hear me!"[199] On the contrary, Calvin finds that the certainty which the doctrine of election brings, viewed through the promise of grace, is pictured rather by these words from Bernard:

O place of true rest, which may not unworthily be called a bed-chamber, where God is seen, not as disturbed with anger or distracted by care, but where his will is proved to be good and acceptable and perfect. This view does not terrify, but soothes; it incites no restless curiosity, but allays it; it does not fatigue, but tranquilizes the senses. Here is true rest. A tranquil God tranquilizes all things, and to see him at rest is to be at rest.[200]

[196] Com. Jn. 6:40 (CO XLVII.147c–d); cf. 8:47 (p. 210b–c).
[197] Com. Jn. 17:6 (CO XLVII.379c).
[198] III.xxiv.5 (OS IV.416.3).
[199] *Ibid.* (line 32).
[200] III.xxiv.4 (OS IV.415.19–26).

We shall return to the consideration of election later in this chapter.

2) *Faith and hope.* As the object of faith is a "promise," the certainty of it rests more in hope than in possession, "for faith is a certain and secure possession of those things which are promised to us by God."[201]

Christ left nothing incomplete of all our salvation; but from this it is falsely inferred that we already possess the benefits procured by him, as if the saying of Paul were false that our salvation is hidden in hope. . . . Therefore, although Christ offers us in the gospel a present plenitude of spiritual blessings, yet the fruition of them is concealed under the custody of hope, till we are divested of our corruptible bodies and transfigured into the glory of him who has gone before us. In the meantime the Holy Spirit commands us to rely on the promises.[202]

"Hence it is that he dwells in our hearts, and yet we are strangers in regard to him, for we walk by faith, not by sight."[203]

The whole Christian life takes place in the interim between the final revelation of God's promise in Christ and the transformation of it from promise to reality in eternal life. The Christian lives in the paradoxical situation of having, yet not having; possessing, yet poverty stricken; certain of his salvation, yet with an expectancy that incites him to activity rather than lulls him to complacency. The "inner contradiction in history," reintroduced into American theology by Reinhold Niebuhr under the terminology "sin is overcome in principle, but not in fact,"[204] need never have been reintroduced had the words of Calvin about faith and hope been kept in mind.

The Spirit of God shows us hidden things, the knowledge of which cannot reach our senses: promised to us is eternal life, but it is promised to the dead; we are assured of a happy resurrection, but we are as yet involved in corruption; we are pronounced just, yet sin dwells in us; we hear that we are happy, but we are as yet in the midst of many miseries; an abundance of all good things is promised to us, but still

[201] III.ii.41 (OS IV.51.8–10).
[202] II.x.3 (OS III.400.28–401.4).
[203] *Ibid.* (p. 401.14–16).
[204] *Nature and Destiny of Man,* II, 49. Minear, *The Eyes of Faith,* p. 56, suggests that Niebuhr use the more Biblical terms "promise" and "fulfillment."

we often hunger and thirst; God proclaims that he will come quickly, but he seems deaf when we cry to him. What would become of us were we not supported by hope and did our minds not emerge out of the midst of the darkness above the world through the light of God's word and of his Spirit? [205]

The same eschatological orientation appears in the following:

Now wherever this living faith shall be found, it must necessarily be attended with the hope of eternal salvation as its inseparable concomitant, or rather must originate and produce it; the want of this hope would prove us to be utterly destitute of faith, however eloquently and beautifully we might discourse on it. . . . Hope is no other than an expectation of those things which faith has believed to be truly promised by God. . . . Faith is the foundation on which hope rests, hope nourishes and sustains faith. . . . Hope, while it is silently expecting the Lord, restrains faith, that it may not be too precipitate; it confirms faith, that it may not waver in the Divine promises or begin to doubt of the truth of them; it refreshes it, that it may not grow weary; it extends it to the farthest goal, that it may not fail in the midst of the course or even at the entrance of it.

The assistance of hope is necessary because "the Lord, by deferring the execution of his promises frequently keeps our minds in suspense longer than we wish. . . . Sometimes he not only suffers us to languish but also openly manifests his indignation." [206]

Peter Brunner writes,

The "interim" in which faith knows itself to be, can never be done away with [according to Calvin] during the temporal existence of men. Never in the life we know can promise become fulfillment as an ascertainable, recognizable fact. Man stands ever under the sign of promise, even when he believes in the gospel and in Christ. Of course the gospel is the fulfillment of all promises. But we are not Christ. In him the whole of salvation is completely finished, but we do not yet possess this salvation; the gospel is for us promise, not fulfillment. Whoever overlooks this and transforms the sign of promise into the sign of fulfillment falls prey to "a devilish presumption." [207] . . .

[205] Com. Heb. 11:1 (CO LV.143d–144a).
[206] III.ii.42 (OS IV.52.26–30, 53.1–27 *passim*).
[207] *Vom Glauben bei Calvin*, p. 154.

Faith reaches forward toward something that remains always in the future, that lies beyond everything given here and now. . . . Faith is therefore no immediate having, but a possession of what we cannot "possess" because it does not yet exist for us.[208]

The certainty of faith, thus, is not a simple certainty. While it is a sure knowledge of one's own salvation in Christ, it is always involved in mystery and paradox—in the ultimately unfathomable mystery of gratuitous election and the temporary paradox of history in which the salvation already won by Christ remains, because of sin, a hope based on a "promise" rather than a possession. The gratuitousness of faith reminds the believer through the doctrine of election of the ultimate unknowability of the ways of God with man, its promissory character points him to the not-yet-known which will later be revealed. The "gratuitous promise in Christ," to whom alone the eyes of faith are directed, although conditioned by both mystery and paradox, nonetheless gives the believer a knowledge and an assurance in which he can confidently rely.

Calvin's Definition of Faith

We have now progressed far enough to appreciate, so far as the problem of knowledge is concerned, Calvin's formal definition of faith. This carefully wrought statement appeared in the *Institutes* first in the edition of 1539 and was never altered afterward, although the material on faith had grown a great deal by 1559. It contains all the elements we have covered. For emphasis, the key words or phrases to which we have already devoted individual analysis are marked with asterisks:

Now we shall have a proper definition of faith if we say that it is a steady and certain* knowledge* of the Divine benevolence* toward us,* which being founded upon the truth* of the gratuitous* promise* in Christ* is both revealed* to our minds* and sealed* in our hearts by the Holy Spirit.* [209]

[208] *Ibid.*, p. 156.

[209] "Nunc iusta fidei definitio nobis constabit si dicamus esse divinae erga nos benevolentiae firmam certamque cognitionem, quae gratuitae in Christo promissionis veritate fundata, per Spiritum sanctum et revelatur mentibus nostris et cordibus obsignatur." III.ii.7 (OS IV.16.31–35).

Albrecht Ritschl misses the word trust (*fiducia*) in Calvin's definition and sees in its absence an evidence of Calvin's having intellectualized Luther's concept.[210] This objection is not justified when the definition is read in the light of Calvin's whole teaching of faith. In our last section we have used the term "certainty" as most appropriate to the subject in hand: knowledge. The whole discussion might have been given under the title of "trust" with only a slight change in emphasis, for certainty as we have seen is not that of a provable proposition, but of individual confidence and trust in the mercy of God. "To separate faith from trust (*fiducia*) would be equal to an attempt to separate heat and light from the sun." [211] Of a piece with this refusal to intellectualize faith by isolating the element of knowledge in it from the total reaction of the individual, is Calvin's quarrel with the scholastic distinction between "formed" and "unformed" faith. He refused to admit that any mere knowing, without the total response in love, could be called faith.[212]

We must now look at two important elements of faith that cannot be seen in the formal definition.

Beyond Calvin's Formal Definition

CALVIN'S PICTURE OF EXISTING FAITH.—Calvin's doctrine of faith as expressed in the formal definition is *sachbezogen,*[213] or de-

[210] *Die Christliche Lehre von der Rechtfertigung,* III, 128.

[211] Com. Eph. 3:12 (CO LI.183d).

[212] III.ii.8, *passim.*

[213] This uniquely German term characterizes for Peter Brunner (*Vom Glauben bei Calvin,* pp. 113 ff.) Calvin's doctrine of faith as looking always toward its *object,* so that "of the few things that he says about what goes on in the believing subject, the psychological side is of the least importance." "In this connection Calvin's silence about his conversion stands in a new light. Not as if Calvin were not conscious of deep experiences and agitations of the soul, but they are not important to him; especially where he speaks of the Christian religion, because the main thing for him is, not the experience, but the object (*Sache*)." P. 114. Calvin asks "what" faith believes, not "how," in contrast to emotional mysticism, pietism, and Schleiermacher. This is generally true as far as it goes, but it does not go far enough to account for the fact that in Calvin's theology trust and certainty are not synonymous with peace of mind. The only way P. Brunner can account for this, in so far as he recognizes it at all, is in terms of "holy fear," *timor religiosus,* again God's infiniteness and man's finiteness: "It must not be forgotten that in faith the God who reveals himself as mercy and love in his saving will toward us, is a hidden God, and an incomprehensible Deity (*ein ver-*

termined by its objective relations. We have already studied this objective aspect, but some further considerations are necessary. Calvin is a better psychologist of faith than any of the elements of his teaching as represented by the terms of the formal definition would lead us to believe. When Calvin defined faith as a "steady and certain knowledge," he was describing it essentially and therefore normatively. He was conscious that these two words do not give an adequate phenomenology of believing. There is more to say, and there are modifications to be made when we turn our attention to the believer himself, to that aspect of faith that is related to the believing subject and determined by the exigencies of individual experience. For what believer recognizes himself as pictured in this definition, except for some few moments of his existence? These considerations will not modify the definition itself, but they show Calvin's awareness of problems of believing that are more intricate and personal than can be expressed even by the paradox of promissory possession.

It is well enough to maintain "that for faith to waver is absurd" [214] and that faith is a "confidence which banishes all fears and anxiety," [215] and the like.

> But someone will object that the experience of believers is very different from this; for in recognizing the grace of God toward them they are not only disturbed with inquietude, which frequently befalls them, but sometimes also tremble with the most distressing terrors. The vehemence of temptations to agitate their minds is so great that it appears scarcely compatible with that certainty of faith of which we have been speaking. We must therefore solve this difficulty, if we mean to support the doctrine we have here advanced.[216]

Now the attention is turned wholly toward the actual believer, and we see immediately that the certainty of which Calvin has

---

borgener Gott und ein unbegreifliches Numen)," p. 144. But trust and holy fear are for Calvin quite compatible in faith. What comes between trust in God and real peace of mind is not "holy fear," but sin. P. Brunner never refers to Calvin's explanation of this in III.ii.17, 18, and never cites from the commentary on the Psalms to which III.ii.17 (especially as enlarged in ed. '59) is a little index on the theme. Cf. *Vom Glauben*, pp. 113–146.

[214] Com. Jn. 3:33 (CO XLVII.73d); and III.ii.15–16.

[215] Com. Rm. 8:33 (CO XLIX.163d). [216] III.ii.17 (OS IV.27.19–25).

made so much does not in fact issue in psychological serenity. He continues:

When we inculcate that faith ought to be certain and secure, we conceive not of a certainty attended with no doubt or of a security interrupted with no anxiety; but we rather affirm that believers have a perpetual conflict with their own distrust and are far from placing their consciences in a placid calm, never interrupted by any disturbance. Yet on the other hand, we deny, however they may be afflicted, that they ever fall and depart from that certain confidence (*fiducia*) which they have conceived in the divine mercy.[217]

The final words of this quotation vindicate the definition. But what goes before is extremely important as a picture of the believer's state of mind. Calvin has not read the Psalms in vain.

It is an uncommonly revealing biographical note that Calvin, the so-called heartless logician, considered David, the fighting king and poet of the troubled soul, his own nearest counterpart in the Bible.[218] Probably Calvin's boldness to identify himself rather too unabashedly with David in the preface to the commentary on the Psalms is understandable in terms of some similarities between the Geneva church and the chosen people of the Old Testament in the time of David and in other periods. The second great leader of the Reformation, like the second king of Israel, saw himself the head of a tiny church-state, chosen by God for his purposes, yet beset by enemies and traitors, and in spite of some glorious gains, quite unimpressively small on the world's face. Calvin lived to see the Reformation both grow and retract, to see his dream of a united church fail of realization, and for all his victory in Geneva, the city was until his death as much a place of refuge for Protestants harassed out of other lands as a base for new advances. The future of the reformed church like that of the people of God in the days of the prophets, according to Calvin, rested in a "faithful remnant" and an eschatological hope, not an assured success in history. Calvin thought himself specially ele-

[217] III.ii.17 (OS IV.27.25–36).

[218] Com. Ps. "To the Readers" (CO XXXI.19d). Calvin attributed a large number of Psalms to David, although always after some critical investigation. Cf. Com. Ps. 42 and 43 (CO XXXI.425, 436).

vated by God (under the lash of threats by Farel and Bucer) to a place of leadership. And it is explicitly by virtue of this position, the responsibilities of leadership, and chiefly his experience of despair over the power God allowed to his (the church's) enemies, that he considered himself a good interpreter of the Psalms. In the preface he calls attention to his own experience as the clue to his understanding.[219] Here occurs one of the few biographical references in all his theological writings—an interweaving of his life story and his self-identification with King David.[220] Of whose soul but his own was the definer of faith as "certain knowledge" speaking when in this same context he called the Psalms "an anatomy of all the parts of the soul,

> for there is not an emotion of which any one can be conscious which is not reflected as in a mirror. Or rather the Holy Spirit has here drawn to life all the griefs, sorrows, fears, doubts, hopes, cares, anxieties, and in short all the turbulent emotions with which the minds of men are used to be agitated.[221]

Knowing full well that God's providence rules in history and his own election is as certain as the mercy of God, Calvin writes and confesses, "whenever the minds of the saints are overspread with this darkness [repeated calamity] there is always some unbelief mingled in that prevents them from emerging immediately into the light of new life." [222] Obviously this unbelief is not to be honored by a place in faith's definition, for it comes from sin, but Calvin recognized its existence in every believer.

"Experience" and "the present appearance of things," which

[219] "Now, if my readers derive any fruit and advantage from the labor which I have bestowed in writing these commentaries, I would have them to understand that the small measure of experience which I have had by the conflicts with which the Lord has exercised me, has in no ordinary degree assisted me, not only in applying to present use whatever instruction could be gathered from these divine compositions, but also in more easily comprehending the design of each of the writers. And as David holds the principal place among them, it has greatly aided me in understanding more fully the complaints made by him of the internal afflictions which the church had to sustain through those who gave themselves out to be her members, that I had suffered the same or similar things from the domestic enemies of the church." *Ibid.* (p. 19c). At the end of the preface he returns to the same idea (p. 33b–c).

[220] *Ibid.* (p. 27c, 31a, c).

[221] *Ibid.* (p. 15c).

[222] Com. Ps. 22:16 (CO XXXI.228b).

in some respects confirm faith, try it sorely in others.[223] Of the time when the psalmist cried out "My God, my God, why hast thou forsaken me," Calvin writes (biographically?),

This same is what everyone of the faithful experiences in himself daily, for according to the carnal sense he thinks himself cast off and forsaken by God while yet he apprehends by faith the grace of God. Thus it happens that contrary states of mind are entangled and confounded in their prayers. For the carnal sense cannot but conceive of God as either propitious or hostile according to the present appearance of things. When, therefore, he suffers us to be hurled into grief and almost to be consumed, we must necessarily feel according to our carnal apprehension as if he had quite forgotten us. When such perplexity overcomes the whole mind of a man, it submerges him in profound unbelief, and he no longer aspires to a remedy. But if faith aid in opposition, the same person who from the state of things regarded God as incensed or alienated beholds his hidden and secret grace in the mirror of the promises. They alternate between these two contrary states of mind when on one hand Satan, exhibiting the signs of the wrath of God, urges them to despair and endeavors to cause their downfall; but on the other hand, faith, recalling them to the promises, teaches them to wait patiently and trust in God until he again show his fatherly countenance.[224]

The certainty of faith as conceived, shall we say, theologically, in Calvin's definition, is less than undisturbed peace of mind when described in fact, psychologically and autobiographically. In this life man, even John Calvin, is never quite faith-full.

The pious heart therefore perceives a division in itself, being partly affected with delight through a knowledge of the divine goodness, partly distressed with bitterness through a sense of its own calamity; partly relying on the promise of the gospel, partly trembling at the evidence of its own iniquity; partly exulting in the apprehension of life, partly terrified by death. This variation happens through the imperfection of faith [not "holy fear"]; since we are never so happy in the course of the present life as to be cured of the disease of distrust and entirely filled and possessed by faith.[225]

[223] Cf. Com. Ps. 43:3 (CO XXXI.435a). Cf. *ibid.*, 42, 43 (CO 425–435 *passim*).
[224] Com. Ps. 22:2 (CO XXXI.220c–d). [225] III.ii.18 (OS IV.29.7–15).

Then the question reasserts itself: must we not say that

> faith consists not in a certain and clear, but only in an obscure and perplexed knowledge of the divine will toward us? By no means. For if we are distracted by various thoughts, we are not therefore immediately divested of faith, neither, though harassed to and fro by the agitations of distrust, are we therefore plunged in its abyss; nor, if we be shaken, are we therefore dislodged from our place. For the invariable issue of the contest is that faith at length surmounts those difficulties, from which, while it is encompassed with them, it appears to be in danger.[226]

Faith will never finally be blotted out in the elect, no matter what doubts attack, for it is God's work rather than man's, and man is thus held by God, not by his own efforts. But, as in Calvin's doctrine of providence, the final determination by God is not meant to release man from a present effort. The certainty of final outcome is not seen as nullifying the seriousness of the soul's struggle. This struggle, too, is the implementation of God's work in man, His chastening.[227] In the trials of experience, faith grows. Certainty is never "carnal security," [228] but an active, existential, struggling certainty. Faith dies if the believer refuses to exert himself, thus refusing the education which God in his providence has given to him. Thus, we see the intricate movement of Calvin's doctrine of faith, both *sachbezogen* and *menschbezogen,* the "knowledge of *God* and *ourselves,*" being an existential comprehension of our own state and of our relation to the holy and merciful God. If the bare words of his definition of faith make it "steady and certain knowledge," according to Calvin, we must notice that such faith never is realized. We could formulate a description of existing faith for him as a "steady and certain knowledge invariably attacked by vicious doubts and fears over which it is finally victorious."

FAITH AS MYSTICAL UNION WITH CHRIST.—As we have just dealt with some negative psychological aspects of faith that are not clear in the words of the formal definition, so now we shall go

[226] *Ibid.* (lines 19–26).
[227] Com. Gen. 32:24 (CO XXIII. 442b–443b).
[228] III.xxiv.7 (OS IV.418.33).

beyond the definition on its positive side to indicate the place of knowledge in faith with reference to the total work of the Spirit, the goal of which is "mystical union with Christ."[229] We shall by no means treat this subject in detail or even undertake the difficult task of defining exactly what Calvin means by this phrase which he took over from classical mysticism.[230] We shall go only far enough to show that the noetic aspect of faith is imbedded inextricably in a total work of the Spirit that includes both will and intellect and finally body as well as soul. Further, we shall emphasize that this is a present, not exclusively eschatological, aspect of faith.

We have discussed in the preceding section the mixture of knowledge and doubt in the believer, and before that the limits of the believer's knowledge. While these were attributed partly to the promissory character of faith and the height of the mysteries revealed, they were chiefly credited to the persistence of sin in the believer, which continues throughout the present life. But Calvin is very careful about how this is understood, lest the result be an underevaluation of God's present work in the Christian. It must not be construed as if faith itself were a "doubtful opinion" or a "confidence mixed with unbelief."[231] And by no means dare we say with some "semipapists" that doubt is in man, while hope resides apart from man in Christ, so that fears come in trusting self and peace from trusting Christ. This is to overlook that Christ is really in us and that hope therefore really belongs to us more than do the inevitable doubts that sometimes attack us. Doubts may be outwardly, but never inwardly, predominant, for Christ dwells in us.

Although the complete fulfillment of the promises is in the distance, "we are to expect salvation from him [Christ], not be-

[229] Doumergue begins his analysis of Calvin's doctrine of faith with some pages on "the guidance of the Holy Spirit and the mystical union of the Christian with Christ." *Jean Calvin*, IV, 240–242. He rightly uses "mystical union" as the theme of his whole Book IV on "The Christian Life," which includes his analysis of the *Institutes*, Book III, with the exception of the doctrine of predestination, cf. pp. 252, 272.

[230] Jacobs says Calvin took over this term first in the fight against Osiander, *Prädestination*, p. 128.

[231] III.ii.24 (OS IV.34.10–12).

cause he appears at a distance from us, but because, having ingrafted us into his body, he makes us not only partakers of all his benefits but also of himself."[232] The completion of faith is hope, but this must not be construed as if the believer were left during the interim of this life to fight his battles entirely alone until a final eschatological rescue by God,

as if when I say that Christ is received by faith, that I mean he is received merely in the understanding and imagination. For the promises offer him, not so that we stop at the mere sight and bare knowledge, but that we enjoy a true communication (*communicatione*) of him.[233]

If you consider yourself, condemnation is certain, but since Christ with all his benefits is communicated to you, so that all that he has becomes yours, and you become a member of him and one with him—his righteousness covers your sins, his salvation supersedes your condemnation, he interposes with his merit, that your unworthiness may not appear in the Divine presence. Indeed, the truth is that we ought by no means to separate Christ from us or ourselves from him, but we must hold strongly with both hands to that alliance by which he has cemented us to himself. . . . *Christ is not without us, but dwells within us; and not only adheres to us by an indissoluble connection of fellowship but also by a certain wonderful communion coalesces daily more and more into one body with us, till he becomes altogether one with us.*[234]

The knowledge of Christ is part of a wider, more comprehensive communication of him. It is true that only when "inwardly instructed" by the "illumination of the Spirit" is Christ known by "the experience of faith."[235] To "know" Christ, however, does not mean speculative knowledge, but enjoying "the sacred and mystical union between us and him; but the only way of knowing this is when he diffuses his life into us by the secret efficacy of the Spirit."[236]

[Christ] now describes the way of bestowing life, namely, when he illuminates the elect in the true knowledge of God: for he does not

232 *Ibid.* (lines 28–31).
233 IV.xvii.11 (OS V.354.10–15)
234 III.ii.24 (OS IV.34.32–40; 35.7–11, italics added).
235 Com. Jn. 14:17 (CO XLVII.329d–330).
236 *Ibid.*, 14:20 (p. 331b).

now speak of that enjoyment of life for which we hope, but only of the manner in which men attain life. And that this idea may be correctly understood, we must first remember that we are all in death until God, who alone is life, illuminates us. Where, however, he has shone, because we possess him by faith, at the same time we enter into possession of life; thus it is that this knowledge of him is truly and justly said to be saving. Almost every one of the words has its weight, for it is not every kind of knowledge of God that is here described, but that which transforms us into the image of God from faith to faith, and indeed that which is the same with faith, by which, having been ingrafted into the body of Christ, we are made partakers of divine adoption and heirs of heaven.[237]

The union with Christ in faith is elsewhere explained by the eating of the flesh of Christ, which here "does not relate to the Lord's Supper, but to that perpetual communication which we obtain apart from the use of the Lord's Supper." [238] This perpetual communication of the flesh of Christ is the spiritual reality of which the elements of the Supper are related as "symbol" to the "thing itself," [239] or "corporeal sign" to "spiritual truth." [240] Elsewhere on this same idea he comments,

For there are some who define in a word, that to eat the flesh of Christ and to drink his blood is no other than to believe. But I conceive that . . . we are quickened by a real communication of him, which he designates by the terms of eating and drinking, that no person might suppose the life which we receive from him to consist in simple knowledge.[241]

These terms, then, are not metaphors for believing, but show that faith does much more than know of a future salvation: it participates in present life. This life is communicated by a miraculous property of the flesh of the risen Christ, which, although at an immense local distance from us,[242] is endued with a plenitude of life to communicate to us.[243] This is the deepest significance of the

[237] Com. Jn. 17:2 (CO XLVII.376c); cf. 6:47 (p. 151b). Note the relation between "light" and "life," Com. Jn. 1:1–4.

[238] Com. Jn. 6:53 (CO XLVII.154c).

[239] IV.xvii.10 (OS V.352.9–10).

[240] *Ibid.*, par. 11 (353.1; 354.1).

[241] IV.xvii.5 (OS V.347.5–10).

[242] IV.xvii.10 (OS V.351.26).

[243] *Ibid.*, par. 9 (350.25).

incarnation: the communication of life to us by the flesh of Christ, [244] "for the flesh of Christ is like a rich and inexhaustible fountain which transfuses into us the life flowing forth from the divinity into itself." [245] "Let our faith therefore receive what our mind is not able to comprehend, that the Spirit truly unites things separated by space," [246] namely, the flesh of Christ and our souls. The sacrament is effective by faith—not that Christ "is" the elements or even less that receiving it is mere occasion to think on Christ—but faith is the mouth by which we eat Christ, by which our spirits feed on his flesh and blood.[247] Again, "faith intervenes as the medium by which we are spiritually ingrafted into the body of Christ." [248] In another figure,

I attribute, therefore, the highest importance to the connection between the head and the members; to the inhabitation of Christ in our hearts; in a word, mystical union, so that being made ours, he makes us partakers of the blessings with which he is endued. We do not then contemplate him at a distance and without us, that his righteousness may be imputed to us; but because we have put him on and are ingrafted into his body he deigns to make us one with himself, therefore we glory in having a fellowship of his righteousness.[249]

Calvin also, following Paul in I Corinthians 15:45, describes the life of Christ in the believer in the metaphor of the soul. On Galatians 2:20, he writes,

This explains what he meant before by "living unto God"; namely, that he does not live by his own life, but is animated by the secret power of God so that Christ may be said to live and grow in him. For as the soul enlivens the body, so Christ imparts life to his own members. This is a noteworthy idea, that believers live outside themselves, that is, in Christ, which is not possible except they have a true and

[244] *Ibid.*, pars. 8–11, and the balance of the chapter. Calvin heatedly rejects the confusing of Christ's infinite essence with the communication we have of him in his redemptive work, making clear that the union is by Christ's flesh, that is, Christ as accommodated to our state in his redemptive work; and further that this property of communication is not an essential attribute even of Christ's flesh, but a miracle for the sake of man's redemption. Cf. III.xiii.2 (OS III.451.20 ff.) and II.xii.1–2.

[245] IV.xvii.9 (OS V.351.1–2).

[246] *Ibid.*, par. 10 (351.30).

[247] *Ibid.* (p. 351.20).

[248] II.xiii.2 (OS III.453.4).

[249] III.xi.10 (OS IV.191.27–35).

substantial communication with him (*veram cum ipso et substantialem communicationem habeant*).[250]

Again, on Ephesians 5:28–32 he describes the "mystical communication we have with Christ" (*de mystica communicatione quam habemus cum Christo*).[251] For "if we are true members of Christ, we share his substance, and by this participation unite in one body."[252] Calvin denies that this passage refers to the Lord's Supper, but rather to the reality which the Supper represents. Farther on,

Such, therefore, is the union between Christ and us, by which he, so to speak, transfuses himself into us. We are "bone of his bone and flesh of his flesh," not because like ourselves he is man, but because by the power of his spirit he ingrafts us into his body so that we derive from him our life.[253]

The mystical participation is not to be analyzed but rather experienced.

I am not ashamed to confess with Paul my ignorance and admiration. How much more satisfactory than to diminish by my carnal understanding what Paul pronounces to be a deep mystery. Reason itself teaches that what is supernatural is certainly beyond the capacity of our abilities. Let us therefore rather labor to feel Christ living within us than to discover the nature of that communication.[254]

There is no question here of classical mysticism, of essential union and the swallowing up of personality. Calvin guards against this by attributing the union to the body of Christ, and then not to any essential attributes of the body, but to special properties granted as part of the method of redemption, as we have seen. While the union is conceived largely in terms of obedience, there is more to it than this. If knowledge (the precondition of obedience) is the highest, most important level of the life communicated by Christ, the lower levels, even physical life, are not excluded. Calvin is a theologian uncommonly wary of identifying

250 (CO L.199a–b).
251 (CO LI.225c).
252 *Ibid.* (225d).
253 *Ibid.* (226d).
254 *Ibid.*, 5:32 (227a–b).

the sign and the thing signified, yet he is very bold in asserting the reality behind the sign. This is true here. The participation of the believer in the life of Christ is no mere metaphor, but is linked with the phenomena of being alive, both in soul and body: the Logos of redemption is still the Logos of creation, whose light is the life of men.[255] Calvin recognizes a kind of hierarchy of the forms of life, "universal life," which we share with the beasts, "human life," by which we are sons of Adam, and the "supernatural life," which only the faithful obtain,[256] and all are included in the renewal of faith and regeneration. Part of Calvin's argument against the idea that the soul sleeps between bodily death and the resurrection in the early tract *Psychopannychia,* is the real "life" relationship between Christ and the believer, such as signified in Colossians 3:3 and Galatians 2:20. He maintains in some detail that the life of Christ and our lives are so closely identified that "if he has no end of life, neither can our souls ingrafted in him be ended by any death."[257] "Is there any obscurity in the promise that he will remain in all who are united to him by faith, and they in him? (John 6:56) Therefore, if we should deprive our members of life, let us dissever them from Christ."[258] True faith perceives that eternal life is already begun in the believer and can by no means be suspended.[259]

Elsewhere Calvin links the process of regeneration to the resurrection of the body. The spiritual body of the resurrection is not a spiritual substance, different from the animal body, but is deservedly called spiritual, because it will then receive its life from the quickening or life-giving Spirit rather than from eating and drinking![260] This is the way in which we are finally "conformed into the image of Christ," in the completing of our present spiritual regeneration.

For we now begin to bear the image of Christ and are every day more and more transformed into it, but this image consists in spiritual re-

[255] Com. Jn. 1:4 (CO XLVII.5b–c).
[256] Com. Eph. 4:18 (CO LI.205b–206a); cf. *supra,* p. 7.
[257] (CO V.193d).
[258] *Ibid.*
[259] *Ibid.* (194b).
[260] Com. I Cor. 15:44 (CO XLIX.557c–d).

generation. But then it will be fully restored both in body and soul, and what is now begun will be perfected, and accordingly we will obtain in reality what we as yet only hope for.[261]

Finally

we must be renewed in respect of our bodies, for our bodies being liable to corruption, cannot inherit the incorruptible kingdom of God. . . . "Flesh" and "blood," however, we must understand according to our present condition, for our flesh will be a participant of the glory of God, but as renewed and quickened (*innovata et vivificata*) by the Spirit of Christ.[262]

And so Calvin's Book III on the activity of the Spirit in applying Christ's work to men, having been introduced comprehensively with the teaching about union with Christ, proceeds through illumination, regeneration, justification, election, and culminates in the doctrine of the resurrection of the body (III.xxv). The key term is "faith," "the principle work of the Spirit," [263] and within faith, knowledge, for knowledge is the highest thing in creation. Yet knowledge is but one aspect of the total impartation of life by which the believer begins now in this earthly existence to share in that eternal life that will one day be his completely when the mystical union is perfected.

The purpose of this brief discussion, suggestive rather than complete, of mystical union with Christ according to Calvin, is to hint at aspects of faith which do not come directly into the question of knowledge, that faith may not be thought of as mere knowledge, however limited the scope of the present essay. Even in its noetic aspect, faith is not for Calvin, the approval of propositions about God, but an existential awareness. "By faith, that is to say by the spiritual, mystic union with Christ, man becomes a new creature." [264] To select the knowledge aspect of faith as we have done is a functional analysis comparable to a physician's injection of a substance into the blood stream so that it alone is seen in the fluoroscope. We must not thereby mistake what we have seen for an exhaustive description of the whole.

261 Com. I Cor. 15:49 (CO XLIX.560b). 262 *Ibid.*, 15:50 (560c).
263 III.i.4 (OS IV.5.14). 264 Doumergue, *Jean Calvin*, IV, 272.

The Content of the Knowledge of God the Redeemer

In the case of the revelation of God the Creator, we found two sources of knowledge, creation and Scripture, which conveyed up to a point identical information about God, and we also noted a certain special content of the Scriptural revelation. It was possible to list some attributes of the Creator and to describe something of his will in creation. The present chapter has shown the revelation of God the Redeemer to center in a single main theme of Scripture. Its knowledge content is both easier to epitomize and more difficult to give in detail than the knowledge of the Creator. It is, simply, Christ. But this special theme is encased in the whole of Scripture, it is involved in successive forms of historical presentation, and it ramifies into the subjects of the person and the work of Christ, the whole of the so-called *ordo salutis* and the "external means" of fellowship with Christ: the church and the sacraments. Our present purpose will have been served if we pay particular attention to knowledge content, to what the believer knows when he knows God through faith in Christ.

God's attributes are for the most part, as Warfield says, "in solution" in Calvin's theology, rather than "in precipitate."[265] This is even more true of Calvin's soteriology than of his doctrine of God the Creator. We shall here, however, "precipitate" the two most prominent attributes of God the Redeemer, that is to say, of what the work of redemption makes known to us of God. To say "two," however, is already to falsify the case, for it is the very unity, mysterious[266] unity, of the "two" which we mean, following Calvin, to emphasize. The two are really one. And further, although the term "attributes" serves to orient us somewhat with reference to the attributes of the Creator, it is not strictly applicable here, for these are not capable of clear definition and delimitation.

Both aspects of the subject now before us have been prominent throughout the foregoing analysis of knowledge in faith, in

[265] *Calvin and Calvinism*, p. 143.

[266] In the sense of the New Testament μυστήριον, suprarational reality.

which we have observed Calvin binding together in a single conception of amazing scope the entirely personal, existential assurance of salvation through the Holy Spirit's application of the work of Christ in faith, with the most utterly objective *jenseits* of all theological ideas: the eternal decrees. The faithful man, in which Christ now dwells, is the elect man, chosen of God in Christ before creation for a salvation that is still largely in the future. He knows God to be merciful, absolutely and forever merciful, in the present certainty of his own personal salvation. But he knows this mercy as utterly gratuitous, because it rests, not in any conditionedness of creation or any merit of sinful man, but in the eternal counsel of God. Gratuitous mercy, then, is the two-in-one attribute of God to which we are pointing. These two words represent the two poles of saving knowledge "of God" as Redeemer and "of ourselves" as redeemed. Both poles are on one axis: Christ. Apart from Christ, neither God's forgiving mercy nor his gratuitous decree is known. Through Christ, both are known and inseparable. The gratuitousness of mercy is revealed in election,[267] and the benevolence or mercy-quality of election is seen in the assurance that faith has of personal salvation.[268] The only mercy man finds in God apart from Christ is the mercy of delayed but inevitable punishment,[269] and there is no faith or hope in this. Apart from Christ there is no election—there is even for the Christian only the "labyrinth" or "abyss" of the double decree, which can only throw man into the worst kind of doubts.[270] There can be no faith or hope in the mere decree, these come only to the believer in his confidence of his salvation. "Hence, all who inquire apart from Christ what is settled respecting them in God's secret decree are mad to their own ruin."[271]

The various terms denoting the gratuitous mercy of God in

[267] "We shall never be clearly convinced, as we ought to be, that our salvation flows from the fountain of God's gratuitous mercy, till we are acquainted with his eternal election, which illustrates the grace of God by this comparison, that he adopts not all promiscuously to the hope of salvation, but gives to some what he refuses to others." III.xxi.1 (OS IV.369.10–14).

[268] *Supra,* p. 188; and III.xxii.10 (OS IV.391.25 ff.).

[269] This is the mercy of the Creator, *supra,* p. 78.

[270] III.xxiv.24 (CO IV.414.36).

[271] Com. I Jn. 4:10 (CO LV.354a).

Calvin's theology exist throughout his writings in countless variations. A few random examples will suffice for our purposes: "gratuitous mercy,"[272] "gratuitous favor,"[273] "gratuitous goodness,"[274] "mere good pleasure,"[275] and "gratuitous love."[276]

"Gratuitousness" is a word indicating God's Godhood, his otherness, his transcendence, his unconditionedness, his absolute freedom or sovereignty, his final incomprehensibility, his holiness—all these, expressed as will.[277] Yet he is no philosophical absolute and no arbitrary God. For this word is only part of a phrase. The second term has to be said along with it, for there can be no certain redemption from either a faceless absolute or a *Willkürgott*. God is transcendent and incomprehensible, but not utterly so, for his

[272] III.xxi.7 (OS IV.378.35) "gratuita misericordia"; II.xvii.1 (OS III.509.22) "ex mera Dei misericordia"; Com. Rm. 8:3 (CO XLIX.137d) "gratuita misericordia," and 3:25 (p. 62b); Com. Gen. 12:1 (CO XXIII.174a) "Abrae vocatio insigne gratuitae Dei misericordiae exemplum est," and 34:25 (p. 461c) ". . . gratuitam suam misericordiam asseruit Dominus."

[273] III.xxi.7 (OS IV.378.13) "gratuitum favorem"; II.xvi.2 (OS III.483.33) "sponte ac gratuita sua indulgentia"; Com. Rm. 4:3 (CO XLIX.70b) "gratuito Dei favore"; Com. Ps. 8:4 (CO XXXI.91c) "gratuitum Dei favorem"; Com. Gen. 32:10 (CO XXIII.440b) "ex gratuito Dei favore," 39:21 (509a) "gratuito Dei favore."

[274] II.vii.4 (OS III.330.10) "nisi gratuita sua bonitate"; Geneva Catechism, ed. 1545 (CO VI.42b) "Deum gratuita sua bonitate"; Com. Gen. 17:15 (CO XXIII.244d) "gratuita Dei bonitas"; Com. Lev. 22:27 (CO XXIV.594a) "gratuitae Dei bonitati"; Com. Ex. 34:5 (CO XXV.114a) "quia scilicet nihil ei magis proprium quam bonitas et gratuita beneficentia"; Com. Lk. 1:74 (CO XLV.49b) "gratuita Dei bonitas"; Com. Rm. 5:5 (CO XLIX.92a) "grauita Dei bonitate"; and Com. Ps. 18:2 (CO XXXI.170d) "gratuita bonitate."

[275] III.xxi.5 (OS IV.375.32) "mero Dei beneplacito," and II.xvii.1 (OS III.509.18); Com. Rm. 8:28 (CO XLIX.159c) "arcano Dei beneplacito"; Com. Eph. 1:5 (CO LI.149b) "sed illi una causa est beneplacitum aeternum, quo nos praedestinavit."

[276] III.xxi.5 (OS IV.374.26) "gratuitam amore Dei," and (p. 375.8); II.xvi.3 (OS III.484.30) "Sic mera ac gratuita nostri dilectione excitatur ad nos in gratiam recipiendos"; Geneva Catechism, ed. 1545 (CO VI.50b) "ex gratuito Dei amore"; Com. Ps. 18:2 (CO XXXI.170d) "liberalis et spontanei amoris"; Com. Jn. 1:13 (CO XLVII.12d) "gratuito amore." Com. Rm. 1:7 (CO XLIX.12c) "Certe penes nos salutis nostrae laudem non statuit Paulus, sed ex fonte gratuitae Dei et paternae erga nos dilectionis totam derivat. Hoc enim princium facit, quod nos Deus amet. Quae porro illi amoris causa, nisi mera sua bonitas, . . ." and 8:28 (159b) "gratuito amore," and 5:15 (98d) "Dei bonitatem vel gratuitum amorem"; Com. I Jn. 4:9 (CO LV.353a) "gratuitus Dei amor," and 4:10 (353c), "Gratis nos Deus amavit. Cur? quia antequam nati essemus."

[277] Cf. Otto, *The Idea of the Holy*, pp. 90 ff., pp. 105 f.

mercy is revealed in Christ along with his gratuitousness. He is the loving and patient Father, self-giving and self-sacrificing, the gracious rescuer of undeserving sinners. The second term of this phrase exhibits some variation: mercy, favor, goodness, pleasure, love. The broadest is goodness, and within this goodness, there is (from the human point of view) a polarity: God's own inviolable goodness, that is, his enmity toward evil, which is expressed in his justice, as against his special goodness or his mercy *erga nos*. Were not his goodness really, inviolably good (just), there would be nothing special and nothing merciful in salvation. But, then, is not his justice violated by his mercy toward us? Calvin refuses to separate the two. He holds that although God satisfied his own justice before our eyes by the imputation of Christ's merits to sinners—even this is not an absolute necessity of God's just goodness, but the method he gratuitously laid down for the salvation of those he gratuitously loves.[278] Christ's suffering provides no final rationale for understanding how justice and mercy are related within God: as if there were such a problem in God.

Gratuitous-goodness, gratuitous-mercy, or gratuitous-love—any one of these is the appropriate epithet for God the Redeemer in Calvin's theology. We can, since Nygren, express this characteristic of God in a single term, ἀγάπη. However, if we wish to keep to the idiom of Calvin, the word-pair is more accurate. Apart from this double word on the one hand and the legal-ethical use of *caritas* on the other, Calvin had no precise terminology of love, as a glance at the indifferent, side-by-side usage of *amor, dilectio,* and *caritas* in the Commentary on I John 4:7–16 will show.[279] In view of the various medieval confusions about the term, we can hardly ask more of Calvin. Nygren himself, in establishing the uniqueness of Christian love, transliterated as agape, has recourse constantly to precisely the adjective Calvin used: "Agape is sovereign," "uncaused love," "spontaneous and unmotivated" love; or

[278] "Because it was out of mere good pleasure that He appointed him Mediator to procure salvation for us. . . . For Christ could merit nothing except by the good pleasure of God." II.xvii.1 (OS III.509.18, 25); III.xxii.1 (OS IV.380.21 ff.). Cf. Seeberg, *Lehrbuch der Dogmengeschichte,* IV/2, pp. 575 f.

[279] (CO LV.352b–356d). Compare not only usage in the comments, but his choice of words in his Latin text of Scripture.

he speaks of the "absolute sovereignty and groundlessness" of Christian love.[280] The linkage with election also agrees with Nygren, although he treats the subject, it seems, as little as possible.

> Here lies the deep truth of predestination. Man is to love God, not because he finds fuller and completer satisfaction of his need in God than in any other object of desire [this is "eros"], but because God's "uncaused" love has empowered and constrained him, so that he can do nothing else than love God.[281]

Nygren's historical survey stops with Luther, but it is in Augustine's predestination [282] and Luther's justification by faith [283]—exactly where their influence on Calvin was strongest—that Nygren finds two of the best expressions of agape after the Apostle Paul. In the single word "agape" we see graphically the unity behind Calvin's double word. Both signify the same thing. Calvin, like Luther,[284] and in part like Augustine, was a theologian of agape, gratuitous love. God the Redeemer is above all the God of grace. Seeberg writes,

> But now as over against sin, God becomes active and is revealed as the gracious one in Christ. Therefore, the specifically Christian knowledge of God is to be sought in salvation or in grace. God is gracious to the sinner without grounds (*umsonst*), without any merit on his side. But it is in the choosing of only a part of mankind—and this entirely of God's own accord (a thing He particularly makes known)—that the essence of grace is recognized most clearly as *gratuitus amor* and *mera dei liberalitas* and through which man comes best to a certainty

[280] *Agape and Eros,* Part I, for example, pp. 52 f., 61, 73, 117, 158; and Part II, Vol. II for example, p. 252, 255, 479, 502, 513, etc. Cf. Emil Brunner's terminology, "grundlose, unmotivierte, unbegreifliche Liebe," *Dogmatik* I, 194.

[281] *Ibid.,* Part I, p. 168.

[282] *Ibid.,* Part II, Vol. II, p. 338; also pp. 250 ff., 336.

[283] *Ibid.,* Part II, Vol. II, pp. 498–503. By "faith alone," Luther was not excluding love from faith, but *caritas* with its eros motif, while emphasizing the gift aspect of faith or its agape quality. See also pp. 482 ff.

[284] This is not to overlook the differences between Luther's and Calvin's conceptions of the love of God. Köstlin points out that there are no such words about love filling the heart of God in Calvin as in Luther and that while the fatherly love of God is the center of the Christian experience, it is not so clearly the dominant motif as in Luther, "Calvins Institutio nach Form und Inhalt," pp. 424–426. How true this is, does not concern us here; but the reference will serve to show that caution must be exercised.

of grace: *quod non omnes promiscue adoptat in spem salutis, sed dat aliis quod aliis negat.*[285]

It has often been said that the leading characteristic of Calvin's theology is his doctrine of predestination, understood particularly in terms of the sovereignty, the absolute freedom of God, who can damn his creatures for his own glory. But for Calvin, God is never merely sovereign.[286] He is sovereignly good, sovereignly just, sovereignly merciful and gracious.[287] The dimension of sovereignty or gratuitousness is never permitted to condition or to control the mercy of God, so that he might become suddenly and arbitrarily not merciful, not just, and not good. When misunderstood, this very characteristic leads to a concept of God as a divine and arbitrary dictator who can and may do anything—or worse, who has already decided everything and has decided it arbitrarily; in Calvin's theology it is the very apex of trust in God's trustworthiness,[288] nonarbitrariness, the complete unconditionedness and therefore eternal unchanging truth of what he has revealed, namely, his mercy in Christ. This mercy, gratuitous mercy, is the starting point and end point of all or any true knowledge of the true God. For Calvin, God the Redeemer is not the God whose

[285] This fine statement, however, is outweighed in Seeberg's treatment by his search for the "universal metaphysical elements" of Calvin's God idea, *Lehrbuch der Dogmengeschichte,* p. 571, which he finds in the properties of God the Creator as we have outlined them in the last chapter. This God is a metaphysically conceived determiner of all events, thus is seen as the regulator of providence and special providence (predestination), whose every act is for the sake of his "holiness" or "glory" displayed in grace and justice within creation (pp. 575–578) and his "sovereignty" as seen in salvation and damnation (pp. 579–582). The latter two discussions are fatefully located together in Seeberg's study of Calvin's doctrine of God with no attention to the limits imposed upon such a speculative arrangement by the christocentric character of election.

[286] Beyerhaus, *Studien zur Staatsanschauung Calvins,* pp. 48–77, is particularly guilty of this, also Kampschulte, *Johann Calvin,* I, 251–278.

[287] "In a word, with all his emphasis on the sovereignty of God, Calvin throws an even stronger emphasis on his love: and his doctrine of God is preeminent among the doctrines of God given expression in the Reformation age in the commanding place it gives to Divine Fatherhood. 'Lord and Father,'—fatherly sovereign, or sovereign Father—that is how Calvin conceived God." Warfield, "Calvin's Doctrine of God," *op. cit.,* p. 176; cf. Doumergue, *Jean Calvin,* IV, 88 ff.

[288] The three functions of the doctrine of predestination are to promote humility, to give the believer a sense of his obligations to God, and to bestow a "firm confidence (*fiducia*)," III.xxi.1 (OS IV.369.33–35).

mercy may be withdrawn. Nor is he the God who deals with men solely in terms of the double decrees. Either of these ideas is spoiled by a separation in which one takes away from what it gives the other, that is, when mercy is sentimentalized or predestination is abstracted and depersonalized. The redemptive message of the Christian faith is not—we speak for Calvin—to make known the double decree as the mode of God's dealing with men, any more than to make known a conditioned, problematic mercy of God, but rather to proclaim the grace of God, his gratuitous mercy: merciful because it brings salvation to sinners; gratuitous because the salvation is undeserved.

Now problems loom up. Is it not curious to call Calvin a theologian of love? Where is love in the best-known statement in his theology, namely:

> Predestination we call the eternal decree of God by which he has determined in himself what he would have to become of every individual of mankind. For they are not all created on equal terms, but eternal life is foreordained for some and eternal damnation for others. Every man, therefore, being created for one or the other of these ends, we say he is predestinated either to life or to death.[289]

These words, like the definition of faith, were carried unchanged from the edition of 1539 into the final redaction. They must be taken seriously, but they must not be taken out of context. The context, without exception, both formally and theologically, is Calvin's soteriology, and in 1559 the doctrine comes at the end (but for the doctrine of the resurrection) of the *ordo salutis*.[290]

For Calvin the doctrine of double predestination does not in any way change the picture of the God of gratuitous love. Rather it emphasizes it. We cannot here enter into a thorough study of the doctrine of the decrees and his basic formulation of it, but we can show the fact that and the way in which, within that formulation, the element of reprobation is subordinate to that of election, despite their apparent equality in the above statement. Our

289 III.xxi.5 (OS IV.374.11–17).

290 Calvin had no *ordo salutis,* strictly speaking, but this is a convenient term to refer to those elements of his teaching (*Institutes,* Book III) to which orthodoxy applied the term.

grounds are two, epistemological and logical. Just one remark, however, about the general structure of the doctrine is necessary in terms of the distinction we have made concerning Calvin as a formal (inerrant words) and as a material (Christ) Biblicist, before proceeding to our two arguments.

We have already shown that Christ is the whole basis of election, whether spoken of in terms of the decree or of faith. We cannot, however, attribute Calvin's doctrine of reprobation to a contrasting and inconsistent formal Biblicism.[291] Its relation to election is an inner one attaching to it as the ultimate in gratuitousness rather than coming to it from without, as it were, from another different theme of Scripture, to modify it. Calvin's formal Biblicism gives him almost as much trouble as assistance in formulating his doctrine, because when every word is taken seriously, some Scriptural characters are both reprobate and elect! The whole tortuous teaching about the "degrees"[292] (*gradus*) of election is simply Calvin trying to extricate his doctrine from the implications of his own inerrancy view of Scripture. On the basis of mere formal Biblicism, Calvin realizes that he would have to say that Esau was first elect in the choosing of all the descendants of Abraham, then rejected when Jacob was blessed.[293] The same is true of Judas, who in John 17:12 is first numbered among "those that thou gavest me," then excepted as "the son of perdition" who is "lost." Calvin escapes with great difficulty here, by calling it a catachresis and denying that the verse can be read according to the rules of grammar. Judas was elect merely to the apostleship, he concludes.[294] In fact, these lower "degrees" of election are indistinguishable from Providence, since they have to do with holy history, not with individual salvation. They illustrate for us merely that Calvin's doctrines of both election and reprobation met with difficulties when he exegeted the inerrant word. Their relation is not that they come from opposite sides of the cleft

[291] Note that it was not election as opposed to reprobation that we called elements of a possible *complexio oppositorum, supra,* p. 38, but the doctrine of the decrees in general as against that of human responsibility.

[292] III.xxi.5, ff., for example (OS IV.376.23) or par. 6 (377.3).

[293] III.xxi.6.

[294] (CO XLVII.382d); cf. II.xxii.7, and III.xxiv.9.

in his doctrine, to which we pointed in the first section of the present chapter.[295]

First, the epistemological ground for our thesis that reprobation occupies such a secondary (although necessary) role, according to Calvin, that it does not modify the view of God as gratuitous mercy revealed to the elect man in faith. It is simply this: the doctrine of reprobation is known only to the believer who knows himself as elect to salvation and looks upon his neighbor as potentially elect. That is to say, the doctrine of reprobation enters into neither the relation to God nor the relation to one's fellow man, neither the worship nor the ethics, of the only one for whom it is a doctrine: the believer.

Calvin teaches the supralapsarian decree of reprobation, that before creation each of the reprobate was determined by God for his end.[296] That is all. No more can be said on the subject.[297] This is a flat, isolated, although necessary statement for him. Beyond this he has no positive teaching. There are in Calvin's theology no ethical, ecclesiastical, or soteriological corollaries to the doctrine of reprobation. It brings about no harmonizing modifications in other doctrines. Calvin formulates the doctrine, then exclaims with Augustine, "O depth! Do you seek a reason? I will tremble at the depth. Do you reason? I will wonder. Do you dispute? I will believe."[298] It is presupposed that the man who can state the supralapsarian decree, the one to whom it has been revealed, is always and can only be, the Christian who knows God in Christ as the God of mercy. It is from the start God's mercy, gratuitous mercy, to be received, not questioned, whatever the logical implications of reprobation may seem to be to the finite, sinful reason. This decree may not be scrutinized, and God may not be questioned on the basis of it. If the decree of election is to be explained only by God's mercy revealed in Christ, the decree of reprobation is not to be investigated at all. Calvin advises the believer rather to "contemplate the evident cause of damnation in corrupt human nature, which is nearer to us, than inquire after a hidden and

[295] *Supra*, p. 159.

[296] For example, III.xxiii.4, 7.

[297] "I reply with Paul that no account can be given of it, for its greatness far surpasses our understanding." III.xxiii.5 (OS IV.398.26–28).

[298] III.xxiii.5 (OS IV.399.19–20).

altogether incomprehensible one in the predestination of God."[299] When the believer looks to God, it is not to examine God on the basis of this decree, which does not concern the believer himself, but on the basis of faith in Christ. Sin on the one hand and God's gratuitous mercy on the other, enter into his own existential relation to God and his fellow men in a way that reprobation never does and never can.

Reprobation is exclusively the elect man's view of damnation,[300] parallel to what we saw formerly when we noted that the verdict of "inexcusability" is derived from special revelation, although applied to recipients of general revelation. But while it is the elect man's view of damnation, eternal reprobation is emphatically not the elect man's view of his neighbor. The "others" who are reprobate are an abstraction, not living persons with names. Calvin does not hesitate to list Judas or Saul or Esau among the reprobate in the past tense, nor does he hesitate to say that the world of his own day is full of the reprobate as a general category. But he can never speak of the reprobate concretely as individuals in the present or future tense. Our neighbor, which includes every living individual, is a sinner, of course, but the Christian sees and honors and loves in him the image of God, which Christ has given him eyes to see.[301] He also preaches to him, without exception, the Gospel.[302] Empirically there are no reprobate individuals in the world at which one can point the finger. The doctrine of the double decree "must by all means

[299] III.xxii.8 (OS IV.403.7–10); cf. III.xxiii.3.

[300] A statement of Albrecht Ritschl, quoted by Bauke, *Die Probleme der Theologie Calvins,* p. 85, expresses the same idea when he says the doctrine of the decrees is "an important appendage (*Anhängsel*) of Calvin's doctrine of redemption, derived, however, from the authority of Paul." Bauke rightly insists that the term "appendage" is incorrect, because the doctrine has a Biblical content. But the point is clear; the decrees are to be looked at only from the point of view of redemption. This Ritschlian idea is completely rejected by Seeberg, who sees predestination as a special brand of providence, and both together as part of a causal relationship between God and the world. Therefore, following Bohatec and Scheibe, he calls it the "central doctrine" of Calvin's theology. *Lehrbuch der Dogmengeschichte,* pp. 580 f.

[301] III.vii.6, and II.viii.55, *passim.* Note especially (OS IV.157.18–22 and III.393.33–394.9, quoting Augustine).

[302] Com. Mt. 7:6 (CO XLV.216a–b).

be preached . . . that he who has ears to hear of the grace of God may glory in God and not in himself."[303] But

If anyone address the people in this way, "If you do not believe, it is because you are already divinely destined to destruction"—he not only cherishes slothfulness but also encourages wickedness. If anyone extend the declaration to the future, that those who hear will not believe because they are reprobate, that would be imprecation rather than doctrine."[304]

Because we do not know who belongs or does not belong to the number of the predestinated, it becomes us to desire the salvation of all. Thus, whoever we meet we shall endeavor to make him a partaker of peace. But our peace shall rest upon the sons of peace.[305]

Although the nonelect are in the institutional church and in the world, "the reprobate" remains an abstract category. In the knowledge "of God" it is never the knower that is reprobate, and in the correlate knowledge "of ourselves" we cannot apply this category to any living individual: we act toward and preach to all men alike, "desiring their salvation." It must be admitted that the doctrine of reprobation, when its theological locus is seen in Calvin's soteriology as a part of the knowledge of God the Redeemer, belongs to the believer's knowledge of God in faith as a limiting concept at the border of the mystery surrounding his own election. By no means does it alter the picture of God as gratuitously merciful as long as we stay within Calvin's formulation of it.

Secondly, there is a logical or systematic peculiarity within the doctrine of reprobation itself that robs it of the right to be set parallel to election as if, according to Calvin, these were two modes of God's dealing with men that are of equal directness and of equal strength in the believer's knowledge of God.

To define this difficulty thoroughly would require a complete study of the relation of sin to reprobation, particularly in reference to Calvin's use of the Aristotelian terminology of essential and accidental relationships and of primary and secondary causation,

[303] III.xxiii.13 (OS IV.408.35–409.2).
[304] *Ibid.*, par. 14 (409.6–11).
[305] *Ibid.* (409.30–34, quoting Augustine).

Without going deeply into this involved subject, I believe that Calvin's case does not rest upon the success of his Aristotelian distinctions. These lame, theodicy-like formulations [306] are used much like the *indicia* of Scriptural inspiration, as aids to the man of faith, not as prior grounds on which faith rests. Whether or not these devices are adequate to his purpose, it is clear that Calvin is trying to show that God takes direct responsibility for all good in creation, including the essential created goodness of Satan, but that evil, while it never happens outside of his omnipotence, cannot be attributed to his intent, for his will is good.[307] The wrath of God is not such a basic characteristic of his relation to men as is his mercy,[308] and Calvin insists that although in a sense God hates sinners as his enemies, he also always loves and wills the good of all that he has created.[309] Finally, the damnation of the reprobate is not so directly a contribution to the glory of God as is the salvation of the elect, for he reprobates them in such a way that they fall by their own fault, and their punishment, not their sins, redounds to his glory.[310]

Aside from the questionably used Aristotelian terms, there is no further relating of God's will to sin in Calvin's theology, except for the flat contradiction that God wills against his will.[311] The point is that good and evil, God's will and sin, election and reprobation, are never for Calvin clear parallels, because God stands in a direct and essential relation to the good and in an indirect and accidental relationship to all that is not good.

In accordance with what we have just said, there is also a harmonious relationship between the doctrine of the Trinity and the decree of election, but no trinitarian frame whatsoever for the doctrine of reprobation. Faith and election are related positively in the gratuitous love of God through Christ, the Eternal Son, who is also the Logos of creation and the Incarnate Word of redemption. Faith and election are two sides of the same coin,

[306] Particularly in the doctrine of providence, I.xvi–xviii, also II.i.10–11.

[307] I.xviii. 3–4.

[308] Com. Rm. 1:18 (CO XLIX.23a).

[309] II.xvi.4 (OS III.485.29 ff.), quoting Augustine.

[310] III.xxiii.8 (OS IV.402.31 ff.) and par. 9.

[311] I.xviii.3 (OS III.225.18–20) "ut miro et ineffabili modo non fiat praeter eius voluntatem quod etiam contra eius fit voluntatem."

completely congruent, both to be understood through Christ, and both ramifying into all areas of Calvin's theology, especially his ethic. This relationship, which Jacobs calls "analytic," is replaced in the doctrine of reprobation by a "synthetic," un-unified and un-unifiable relationship.[312] Sin and reprobation are not congruent: sin occurs among the elect as well as the reprobate, and Adam himself, by whom sin and death came into the world, is considered by Calvin among the elect.[313] Nor is Satan the cause of sin either temporally or in the dimension of reprobation. Men are not reprobate in Satan as they are elect in Christ. Satan is himself one of the condemned creatures, deserving the punishment which has been decreed for him, just as other creatures deserve theirs. The figure of Satan does not supply a middle term relating the will of the trinitarian God on the two levels of eternal decree and actual sin in the way that Christ, the God-man, Eternal Logos incarnate in a person, relates positively the will of God in the "obedience of faith" and election.[314] There is no such middle term in the doctrine of reprobation. From this arises its systematic harmlessness. It cannot be a principle of systematic thought for Calvin, for it has no independent status whatsoever. Reprobation is an isolated doctrine for Calvin, literally in its place in the *Institutes,* in its comparative rarity in Calvin's commentaries and sermons,[315] as well as in its theological scope. It has no power within Calvin's theology to nullify or to limit preaching, or to weaken the ethical imperatives—in fact, it has no power to do anything but emphasize the incomprehensibility and supernaturalness of the whole work of salvation, that is, the utter gratuitousness of God's love.

If Calvin has more than once formulated the doctrine of the

[312] The subordination of the doctrine of reprobation is very well shown in Jacobs, *Prädestination,* pp. 156 ff.; cf. the whole discussion from p. 119 to the end of the book. Seeberg *Lehrbuch der Dogmengeschichte,* Vol. IV, part 2, notes the positive relation between election, faith and the Christian life, pp. 602 f., but makes no reference here to reprobation. The silence confirms our point, but can scarcely be permitted to Seeberg, who sees the decrees as a causal relationship between God and man and as a controlling idea in the knowledge of God.

[313] Com. Gen. 4:25 (CO XXIII.103c).

[314] Jacobs, *Prädestination,* p. 156–157.

[315] *Ibid.,* p. 56.

double decrees in such a way as to preclude gratuitous love as the exhaustive description of God in his redemptive activity "toward us," we must remember to keep these statements in the context of soteriology and in the isolation in which they stand in his theology as a whole. Calvin's doctrine of the decrees, especially the decree of reprobation, cannot by a process of extrapolation be lifted out of its context and set above the doctrines of creation and redemption without being transmuted into a rationalistic metaphysic which would then change the nature of his entire theology. This process is just what Beza and subsequent Calvinistic orthodoxy brought about, an extreme but well safeguarded formulation becoming the dominant theme among the epigoni, as has more than once happened in the history of thought. This doctrine, if kept in the place where Calvin put it, may well serve its assigned function of expressing and promoting humility in the believer. It must never be pursued in such a way that "being excited to presumption, we attempt with nefarious temerity to scrutinize the inaccessible secrets of God."[316] As the believer is not empowered to view the revelation in creation without the "spectacles" of Scripture, so he is not allowed to view the doctrine of the decrees apart from Christ. In both instances the *ordo cognoscendi* is the limiting and controlling factor, prohibiting the believer from trying to reconstruct and comprehend the *ordo essendi* as if he were not both finite and sinful. And even the *ordo essendi,* so far as it is knowable to the believer, exhibits a unified, coherent relationship in the doctrine of God's election to salvation in Christ, but an isolated, fragmentary doctrine of reprobation.

I here disagree with a majority of contemporary theologians who see a predominant speculative and metaphysical motif in Calvin's formulation of the doctrine of reprobation. Certainly as metaphysical speculation his whole doctrine of the double decree is untenable. But it seems to me unlikely that we have here a sudden abandonment of Calvin's whole method for a single experiment in philosophy, especially when he denied it so continuously. A sounder critique would seem to be that here is a radical, one might

[316] III.xxiii.12 (OS IV.406.16–20).

say reckless consistency in the working out of the Biblical teaching of the gratuitousness of divine mercy.[317] At worst it is the *reductio ad absurdum* of a good kerygmatic principle and therefore to be rejected, but it is not an abstract pancausalism.

CONCLUSION.—If Calvin's theology is viewed as a *complexio oppositorum,* here at the center of the knowledge of God the Redeemer and especially in the doctrine of the decrees that opposition is raised to the nth power. Evil is seen not only in the dimension of sin and eternal damnation but also in that of God's eternal decree of reprobation. Good, the only real good, is likewise beheld on the scale of eternity in the salvation of God's elect. And both display God's glory! So put, the *complexio oppositorum* is an impossible combination of God and the devil. No one was more aware of this than Calvin. Small wonder that "the human mind, when it hears these things [the double decree], cannot restrain its petulance, but is as violently aroused as if a trumpet had sounded a charge," and men rush in "to defend God from an invidious accusation." [318] He conceived it his greatest indignity that he was accused of making God the author of sin.[319]

To see opposites combined, however, is to be looking at Calvin's theology from the outside in. To the faithful man, as Calvin describes faith, these are not opposites, except in so far as his mind remains still darkened by sin. Calvin's doctrine of faith, as well as his teaching about the knowledge of God the Redeemer in general, exhibits no process of combining these two elements. It begins, moves, and ends within their mysterious unity. If two elements have to be combined in a speculative synthesis, we have begun with them separately—which, as we have already mentioned, shows that we began with neither of them, because either without the other is no longer itself. God is not the God of the double decree to whom the Christian also predicates mercy because he personally, as one of the elect, knows mercy in Christ. Nor is he a God whose mercy is known, but who must somehow

[317] A criticism of this variety is that of Köstlin; see Appendix III.

[318] III.xxiii.1 (OS IV.393.36–394.1).

[319] Com. Ps. "To the Readers" (CO XXXI.29c).

by devious theodicy be cleared of the charge of causing sin and damnation because of the doctrine of the double decree. God is rather the gratuitously merciful Redeemer in Christ, and to those who know him as such, the elect, the double decree on the one hand illustrates this known character of God, and on the other silences all human voices that would cry out to God in anything but adoration and love. Faith is "knowledge of the Divine *benevolence* toward us . . . founded upon the truth of the *gratuitous* promise in *Christ.*" The knowledge of God the Redeemer has for its content, gratuitous-mercy-known-in-Christ, or agape.

Calvin never ceased to make the divine pity and mercy shine through the doctrine [of predestination] in such wise as to draw forth the spirit of grateful love and glad, self-sacrificing consecration in those who felt the vitalising touch of God upon their souls.[320]

[320] Hunter, *The Teaching of Calvin,* p. 127.

·V·

THE RELATION BETWEEN THE KNOWLEDGE OF GOD THE CREATOR AND THE KNOWLEDGE OF GOD THE REDEEMER

IT IS NOW OUR TASK to relate the two aspects of man's knowledge of God's twofold revelation by bringing together themes of our preceding chapters. We must show the relationship within the Biblical revelation of the two elements of the *duplex cognito Domini:* the knowledge of God the Creator, and the knowledge of God through Christ in the special activity of redemption. We have already seen that the Creator is rightly known only to the recipients of the redemptive revelation, and the redemptive revelation is of significance only when it is known to come from God the Creator. If redemption were to come from some other source than God it would not be real redemption, yet there is no way outside the redemptive revelation itself to identify it as coming from the Creator of heaven and earth. The "spectacles" for seeing the revelation in creation are in fact the special revelation, given as part of the work of redemption. Thus, within the revelation that comes to man by the special means of Scripture, there is a twofold content: (1) that which refers to God in his general activity as the eternal, omnipotent, omniscient, holy, merciful, just, triune God, Maker and providential Sustainer of heaven and earth, and (2) that which shows God in his special work as the gratuitously merciful Redeemer in Christ. The latter revelation is occasioned by sin and is aimed at overcoming sin.

How shall we relate the two elements of the Biblical revelation? The two can be brought into focus if we understand exactly that against which sin is rebellion and that toward which reconciliation is aimed. Most simply, sin is rebellion against the will of God, and reconciliation is the double-sided process of declared forgiveness (justification) and the partial reachievement of obedience (sanctification) through faith in Christ. The term in Calvin's theology by which we can accurately fix what is the will of God in this context—God's orderly will for his creatures, the will against which Adam rebelled, the will on whose standard all men are judged and declared inexcusable, the will that Christ satisfied by his obedience, the will that the believer is increasingly (but only partially) empowered by the Spirit to obey—this will is the eternal, perfect rule of righteousness,[1] which man knows in his conscience, and which, because of sin, is revealed to him again as the moral law.

Because of the way in which the idea of law spans the two orders of the knowledge of God, we have chosen it as a means of setting forth the relationship between the two. Other methods are of course possible. Particularly fruitful would be a study of the relation of the doctrine of the Trinity and Calvin's Christology, or providence and predestination, but the heart of the matter, with regard to the problem of knowledge, lies in the relation of the two chief forms of revelation, law and Gospel, the orderly will of the Creator and the gratuitous mercy of the Redeemer. First we must see in what way law, for Calvin, is to be classed with the knowledge of the Creator.

Law and the Knowledge of the Creator

Law is one of the basic concepts of Calvin's theology. As we saw formerly, it is related closely to the idea of natural order, or God's orderly will in creation. But over against man's freedom God's orderly will is not actualized directly, as in the case of natural events, but through revelation and man's response—that is, God's will has normative value for man. This normative value is at once its legal character, as we pointed out above, especially with reference to the findings of Beyerhaus.[2] Thus described, law is a necessary part of the life of man as a creature and does not imply dis-

[1] III.xvii.7 (OS IV.260.12); Com. Mt. 5:21 (CO XLV.174c); cf. Rm. 2:13 (CO XLIX.37b).

[2] *Supra*, p. 69.

obedience or sin. Here is one of the major aspects of our whole analysis which must be carefully understood lest we see in Calvin's idea of law a "legalism" that does not belong essentially to it. We must first conceive of the law as Calvin did entirely apart from disobedience, before we think of it in the context of sin and redemption or damnation. For Calvin has two concepts of law, just as he has two concepts of nature.[3] One refers to created perfection; the other to the situation induced by the Fall. The first concept of law is not "legal" in the bad sense; that is, it has nothing to do with the conviction or restraint of sinfulness, but like the idea of nature in its first use means simply the orderly, harmonious Creator-creature relationship. This orderly will of God in creation embodying, as we shall see, mutual love between God and man and among men, is the essence of the idea of law for Calvin, from which his other use, like his usage of the term "nature" with regard to depravity, although more frequent, is derivative. If this distinction is understood, Calvin's alleged legalism is much softened. Also the difference between Calvin and Luther will be seen more clearly. That Calvin praises law more highly than does Luther is not indicative, of itself, that he is more "legalistic," because he and Luther used the term with different meanings.[4]

[3] *Supra*, p. 65 f.

[4] "The Lutheran conception of law is distinguished above all by the fact that the Pauline passages in which law is thought of as the correlate of sinfulness are much more emphasized than by Calvin. Luther's experience as a monk, his struggle between law and grace, his impression that law and sin belong together, find scientific expression in his doctrine and were elevated to universal, basic rules of experience in his idea of the structure of the church. This effect of Luther's personality as well as the close connection to the Pauline utterances gives an appearance as if law does not belong to the faithful man and therefore does not exist for him. This conclusion was drawn within the Lutheran area of the Reformation by Agricola. The occasion for this lies indubitably in the basic conception of Luther that the real character of the law is its condemning work and that where this attribute of law is lacking, it is no more properly law. Where Luther finds a free acquiescence in the law, the law disappears entirely or at least it takes on a form to which the universal concept of law is no longer appropriate. Against this Calvin conceives the law under two characteristics which are of different kinds, namely, first, with the effect of condemnation, and secondly, without this effect: the law itself is not removed for the believer, but only the *maledictio legis*. Indeed, Calvin maintains expressly that although the law is written by God in the hearts of the faithful, still they need the objective divine commands as instruction and as a spur to the good. Therefore, while for Luther, the *usus praecipius* of the law con-

The first giving of the law was the prohibition in the garden of Eden. Calvin's comments here are extremely important if we are to appreciate that the idea of law for him is precedent to and in principle unconnected with sin and redemption.

Now Moses teaches that man was the ruler of the earth, with this exception, that he should be, nevertheless, subject to God. A law (*lex*) is imposed on him as a sign of his subjection (*signum subiectionis*), for it would have made no difference to God, if he had eaten indiscriminately of any fruit he pleased. Therefore the prohibition of one tree was a test of obedience. In this way God willed that the whole human race should from the beginning be accustomed to reverence his deity, for certainly it was necessary that man, adorned and enriched with so many excellent gifts, should not break forth into licentiousness. There was, indeed, another special reason, which we mentioned above, lest Adam should desire to be wise above measure; but this is to be remembered as God's general purpose, that he would have man subject to his authority.

This was an

elementary lesson in obedience, that man might know that he had a ruler and lord of life on whose will he ought to depend and in whose commands he ought to acquiesce. And this is, truly, the only rule of living well and rationally, that men should exercise themselves in obeying God.[5]

The prohibition in the Garden, then, was a law, a sign of subjection of the creature under the Creator. A "sign" however, a revelation, not the mere fact of subjection or an instinctive subjection as in the case of the animal creation. It was given as a norm to a man who was free not to sin, to show him the way of obedience.

Calvin further makes clear the relation of the law thus conceived as in its essence something positive in the will of the Creator, as against its negative, accidental functions under the conditions of sin:

---

cerns the sinner, for Calvin the law is related chiefly to the believer for whom, however, the *maledictio* is removed." Lobstein, *Die Ethik Calvins,* pp. 55 f.

[5] Com. Gen. 2:16 (CO XXIII.44d); cf. the same idea, II.i.4 (OS III.231.22 ff., and 232.23 ff.).

It seems, however, as if this does not accord with the judgment of Paul, when he teaches that "the law was not made for the righteous" (I Timothy 1:9). For, if this is so, when Adam was yet innocent and upright he had no need of a law. But the solution is ready. For Paul is not there writing controversially; but from the common practice of life he declares that they who freely run need not be compelled by the necessity of law, as is said in the common proverb, "Good laws spring from bad customs." Nevertheless, he does not deny that God imposed a law upon man from the beginning in order to maintain the right due to himself. If anyone objects with another statement of Paul, where he asserts that "the law is the minister of death" (II Corinthians 3:7), I reply that this is accidentally (*accidentale*) and from the corruption of nature. But then a precept was given man whence he might know that God ruled over him.[6]

The concept of law here is seen to belong to the revelation of God the Creator and to carry no hint of sin or disharmony. It is not something that comes in between God and man, destructive of a personal relation, but is the mode of that relation. This pure, or positive, or essential idea of the law is always distinguished clearly in Calvin's mind from the second conception, which does stand between God and man. Thus, we frequently come across his insistence that while the law (here the Mosaic moral law) means death to sinful man, this is an "accidental" property [7] of the law and that it is "accidentally" and "adventitiously" [8] killing. While on the positive side the law is said by Calvin to lead to "the fulfillment of righteousness that it may form the life of a man after the example of divine purity. For God has so delineated his own character in it that anyone exhibiting in action what is commanded would exhibit in his life, as it were, an image of God." [9] The law "joins a man by holiness of life with his God and, as Moses expresses it, makes him cleave to him"; [10] it contains in its precepts "all the duties of piety and love"; [11] it is a "perfect model of righteousness." [12]

Calvin's high evaluation of the Decalogue is not really directed

[6] Com. Gen. 2:16 (CO XXIII.45a).
[7] Com. II Cor. 3:7 (CO L.42a–b).
[8] Com. Rm. 7:10–11 (CO XLIX.126b, 127a).
[9] II.viii.51 (OS III.390.16–20).
[10] *Ibid.* (lines 26–28).
[11] *Ibid.*, (391.10).
[12] II.vii.13 (OS III.339.8), cf. *passim.*

to the Ten Commandments themselves, but to the perfect idea of law which he sees behind them. He has a threefold process of interpretation which amounts to a universalization of each command, a freeing of it from its accommodated form, so that its eternal truth may be seen. First, the outward commands must be interpreted as requiring inward conformity, because God is a "spiritual legislator." Thus, the "murder of the soul is wrath and hatred." [13] In his Augustinian reading of the last command Calvin draws an absolute picture of inner purity. Even involuntary flutterings of the mind toward wrath or lust or blasphemy are condemned.[14] Secondly, since the negative form of the precepts is partial and accidental, we must take each single prohibition as a synecdoche, further inquire what is the substance of the command, then, assuming that if what is prohibited displeases God, the contrary must please him, we must make of the precept a positive order.[15] Thus, "thou shalt not kill" finally means "that we shall do everything that we possibly can toward the preservation of the life of our neighbors." [16] "Honor thy father and thy mother" means "that since the Lord God takes pleasure in the preservation of his own appointed order, the degrees of dignity ordained by him ought to be held inviolable." [17] On the strength of this Calvin sees the grounds of civil order in the Decalogue.[18] By condemning the worst form of rebellion, God meant to commend all levels of order.[19] Thirdly, the two tables, the first calling for piety or pure worship and love of God, and the second table calling for charity, or love of men, are a brief form of all that God requires of men.[20] This universalizing of the Decalogue, or rather this concept of the Decalogue as a specially accommodated expression of universal, eternal law, is clear also in Calvin's harmony of the last four books of Moses.[21] Here the commands are universalized as just described, and in addition each is used as a general category under which is subsumed its "ceremonial supplements," "political supplements," and "judicial supple-

[13] II.viii.6, 7.
[14] II.viii.49, 50.
[15] II.viii.8, 9.
[16] II.viii.9 (OS III.351.19–21).
[17] *Ibid.*, par. 35 (376.28–30).
[18] *Ibid.* (377.20 ff.).
[19] II.viii.10 (OS III.352.1 ff.).
[20] II.viii.11.
[21] (CO XXIV.261 ff., *passim*).

ments," until the whole legal structure of ancient Israel is seen as an expression of God's orderly will in creation. The "supplements" are passing aspects, appropriate to local conditions.

[The moral law is] the true and eternal rule of righteousness, prescribed to men of all ages and nations who wish to conform their lives to the will of God. . . . [But] certainly all nations are left at liberty to enact such laws as they should find respectively expedient for them, provided they be framed according to the perpetual rule of love, so that although they vary in form they may have the same principle.[22]

A related idea here is that of the conditional salvation offered by the law. Calvin consistently maintains that the fulfilling of the law, if it were possible, would make redemption through Christ unnecessary. This is impossible, but not because in principle the law offers anything but complete salvation. Rather, it cannot happen because of sin.

So we ought also to acknowledge that divine favor is offered to us in the law if we could merit it by our works, but that no merit of ours can ever attain it.[23]

A reward is ready to be bestowed on condition that we perform what is commanded.[24]

We freely acknowledge, therefore, that the perfect obedience of the law is righteousness and that the observance of every particular command is a part of righteousness, since complete righteousness consists of all the parts. But we deny that such a kind of righteousness anywhere exists. And therefore we reject the righteousness of the law; not that it is of itself defective and mutilated, but because on account of the debility of our flesh it is nowhere to be found.[25]

Once more, after several Biblical citations which point to salvation through works,

we certainly do not question that the righteousness of the law consists in works or that this righteousness consists in the worthiness and merit of works. But still it cannot be proved that we are justified by works, unless some person be produced who has fulfilled the law. . . .

[22] IV.xx.15 (OS V.487.6–8, 26–30) and entire paragraph.

[23] III.xvii.2 (OS IV.255.17–19).

[24] *Ibid.*, par. 6 (258.31).

[25] *Ibid.*, par. 7 (260.16–22).

Legal righteousness consists in perfect works; no man can boast of having satisfied the law by works; therefore, there is no righteousness by the law.[26]

Calvin does not quarrel with the idea of works except when it is made the cause rather than the goal of salvation.[27] He values it highly enough to insist that even our works are justified by faith.[28] Calvin devotes III.xvii to showing that the disharmony between the promises of the law and of the Gospel consists in the fact of sin. It is not something ultimate. The present disharmony, however, because of the fact of sin and the incompleteness of sanctification, remains throughout this life.

We have now related three things: (1) Calvin's recognition of law in the original state of innocence, (2) his insistence that the law is in essence positive, and that its restraining and condemning character is an "accidental" (although, since the Fall, inseparable) function of it, and (3) his praise of the law as offering complete (although, because of sin, unobtainable) salvation through the prescription of perfect love to God and man. We must now show further the identical content of the moral law as found in the human conscience, which is an element of the revelation of the Creator, and the moral law as given in connection with the work of redemption.

Subsequent to the Fall of man, God's orderly will for his creatures continues to be revealed universally in conscience, specially in Scripture, particularly the Mosaic moral law and the teachings of Jesus. Here we find two equations: that of the content of the Mosaic law with the law of nature and that of the teachings of Jesus with the Mosaic law. The former is sometimes recognized by interpreters of Calvin, the latter is common.[29] The

[26] III.xvii.13 (OS IV.266.31–33, 267.14–16).

[27] III.xiv.18 (OS IV.237.1 ff., and 248.28 ff.).

[28] "So we may justly assent that not only ourselves but also our works are justified by faith alone." III.xvii.10 (OS IV.263.11–12).

[29] Beyerhaus, *Studien zur Staatsanschauung Calvins,* p. 68; Gloede, *Theologia Naturalis bei Calvin,* pp. 174 f.; Wernle, *Der evangelische Glaube nach den Hauptschriften der Reformatoren,* p. 149. While Lobstein shows that the Decalogue is the norm of the Christian life, thus, that there is a positive relation between law and gospel, he does not show the identity of Mosaic law and conscience. He refers

identity of the Old Testament moral law with the conscience is an identity of content and of purpose, not of the details of form. Calvin's exposition of the Decalogue in I.viii begins with recognition of this identity. "Moreover, the very things contained in the two tables are in a manner dictated to us by that internal law which is inscribed and, so to speak, engraved on all hearts, as we said formerly." [30] "Since it was necessary because of our dulness and obstinancy, the Lord gave us a written Law, which both declares more certainly what in the law of nature was too obscure, and, arousing our indolence, makes a deeper impression on our understanding and memory." [31] Further, in his other long study of the Decalogue he constantly shows parallels to what the heathen know from nature or conscience.[32] Even the hallowing of the Sabbath was "prior to the law [of Moses]," derived from God's having rested on the seventh day of creation. It was "altogether extinct" among the heathen, "almost obsolete" with the race of Abraham, and was "renewed" at Sinai.[33] On the other hand, the ceremonial law is in quite a different class, carrying rather the gratuitous promise than the revelation of the Creator.

The second equation, that of Jesus' ethical teachings and the Mosaic moral law, is coupled often with encomiums upon the eternity and perfection of the law and the summary of the law as love.

And certainly Christ prescribed no other rule of a pious and just life than that which had been laid down by the law of Moses, for the perfect love of God and our neighbor comprehends the utmost perfection of righteousness.[34]

Away, then, with that error that the defects of the law are here corrected by Christ; for it must not be imagined that Christ is a new

---

to the derivation of family ethics from creation, but makes nothing of it. *Die Ethik Calvins,* pp. 45–62, pp. 95 ff.

[30] II.viii.1 (OS III.344.11–14). [31] *Ibid.* (lines 24–27).

[32] A large number of our references, *supra,* pp. 67 ff. come from this study. Cf. Com. Ex. 22:25 (CO XXIV.681a–d); Com. Lev. 18:6 (CO XXIV.661–662); Com. Deut. 19:14 (CO XXIV.676b), and 22:22 (648d).

[33] Com. Ex. 20:11 (CO XXIV.580d–581a).

[34] Com. Lk. 10:26 (CO XLV.610b).

legislator who adds to the eternal righteousness of his father, but rather he is to be heard as a faithful interpreter, that we may know what is the nature of the law, what is its end, and how far it extends.[35] It has been the prevailing opinion that the beginning of righteousness was formerly laid down in the law, but that the perfection of it is taught in the gospel. But nothing was further from the design of Christ than to alter or innovate anything in the precepts of the law. For there God has once fixed the rule of life which he will never retract. . . . That the doctrine of the law not only begins but also brings to perfection an upright life may be inferred from this one principle, that it requires perfect love of God and of our neighbor. Moreover, he who possesses such love, lacks nothing of the highest perfection. Therefore the law, so far as respects the precepts for living rightly, leads men to the farthest point of righteousness. Accordingly Paul declares it weak, not in itself, but in our flesh.[36]

It is clear, therefore, that Calvin equates God's orderly will as revealed in creation with the moral law as given to Moses, and the Mosaic moral law with the ethical teachings of Jesus. He does not quite so clearly equate conscience with Jesus' teachings, yet the terminology of conscience and natural law does occur in the comments on the Sermon on the Mount. Most striking here is the passage on the love of neighbors and of enemies, which is grounded, not on the special work of Christ, but on the "law," the "law of charity" (*lex caritatis*), and on what "nature dictates."[37] These all belong together as expressions accommodated to differing circumstances of the regular, orderly, love relationship of God and his creatures. Gloede cites with approval[38] and Wernle in criticism[39] that Calvin sees no difference between *caritas* and *aequitas* or *iustitia*. I would suggest that a reason for this is his sense for the inherence of order in all right relationships. He does not see form or order as in restraint of the freedom and spontaneity of love but as the mode of their expression. In the Lutheran conception, love and law are in com-

[35] Com. Mt. 5:21 (CO XLV.175a), also 5:27 (179a).
[36] Com. Mt. 5:21 (CO XLV.174c).
[37] Com. Mt. 5: 43, 44 (CO XLV.187d–188d); cf. II.viii.50.
[38] Gloede, *Theologia Naturalis bei Calvin*, pp. 173–178.
[39] Wernle, *Der evangelische Glaube nach den Hauptschriften der Reformatoren*, pp. 149 f.

petition; for Calvin they are by definition the same thing in essence. It is grace or gratuitous mercy in the gospel that is of another order. But before we enter that discussion we must discuss our thesis with reference to the *Institutes* as a whole.

In view of the analysis we have just made, one might expect to find Calvin's study of the Decalogue as part of the "knowledge of God the Creator" in the *Institutes*. That which "declares with greater certainty what in the law of nature was too obscure" and is a "perfect rule of righteousness," only "accidentally" related to sin, would certainly seem to belong there. But in fact it is found elsewhere. An exception to this is that part of the comment on the second commandment in the 1559 edition does not stand with the rest, but receives detailed separate treatment in I.xi–xii. This by no means implies that the second command belongs in a different class from the others, rather, it illustrates the validity of the first table of the law for the Christian apart from specific references to Christ.

Further, although Calvin finds the "third" and chief use of the moral law to be its function as a guide to the Christian, he does not locate his Decalogue analysis in Book III, where he describes the personal ethics of the Christian man (III.vi–x), or in Book IV, under social order (IV.xx). However, both of these analyses are based upon the law.[40] The order prescribed in the law is the indispensable foundation of both personal and social ethics.

Thus, although the law is a part of Books I, III, and IV, the main presentation of it occurs in Book II, "Of the Knowledge of God the Redeemer." Here it is found in its chronological place among the successive forms or accommodations in the history of the revelation of the Redeemer. The moral law is reviewed in connection with the ceremonial—the two together forming the "religion delivered by the hand of Moses." [41] It is, however, the ephemeral ceremonies, not the eternal moral law, which are that part of the "religion of Moses" which bears the "promise in Christ," and which alone deserve, so far as special content is concerned,

[40] *Infra*, p. 235.

[41] II.vii.1 (OS III.326.29).

to be classed as a part of the revelation of God the Redeemer.[42] Thus, it is not the chief theological significance of the moral law or its content that determines the placing of the Decalogue analysis in the *Institutes* of 1559 but rather its accidental or historical link to the "ceremonial supplements." This is not meant to deny ample grounds for placing it thus, but to show that the mere location of this analysis in the final edition is not a reliable index to Calvin's total evaluation of the law. Along with the location, it should be noticed that Calvin sets the moral law first in the content of the knowledge of the Creator[43] and then with reference to redemption.[44] The content relates to God the Creator, the special act of giving it in this form relates to the covenant.

Throughout all the earlier editions of the *Institutes,* as well as in the catechisms, the Decalogue receives isolated treatment. It is a part neither of soteriology nor of ethics, nor is it linked closely to the ceremonial law. The placing of the law chapter first in the *Institutes* of 1536 is not important, since it represents simply a reproduction of the order of Luther's catechism. In the editions from 1539 to 1554 the Decalogue is treated separately as chapter iii, with little reference to Christ, and precedent to the whole soteriology. The exception is that the doctrine of the "third use" of the law is part of this and belongs properly to soteriology. Thus, before 1559 the moral law does not appear as part of Calvin's soteriology, although it does follow the doctrine of sin. This means that the 1559 edition is the only writing that seems opposed to our thesis, and then only in external form. The theological significance of the law remains the same throughout.

Law and the Knowledge of the Redeemer

As the law, whatever its secondary historical form, is the revealed, eternal, orderly will of God the Creator against which man revolted, so it is the goal toward which reconciliation is aimed. But the movement is not in a direct line, as if an incomplete obedience need only be completed or as if grace were a kind of mechanical repair. The breaking of the law was at once

[42] II.vii.16 (OS III.341, 4 ff.) and *passim.*

[43] II.viii.2 (OS III.344.28 ff.). [44] *Ibid.,* par. 14 (355.16 ff.).

the breaking of personal communication with God and the re-establishment of it required a new advance by God toward men—one neither predictable on the basis of law nor to be contradicted by it. Hence we find the same break here that we discovered above, so to speak, between our Chapters III and IV. Yet the two sides are not unrelated.

The language of law and of love which is "the chief thing of the law"[45] is universal. That is to say, it is as broad as creation. Law concerns the regular, the orderly, although it is never in essence impersonal even on the lower level of the *ordo naturae*.[46] All things and all persons are affected by it more or less in the same way. Men obey or disobey and are treated accordingly. The language of the gospel or of redemption, on the other hand, is special and exclusive. All have disobeyed, but all are not treated accordingly. Next to the revealed orderly will of God in Scripture, which makes equal demands on all men, and promises rewards, is the special, gratuitous mercy of God that with awe-inspiring sovereignty rescues some. The commensurability of these two revelations is seen in that Christ, whose work is grounded in God's gratuitous mercy, obeyed the law perfectly, thereby justifying man and releasing the power of the Spirit to foster the believer's obedience of the law. The obedience of Christ, justification, and sanctification have as their presupposition and goal the perfect law-love-creation ideal—although they have as their occasion sin, and as their actual impulse the gratuitous mercy of God, and neither a perfect perception of nor a perfect fulfillment of the law is possible in the present life. On the other hand, gratuitous love lies behind both law and gospel, creation as well as redemption. We shall first look at the redemptive work of Christ's obedience, justification, and sanctification within the frame of law and then at law as having its ground in God's gratuitous mercy.

CHRIST'S OBEDIENCE.—Christ merited our salvation by obeying the law.

For hence we conclude that we must seek from Christ what the law would confer on anyone who fulfilled it; or, which is the same, that we

[45] III.xi.17 (OS IV.201.20).

[46] *Supra*, p. 66.

obtain by the grace of Christ what God promises in the law to our works, "which [precepts] if a man do, he shall live in them" (Leviticus 18:5).[47]

For if righteousness consists in an observance of the law, who can deny that Christ merited favor for us when by bearing this burden himself he reconciled us to God, just as if we were observers of the law? . . . For what was the design of this subjection [of Christ to the law] but to procure righteousness for us by undertaking to perform that which we could not do? Hence that imputation of righteousness without works of which Paul treats (Romans 4) because that righteousness which is found alone in Christ is accepted as ours.[48]

JUSTIFICATION.—This is the result of Christ's work and has the same legal tone. It means a forensic declaration or imputation of righteousness against the background of the law of God the Creator.

Therefore he is said to be justified by works in whose life appears such purity and sanctity as to deserve an attestation of righteousness before the throne of God or by the integrity of his works can answer and satisfy his judgment. On the other hand, he is justified by faith who, being excluded by the righteousness of works, apprehends by faith the righteousness of Christ, invested in which he appears in the sight of God, not as a sinner, but as a righteous man. Thus, we simply explain justification to be an acceptance by which God receives us into his favor as if we were righteous. And we say it consists in the remission of sins and the imputation of the righteousness of Christ.[49]

[The sinner] . . . having obtained the remission of sins, is justified by the intervention of the righteousness of Christ; and although regenerated by the Spirit of God, he thinks upon the everlasting righteousness reserved for him, not in the good works to which he devotes himself, but solely in the righteousness of Christ.[50]

[47] II.xvii.5 (OS III.513.17–21); cf. Com. Acts 13:38 (CO XLVIII.306b).

[48] II.xviii.5 (OS III.513.24–33). "Another part of our reconciliation with God was this, that man who had ruined himself by his own disobedience ought to remedy this condition by obedience, satisfy the judgment of God, and suffer the punishment of sin. Therefore our Lord appeared as true man, he put on the character of Adam and assumed his name to act as his substitute in obeying the Father, to lay down our flesh as the price of satisfaction to the just judgment of God and in the same flesh to suffer the penalty which we had deserved." II.xii.3 (OS III.439.21–28).

[49] III.xi.2 (OS IV.183.1–10).

[50] *Ibid.*, par. 16 (200.19–23).

The result of justification is "Christian liberty,"[51] which for Calvin is nothing more than peace of conscience,[52] the same conscience that is the ground of inexcusability.[53] This liberty is not freedom from the requirements of law as expressed in conscience and the Decalogue, but freedom from guilt before God even though these requirements have not been fulfilled.

> The first part of Christian liberty is that the conscience of believers, when seeking an assurance of their justification before God, should raise themselves above the law and forget all the righteousness of the law.[54]

> Still, it cannot be rightly inferred from this that believers have no use of the law. It ceases not to teach, exhort, and urge them to good, although it is not recognized by their consciences before the tribunal of God.[55]

Thus we come to sanctification and the "third use" of the law.

SANCTIFICATION.—The inseparable accompaniment of justification, this consists in the "mortification of the flesh" and the "vivification of the Spirit."[56] It involves repentance and regeneration, "the end of which is the restoration of the Divine image within us,"[57] which is the restoration of "righteousness and true holiness."[58] This consists in "piety toward God" and "charity toward men," in a word, the observance of the law.[59]

Jacobs rightly observes that "the life of a Christian man," in III.vi–x, is an extension of the Decalogue commentary.[60] Calvin says so himself:

> We have said that the end of regeneration is that the life of the faithful may exhibit a symmetry and agreement between the righteousness of

[51] III.xix. The entire content of this chapter "Of Christian Liberty" is closely related to II.vii–viii and III.vi–x.

[52] III.xix.1–3, especially (OS IV.282.11 ff., 283.25 ff.).

[53] The formal definition of conscience and the distinction between responsibility to divine and human government, *supra*, p. 59 came from this chapter on justification.

[54] III.xix.2 (OS IV.283.4–7).

[55] *Ibid.* (lines 20–24).

[56] III.iii.5 (OS IV.60.1 ff.).

[57] *Ibid.*, par. 9 (63.11 ff.).

[58] *Ibid.* (65.5 f.).

[59] III.iii.16 (OS IV.72.29–39).

[60] "The discussion of the doctrine of sanctification, the so-called ethic of Calvin, is the expansion (*Entfaltung*) of the doctrine of the *tertius usus legis*," *Prädestination und Verantwortlichkeit bei Calvin*, p. 103.

God and their obedience, and that they may confirm the adoption which they have received as sons. But although the law contains in itself that newness by which the image of God is restored in us, yet since our tardiness needs much stimulation and assistance, it will be useful to collect from various places of Scripture a rule for the reformation of life, lest any with a heartfelt desire for repentance should in their zeal go astray.[61]

These are the opening words on the Christian life. The following chapter opens in the same way, with a reminder that the law is at the base of it. "Although the law of the Lord contains a most excellent and well arranged rule for the conduct of life, yet it has pleased the heavenly teacher to train his own [people] in a still more accurate fashion to the rule which is prescribed in [Mosaic] law."[62] Included subsequently are worship, self-sacrifice, alms giving, loving all men because of the image of God in them, industriousness and patience, and all are parts of God's "most orderly righteousness (*ordinatissima iustitia*)."[63] "The doctrine of the law remains, therefore, through Christ inviolable; which by tuition, admonition, reproof, and correction forms and prepares us for every good work."[64]

The third use of the law, which is the principle one, and which is more nearly connected with the proper end of it [than its condemning and its political functions] relates to the faithful. . . . For they find it an excellent instrument to give them from day to day a better and more certain understanding of the Divine will to which they aspire, and to confirm them in the knowledge of it. It is as though a servant were already influenced by the strongest desire of gaining the approbation of his master, yet it is necessary for him carefully to inquire and observe the orders of his master in order to conform to them.[65]

Mortification and vivification are possible because of the salvation gratuitously offered by the method of Christ's obedience, but the aim to which they tend is the proper obedience of the divine will under the tuition of the moral law, while free from its curse.

Christ's obedience, then, is a fulfilling of the law, which re-

[61] III.vi.1 (OS IV.146.14–21).
[62] III.vii.1 (OS IV.151.3–6).
[63] *Ibid.*, par. 10 (161.14).
[64] II.vii.14 (OS III.340.10–13).
[65] II.vii.12 (OS III.337.23–24, 29–34).

moves its curse. Justification is the imputation of his righteousness to the elect sinner. Sanctification is the Spirit's work, bringing the believer again into harmony with the law. Whether the life eternal is a life under the law and what form of the law will rule are speculative questions, but Calvin implies that the answers are affirmative, and there is nothing in the essence of his idea of law and love, or orderly, universal love, to controvert it.

> Thus, I think the written law with its exposition will pass away. But because I hold that Christ spoke simply, I shall not feed the ears of readers with such amusements. Therefore let it suffice for us to hold that heaven and earth shall sooner fall to pieces and the whole frame of the world become a mass of confusion than that the stability of the law shall give way.[66]

The last judgment will be a "real restoration (*instauratio*) of a just order."[67] Christ "renews" and "restores" the world by his work.[68] Similarly the superiority of love over faith and hope in I Corinthians 13 is its "perpetuity," for "faith and hope belong to the state of imperfection, but love will remain even in a state of perfection."[69] Finally, when redemption is complete, the temporary and sin-occasioned office of Christ and his kingdom will be brought to an end, and Christ will enjoy again only that glory which he enjoyed before creation.[70] But even if we do not press the point with reference to eternal life, still, harmony with God's law through Christ's work, justification, and sanctification is the immediate goal of redemption.

But if redemption belongs as just described to the *lex-caritas* scheme of creation, so that the God of gratuitous mercy is seen to work within the frame of his eternal, orderly will—so also the whole creation rests upon the gratuitous mercy of God. For there is no other motive for God's having created and sustained creation, for the giving of life, law, or any other gift of God originally or again in redemption, apart from God's incomprehensible, groundless love. In addition to Christ,

[66] Com. Mt. 5:18 (CO XLV.172b) and *passim*.
[67] Com. Rm. 3:6 (CO XLIX.50d). [68] Com. Rm. 4:13 (CO XLIX.77a, c).
[69] Com. I Cor. 13:13 (CO XLIX.515d).
[70] II.xiv.3 (OS III.462.9–23); cf. II.xv.5 (479.5 ff.) and I.xiii.26 (OS III.147.14 ff.).

we have the love of God toward us testified to also by many other proofs. For if it be asked, why the world has been created, why we have been placed in it to possess the dominion of the earth, why we are preserved in life to enjoy innumerable blessings, why we are endued with light and understanding, no other reason can be adduced, except the gratuitous love of God.[71]

God's "paternal love" brought into being the world gratuitously, providing all things for the sake of man, creating by a method instructive to man in such a way that (exactly as in the case of faith) man can only receive and worship; he must not question further or ask for any other cause.[72] Creation itself is in its essence just as incomprehensible, just as much a work of God's love, as the redemption which is aimed at restoring it.

The Dialectical Relationship

Man owes his creation and his redemption to the gratuitous love of God. Yet he owes his need for redemption to his sinful rebellion against God's orderly rule in creation, and he discovers that salvation consists in Christ's obedience, justification, and sanctification, which accomplish the removal of guilt and the re-establishment of that orderly rule. The two sides are inseparable: the special, gratuitous quality of God's mercy and the orderly universal inclusiveness of law. Dropping the first produces a legal or rational orthodoxy. Dropping the second produces a radical kind of *sola gratia* that Calvin never envisioned. Calvin held both—for the Creator and the Redeemer are one. Because of sin, however, this remains a statement of faith, not a relation describable by either rational or moral-legal systems of unity. The believer can never build a continuous thought structure relating the creating and redeeming work of God, because of the mystery of gratuitous love that lies behind both and the noetic effects of sin. The relation of the knowledge of God the Creator to the knowledge of God the Redeemer remains a dialectic one, or, as we called it above,[73] a double presupposition. Each presupposes the other, but in a different way: (1) The redemptive knowl-

[71] Com. I Jn. 4:10 (CO LV.352d–353a); I.v.6 (OS III.51.21–26).

[72] I.xiv.1–2.

[73] *V. supra*, p. 46 and p. 147.

edge must be seen to have come from God, the Creator of heaven and earth, the same God to whom Scripture points in the natural order and the moral law, whom Scripture describes as the Triune Creator and Sustainer of the world. This is a logical or conceptual presupposition. It is not a propaedeutic or a first lesson in redemption, for, as we have seen, merely opposing a Christian interpretation of the Creator to a heathen one does not produce faith; we know the Creator only in the gratuitous promise of mercy in Christ—which is the other presupposition: (2) The knowledge of God the Creator comes only to those illuminated by the Spirit in faith, although the knowledge of faith, properly speaking, is not God as seen in his general creative activity, but as seen in the special work of redemption in Christ. Thus, the knowledge of the Redeemer is an epistemological presupposition of the knowledge of the Creator.

Just as the law belongs to God's orderly, eternal, revealed will for his creatures and is the background and goal of redemption, but is not truly known or obeyed except in the special, gratuitous work of Christ—so the doctrine of the Trinity is the frame or the presupposition of Christ's work, yet it is unknown apart from the redemptive revelation. Nowhere does Calvin systematically ascend through the doctrine of Christ to the Trinity, nor does he present the redeeming work of Christ as a speculative working out of the doctrine of the Triune Creator, as did Osiander. Rather he has both doctrines in hand all the time, each presupposing the other. Yet each is related finally in the mysterious oneness of which God himself convinces the believer in faith, not in any systematic, logical, or legal necessity.

So also for the doctrines of providence and predestination. Providence is a description of God's universally although personally active will in creation, while predestination specifically concerns the redemption and condemnation of men. All men have a vague premonition of the former, but only the elect know it for what it really is, and they know it through the "spectacles" of Scripture rather than from universal experience. That is to say, Scripture functions thus only for the faithful, for those who know themselves to be elect. The elect know the providence of

God, and they know it, not directly, but through faith that their Redeemer is the God of creation-providence. Election means nothing unless it is election by the providential World-ruler, yet providence is always seen as blind fate or chance, except to those who know God as having chosen them in gratuitous mercy. Each doctrine is a presupposition of the other.

Only the redeemed truly know the Creator. They, however, know him, not directly in his creative activity, but as the God of their redemption. And redemption, although coming unexpectedly, gratuitously, comes from the Creator and operates within the frame of the orderly will of the Creator. This will is knowable, in principle, from creation itself, but because of sin, is found only as part of the special redemptive revelation.

Calvin's doctrine of the verbally infallible Scripture does more than anything else to obscure the epistemological significance of the *duplex cognitio Domini* in his theology by seeming to present the reader with a set of infallible propositions about both Creator and Redeemer. We have seen, however, that his doctrine of Scripture is in fact not *sui generis,* but a derivative of his doctrine of faith, the *testimonium internum Spiritus Sancti* being but a part of the total illumination of the mind, having as its object, not a book, but Christ the Redeemer. When Calvin's doctrine of Scripture as presented in the *Institutes* is seen as the sole basis on which his whole epistemology is built, which has been the error of orthodoxy, his doctrine of faith naturally becomes secondary and his theology appears static and monolithic. But when his formal doctrine of Scripture is seen to be a buttress for support of the doctrine of the Creator, awaiting fuller treatment in the doctrine of faith proper—which is consonant with the christocentric character of his whole theology—then the qualitative difference between the knowledge of the Redeemer and of the Creator can be appreciated. Calvin cannot be completely exonerated, as we have already shown at length, from having developed the doctrine of Scripture in the *Institutes* in such a way as to give the former impression, yet he did clearly indicate that this was not his intention, and he did have two other motifs working against it, namely, his picture of faith as personal committment to Christ, and his critical handling of the text. Neither of the latter was unambiguously related to the former by Calvin himself—a systematic failure—but the spiritual depth and theological genius of his doctrine of believing trust in the gratuitous promise of love, did in fact rise far above any pedestrian Biblicism. The same doctrine preserved his view of predestination, so far as he was concerned, from being mere metaphysics. His sublime disregard for logical consistency, pointed out by Bauke, was apparently too much for the inevitable scholasticism that was to follow and was to lose the vital christocentric character by making the verbally infallible book an epistemological axiom of theology, and by making the divine election part of the doctrine of God the Creator. Deprived of its christological center, Calvin's theology is a theology of revelatory proposition and contradiction, and this is untenable. But neither is it any longer Calvin's theology. Seen in the light of its christological center, it is a theology of paradox, that is of statements that seem to the finite and sinful mind of man to be contradictions. This is not only tenable, but is of the very nature of Christian theology, which is always theology based upon supernatural revelation, and which always transcends the categories of human reason.

There is, then, no continuum in Calvin's theology between the two orders of knowing and their parallel parts. Or, one should say, there is no observable and theologically formulable continuum. The ultimate harmoniousness and continuity of all God's works is never doubted any more than it is explored. Man must do neither. Yet both aspects are held firmly together in a realm that stands both objectively and subjectively outside the scope of formal theology: the realm of faith, or of what Brunner calls "personal encounter" with God. In terms of human reason, the relation of the two orders of knowledge can best be called a dialectic one—not a dialectic resolved within the thought system as in Hegel, but one of which the final unity lies in the transcendent God and is partially apprehended by faith, as in Kierkegaard.

With this, the analysis of the epistemological structure of Calvin's system is complete. He goes no further. Displaying a reticence that is of the essence of Protestantism, Calvin refuses to join together what are united only in God's mystery. By a strong dual emphasis on both gospel and law (gratuitous redemption and orderly creation), yet with full appreciation that their unity is beyond the comprehension of sinful men, Calvin retains both the evangelical quality of his theology and its catholicity—both its kerygmatic quality and a strong sense of the inherence of form and structure in the universe at large and in all aspects of human life.

·VI·

INFLUENCE OF THE TWOFOLD KNOWLEDGE ON THE STRUCTURE OF CALVIN'S THEOLOGY

The Problem

By the structure of Calvin's theological thought we mean something other than the literary form, the sequence and interrelation of ideas in any given writing, or the material contents as such. And we are not pursuing questions of method, i.e., we are not trying to reconstruct Calvin's procedure as he analyzes a text or constructs the argument of a treatise, although all these matters, so far as they are discernible, are relevant and have been considered. We are interested in making a contribution to exposing and describing the form of the massive thought structure that gives Calvin's theological work the consistency and identity that has powerfully expressed itself in a variety of ways in the corpus of his writings.

Provisionally, at least, the term "system" is set aside both as a question-begging term, and as one that has no generally acceptable meaning. Further, the term "structure" does not, for better or for worse, bear any intentional relationship to the techniques of analysis which go with the name "structuralism" — in which the present writer is not trained.

Although this is a disputed, difficult, and perhaps impossible field of inquiry, it is one that cannot be avoided. All who deal seriously with Calvin's theology or any considerable part of it posit explicitly or implicitly a thought structure. Many elaborate efforts have been made to characterize his mind definitively, and even a hasty survey of the literature of the last sixty years, since Hermann Bauke's *Die Probleme der Theologie Calvins* (1922), shows a confusing and even contradictory variety among the most serious and thoughtful interpreters. While this condition may indicate various shortcomings among the interpreters of Calvin, and also problems created unnecessarily by Calvin himself, it may also give witness to the richness and variety of his theological universe which yields new discoveries as theological climates of opinion change and as historical disciplines probe into formerly untouched areas of inquiry.

A survey of literature is inappropriate here, but some characterizations may be helpful, at least to reveal the writer's frame of reference. Overall there has been a major shift from an aggressively dogmatic interest, fired by neo-orthodox concerns, to more methodologically pure historical approaches. In some respects hermeneutic interest has superseded the dogmatic. The increasing breadth, depth, and openness of Catholic Calvin studies have happily combined both dogmatic and ecclesial interest (in the spirit of Vatican II) with meticulous genetic inquiry. Calvin's relation to classical and patristic studies, to late scholasticism, to humanism and jurisprudence, especially focused on rhetoric, have come a long way, and have still a long way to go — promoting modesty in the writer of such essays as the present one. The recovery, publication, and analysis of a vastly increased number of Calvin's sermons has only begun to make itself felt. Consideration of the interrelation among Calvin's commentaries, treatises, and sermons has advanced greatly and is, of course, dependent upon all aspects of the foregoing. It is with this last that we now begin.

Literary Form and Thought Structure

A prime difficulty for the study of the structure of Calvin's theological thought is that the bulk of his literary corpus is in the form of commentary or exposition of texts of which he was not the author. Thus the choice, sequence, disposition, and interrelation of the elements are determined not by Calvin's mind but by his intent to express the mind of the writer. When the texts before him are biblical texts, such criticism of the ideas contained as he exercised in the commentary on Seneca are intentionally excluded. He means to be wholly the servant of the text he is interpreting.

The process of interpreting the mind of a writer, however, is not at all simple, as Calvin well knew and expressed, for instance, in his letter to Grynaeus,[1] prefaced to his first biblical commentary. A recent, fascinating study of this commentary on the Epistle to the Romans by Benoit Girardin, *Rhétorique et Théologique* (1979), demonstrates in daunting detail how methods of rhetorical analysis mark both the similarities and the differences in the exegesis of Melanchthon, Bucer, Bullinger, and Calvin.[2] Hundreds of rhetorical decisions affect a wide spectrum of procedures, from philological and syntactic matters leading to translation, to tracing the thread of the argument, to deciding upon a disposition of the parts of the discourse, and the assignment of rhetorical figures; indeed, "rhetoric can assimilate everything, transform everything, rule everything; its possibilities are unlimited and its pretensions totalitarian: dominating all discourse."[3] But in this rhetorical "space" theology is not passive; it, too, can play the game, and contest with rhetoric out of its own sui generis requirements. When Girardin compares the teaching about predestination in the Romans commentary and in the *Institutio* of 1539, which were being written at the same time in Strasbourg, he accounts for differences in the type of rhetoric Calvin discerns as appropriate to the purposes of Paul and to his own purposes in the *Institutio.*[4] Again, he studies the subjects of predestination and law in the commentary to determine "how theology (le theologique!) imposes its own law, its mark, and its limits on rhetoric while, however, allowing it (rhetoric) a place."[5] I am not competent to judge this difficult argument in detail, but as one generally familiar with Calvin's teachings, I find that while this material throws fascinating light on almost every word and phrase, the theological yield — that is, the contribution to understanding Calvin's thought — is, for me, rather slight. It appears that theology is the stronger player in this "bricolage." Recognizing the humanistic-rhetorical-juristic elements in Calvin's work appears, at the present state, not to revolutionize the understanding of his teaching.

It is in the treatises, chiefly the *Institutio,* across the years of

[1] *CO* 10 pars prior, 402ff. See the treatment of T. H. L. Parker, *Calvin's New Testament Commentaries* (1971), Ch. III.

[2] Ch. 5 and 6, *passim,* e.g., pp. 266, 324ff.

[3] *Ibid.,* p. 321.

[4] *Ibid.,* pp. 241ff.

[5] *Ibid.,* p. 322.

extension and reordering of the material, that Calvin's own ways of thinking, farther removed from any given biblical text than in the commentaries and sermons, are freer to express his own mentality. Here, too, there are problems to solve, for example as presented by Quirinus Breen. Breen sees Calvin as a syllogistic thinker, who means in the *Institutio* to persuade a general, non-specialist public and to that end uses quite freely a great variety of rhetorical techniques: epideictic, forensic, and deliberative.[6] Ford Battles, on the other hand, finds through the principle of accommodation, not the reduction of logic to persuasive devices, but the "divine rhetoric" itself, thus unlocking "God's beneficent tutelage and pedagogy of his wayward children."[7]

The question that concerns us now, however, is not the role of rhetoric or logical devices in Calvin's thought, but simply to assert that it would seem that freed of the text in close context and seeing the topics derived from many texts gathered together, ordered, and reordered by Calvin over the years, the structure of his thought, his peculiar way of constructing a theology, probably appears best in the *Institutio.* This accounts for the priority of the *Institutio* in what follows.

A Proffered Conception of Structure

The center of Calvin's thought, around which all else moves, is the divine provision for and the divine accomplishment of the salvation of sinful humanity through Jesus Christ to the glory of God alone.[8] That is to say, Calvin's thought has a *soteriological center* which dominates all his theology, but not all elements equally. Although Calvin's soteriology proper is profoundly Christocentric, it is not strictly accurate to say that his thought or theology as a whole is Christocentric. This is true because there is an inherent dialectic

6 "John Calvin and the Rhetorical Tradition," *Church History* 26 (1957) 3-21.

7 "God was Accommodating himself to Human Capacity," *Interpretation* 31 (1977), 1938, 20 *et passim.*

8 We do not mean here to introduce a central dogma or systematic premise, but to describe the strongest element in a field of force within which Calvin does his theological work, whether in the form of biblical commentary, sermons, or theological treatises.

within his soteriology by which it is related to and is set within non-soteriological elements upon which it depends for its meaning.

By asserting that a soteriological or evangelical motif dominates Calvin's thought, we at the same time assert that his theology is oriented by a temporal process, a *from which* and a *to which,* a *no longer* and a *not yet,* but a process in which the "no longer" and the "not yet" overlap, in which the origin (createdness as such) and the ultimate (eschatological) end coexist in the historical life of the church. In other almost synonymous terms, covenant history under the conditions of sin is the matrix of all Calvin's thinking.

The historical matrix of salvation *from* . . . and *toward* . . . issues in a two-sidedness (to be discussed further below) held together in a dialectical process from which nothing in Calvin's thought escapes. By dialectic we mean here the interrelationships of elements of thought belonging to the same universe of discourse that can neither be stated in a continuous logical sequence, nor be systematically related to one another in a rationally consequent system — and yet, cannot be separated from one another or asserted as independently true propositions, without losing their proper meaning.

The theological universe of Calvin, centered in soteriology, is a universe of knowing: it is cognitive or noetic throughout and thus is rightly designated a theology of the Word. His thought is not rooted in an apprehension of being, a grasp of the ontic, or founded on ontological or metaphysical truth formed into propositions. It is founded wholly on a special self-disclosure of the Word of God made effective through the persuasion and conversion worked by the Holy Spirit in faith. Knowledge, thus, is the fundamental and central category of Calvin's theological thought, to which we now turn.

But first, a caveat: For all the foundational place of knowledge in Calvin's thought, and the extensive analysis and classification of kinds of knowledge, ends of knowledge, etc., Calvin is not interested in problems of perception, of knowledge theory, of precision with reference to various options within the faculty psychology of his time, or the like, which one expects to find in a technical epistemology. Probably it is unwise to use the term epistemology in discussing his thought.[9] This tends to be borne out by the detailed analyses of Gerd Babelotzky[10] and the more general observations of Charles Partee,[11] as well as the widely differing estimates of Calvin's knowledge of scholastic philosophy by A. Ganoczy and H. Schützeichel, on the one hand, and K. Reuter and T. F. Torrance, on the other.[12] I suggest that it is Calvin's soteriological focus on "useful" and "practical" knowledge — useful for salvation and practical for the Christian life — that excludes these technical matters from among Calvin's major preoccupations.[13]

Further observations on the knowledge of God in Calvin now follow, arising from this soteriological focus:

1. The term "knowledge of God" throughout Calvin's writings does not refer to the knowledge of observation, or discovery, or remembering, but is an elliptical expression, a shorthand including both divine revelation and its reception in human knowledge. In

[9] Two articles of T. F. Torrance, "Knowledge of God and Speech about Him according to John Calvin," *Regards contemporains sur Jean Calvin,* Actes du Colloque Calvin (Strasbourg, 1964), pp. 140-160, and "Intuitive and Abstractive Knowledge: from Duns Scotus to John Calvin," *Studia-Scholastico,* Congressus Scotisticus Internationalis, 2nd (Oxford, 1966), vol. 4 (1968), pp. 292-305, assert for Calvin the "intuitive" (traced from Scotus to John Major) rather than "abstractive" character of the knowledge of God that functions in Calvin's theology. Intuitive knowledge is construed as experiential encounter with the divine Being, by which "we are given to participate in God's own rationality, in his own self-knowledge or self-witness." Again, concerning the testimonium internum Spiritus Sancti, Torrance comments, "By the word *internum* Calvin does not refer primarily to what is internal to us, but to what is internal to God Himself" (p. 157). Torrance pays no attention to accommodation, or the duplex cognitio Dei, and very little to the cognitio Dei et nostri, which other students of Calvin have found important for understanding him. He mentions no other Calvin interpreters and offers not a single citation to Calvin's works in either of the two articles; hence we mention these prominently placed essays, but find it hard to make constructive use of them. Cf. G. W. Locher, *Testimonium Internum,* Theologische Studien 81 (Zürich, 1964).

[10] *Platonische Bilder und Gedankengänge in Calvins Lehre vom Menschen* (1977), ch. 2.

[11] *Calvin and Classical Philosophy* (1977), Ch. III. Also my own work, *passim.*

[12] A. Ganoczy, *Le jeune Calvin* (1966); H. Schützeichel, *Die Glaubenstheologie Calvins* (1972); K. Reutet, *Das Grundverständnis der Theologie Calvins* (1963); T. F. Torrance, *supra,* n. 9.

[13] Knowledge in Calvin's thought is commonly called "practical" by Lobstein, Pannier, Doumergue, Warfield, and "useful" in various writings of E. H. Harrison, v. "The Idea of Utility in the Thought of John Calvin," in *Christianity and History* (1964), pp. 249-269. I think "existential" is more adequate, as explained in my *Knowledge of God . . .* (*infra,* n. 14), pp. 24-31.

strictest adherence to Calvin's own conceptuality, "The 'knowledge of God' is always man's knowledge of God's revelation (according to the principle of accommodation) and the very revelation of God always in a radical way implies man's self-knowledge (according to the principle of correlation)."[14] Most students of Calvin (T. H. L. Parker,[15] R. Stauffer,[16] *et al.*) rightly change Calvin's language and use the term "revelation." But many (including, astoundingly, Krusche)[17] fail to note that it is only in faith (*Institutio* III.i-ii) where the term "knowledge" is appropriate because here revelation becomes known and fulfills its purpose. The import of this will be developed below.

2. Accommodation. Revelation does not refer to some general streaming of light from the deity but a voluntary, directed "accommodation" of what God wills to make known of himself to the capacities of the human creature. Although largely unnoticed by students of Calvin until the middle of this century (Paul Lobstein treated the concept and found it in passing a possible contribution of Calvin to the then reigning symbolo-fideism of Strasbourg[18]), and never discussed by Calvin as a special topic in the *Institutio,* the importance of accommodation in revelation is beginning to be realized.[19] It is found throughout commentaries and sermons, as well as in the *Institutio.* The most elaborate discussion occurs in Calvin's final academic lectures (January-February, 1563) on the early chap-

14 E. A. Dowey, *The Knowledge of God in Calvin's Theology* (1952, 1965), p. 24. This volume is the background for the present study.

15 *The Doctrine of the Knowledge of God, A Study in the Theology of John Calvin* (1952). "The problem of the knowledge of God is the problem of revelation," p. 13; and note chapter titles.

16 *Dieu, la création et la providence dans la prédication de Calvin* (1978), Chs. 1 and 2.

17 W. Krusche, *Das Wirken des Heiligen Geistes nach Calvin* (1957), Ch. IV, part 3, esp. pp. 261ff.

18 "La connaissance religieuse d'après Calvin," *Revue de Théologie et de Philosophie* (Lausanne) XLII (1909), pp. 53-110; v., pp. 74, 98ff., 108f.

19 The first extended treatment was my own, *Knowledge of God,* pp. 3-17, within which creation, pp. 4ff., and redemption, pp. 9ff., are considered. Another is F. L. Battles, *supra,* n. 7, which presents classical and patristic precedents, as well as numerous examples from Calvin.

ters of Ezekiel. A typical example, carrying the usual anti-scholastic barb, runs as follows:

> God appeared under a visible form to his servant: could Ezekiel on that account do as the scholastic theologians do — philosophize with subtilty concerning God's essence and know no end or moderation in their dispute? By no means, but he restrained himself within fixed bounds. Paul was caught up to the third heavens (II Cor. xii.4), but he says that he heard unspeakable things which he was not permitted to explain. So, therefore, let us be content with sound doctrine, which can sufficiently fortify us against the snares of the devil.[20]

This would appear to be a direct rejection, say, of Thomas' reasoning by analogy.[21] However, Calvin's alternative is not worked out in accommodation theory, but in relentless exegetical inquiry into what happened when oracles were strengthened by miracles, theophany, dreams, visions. His interest is in the identity of the Revealer, the means chosen, the distinguishing marks (as against the devil's miracles), the soteriological content — all with final reference to the power of the Holy Spirit.[22] Encompassing all accommodation is the mediatorial function of the Word in creation, in covenant history, and finally in the Word made flesh,[23] which is God's deepest accommodation or descent from his own mysterious being, and at the same time it is both the high point of human knowledge and the limit of it.

It is the effectiveness of the divine accommodation through the power of the Spirit in faith on which the whole theology of Calvin rests, not the cogency of syllogisms or brilliance of rhetoric. The goal of it is the persuasion, conviction, certainty wrought by the illumination of the Holy Spirit in the hearts of the faithful.

3. The Bible. It is through the instrumentality of Scripture that the saving revelation is made known. Thus, we might expect that for Calvin the promotion of this message in the church would be the highest goal of his calling. And so it is. Practically the whole of

[20] *Prael. in Ezech.* 1:25-26, *CO* XL.57.
[21] *ST* I.xiii.5.
[22] Dowey, *Knowledge of God,* pp. 93-99.
[23] *Ibid.,* pp. 9-17, 157ff.; cf. *Comm. in Joannis* 1:5, *CO* XLVII.7.

Calvin's literary output is so intended. His biblical commentaries (and lectures) are exposition of Scripture. His *Institutio* is the collection and ordering of loci communes drawn from Scripture, separated from the actual commentaries to make them more manageable for readers (perspicua brevitas), and to be used as guides for theological students in the study of Scripture.[24] And to what end? To fulfill the first duty of the pastoral office: "to proclaim the Word of God, to instruct, admonish, exhort and censure, both in public and in private. . . ."[25] The private aspect must not be overlooked, although self-evidently this is not to be expected among Calvin's published works. Nonetheless, as Professor Benoit demonstrated thoroughly in *Calvin, Directeur d'Ames* (1947), a major element of Calvin's letters is pastoral care or spiritual direction. Still, the chief goal of all this biblical work was, bluntly: preaching. Both the *Institutio* and the commentaries stand between the Scripture and the sermon, helping with exposition and application. The sermons proceed by lectio continua, book after book, passage after passage, daily, year in and year out.[26] Professor Stauffer estimates that, taken all together, sermons lost and those still extant, the sermons equal half of Calvin's total output;[27] and much in the letters can be construed as pastoral direction. We may be willing to exclaim with Professor Benoit that "toujours, partout, avant tout, Calvin fut pasteur."[28]

This all is a development of the thesis that Calvin's thought has a soteriological center, located in the historical matrix of life in the church, and that the various literary forms he adopted are all contributory to the proclamation of the Word in the church, public and private. Rightly, Benoit states elsewhere, "Calvin never allowed that theology be a science complete within itself: he saw theology always as standing in the service of faith, as sustaining life."[29]

24 *Joannes Calvinus Lectori, OS* III.6.18–7.3.

25 *Ordonnances Ecclésiastiques, OS* II.328.13f., tr. J. K. S. Reid, *Theological Treatises* (Library of Christian Classics, vol. 22), p. 58.

26 T. H. L. Parker, *Calvin's New Testament Commentaries,* pp. 52ff.

27 R. Stauffer, *Dieu, la création et la providence dans la prédication de Calvin* (1978), p. 10.

28 *Calvin, Directeur d'Ames* (1944), p. 11.

29 "Seelsorge und Theologie in der *Institutio,*" in *Calvin-Studien* 1959, ed. J. Moltmann, p. 1.

The Twofold Knowledge and Faith

We return now to two issues, touched in passing, that are decisive in determining the structure of Calvin's theological thought, once its soteriological center, its fundamentally cognitive character, and the importance of its principle of accommodation are accepted: the twofoldness of revelation, and the primacy of faith (not objective biblical authority) in all true knowledge of God.

Calvin's soteriology has a triple reference: (a) That from which salvation rescues the human race — *the condition of sin.* Sin disrupts human life like a geological fault, causing displacement in all strata — in the relation to God, within human society, and within the individual person. Sin is the occasion for redemption. "If Adam had remained upright," no redemption would have been necessary. (b) The prior condition, from which sin was a fall: *the good creation* in harmony with the Creator. Without this reference, which philosophers lack, neither the depth of sin nor the goodness of creation can be apprehended. (c) *The eschatological consummation* toward which salvation moves, already begun in the restoration of the divine image embodied in the promise of the gospel.

This triple reference, however, issues in a twofold or two-species dichotomy within revelation: (a) the original, primal order of the revelation of the Creator, still extant through the created order itself, and because of sin in the "general" teaching of Scripture, and (b) the revelation of God the Redeemer. It is this duplex cognitio Domini[30] apprehended by faith, within a history not yet consummated, that lies at the root of the dialectical structure of Calvin's thought. We do not refer here to the correlativity of the "knowledge of God and ourselves," which is not abridged anywhere in Calvin's theology and would have

[30] It would be well if the Calvin literature would hold to Calvin's own terminology placed by him prominently in the first two chapters of the *Institutio* of 1559: (1) the "knowledge of God and ourselves," I.i.1, *OS* III.31.6-8, and (2) the "two-fold knowledge" of Creator and Redeemer, I.ii.1, *OS* III.34.21-25. This is done precisely in G. Ebeling, "Cognitio Dei et hominis," *Geist und Geschichte der Reformation,* ed. H. Liebing, K. Scholder (1966), pp. 271-322, esp. pp. 299ff, 304ff., and Dowey, *Knowledge of God,* pp. 41-49 *et passim.* It is confusing when the latter term is transferred to the former distinction, e.g. by Battles in "Calculus Fidei," pp. 86f., 104, and by T. H. L. Parker, *supra,* n. 15, American edition (1959), pp. 118ff.

held even si Adam integer stetisset, but rather to the twofoldness that results from human sin and persists through history.[31]

The duplex cognitio Dei, although formulated exactly for the first time by Calvin in the *Institutio*, 1559, is not an hapax legomenon, but an unvarying element characteristic of his thought from at least 1539 on. In highlighting this distinction as of controlling importance for the understanding both of the structure of the *Institutio* and the structure of his thought as such, I call to the assistance of my own analysis (first offered in 1952) three other witnesses. First, the still unsurpassed essay of Julius Köstlin, "Calvins *Institutio* nach Form und Inhalt, in ihrer geschichtlichen Entwicklung,"[32] then François Wendel's *Jean Calvin — Sources et évolution de sa pensée religieuse* (1950),[33] who adopts and repeats almost verbatim the analysis of Köstlin, and finally B. A. Gerrish, *The Old Protestantism and the New* (1982).[34] Köstlin, Wendel, and Gerrish all hold that the four-part division of the *Institutio* according to the four articles of the Apostles' Creed is less revealing of Calvin's actual disposition of the subject matter than a two-part division: first, the doctrine of the Creator and creation in Book I, and second, salvation throughout Books II-IV. Yet neither Köstlin nor Wendel notes precisely the approximately thirteen times in the *Institutio* of 1559 by which in explicit methodological statements Calvin recalls and clarifies this distinction,[35] and both finally assimilate the entire problem of the knowledge of the Redeemer to the question of Scripture. Paul Lobstein's groundbreaking study, *La conaissance religieuse d'après Calvin* (1909), foreshadows a better understanding, but in a curious way he finds a "scholastic" formal doctrine of Scripture in the *Institutio*, Book I, and a practical, experimental, converting, faithful knowledge through wide reading in the sermons![36] True, but he might have

[31] Cf. Ebeling, *ibid.*, pp. 297-305.

[32] *Theologische Studien und Kritiken* (1868), pp. 6-62, 410-486.

[33] P. 87; English translation, p. 121.

[34] Pp. 199f. and 376f.

[35] These citations are enumerated and commented on in Dowey, *Knowledge of God*, pp. 43-46 and ff.

[36] Lobstein, *supra*, n. 18, pp. 74ff., 92ff., the latter esp. from sermons.

found the same if he had looked ahead to Book III.ii, where such a faith appears as the source of the knowledge of the Redeemer.

Although all Calvin's doctrines are affected by the distinction between the Creator's revelation and that of God as Redeemer, the most important is in the doctrine of knowledge itself. From 1539 on, all editions of the *Institutio* present separate treatments of Scriptural authority and faith. Scripture, confirmed by the testimonium internum Spiritus Sancti, appears in Chapter i, De Cognitione Dei (1539-54), in the context of the revelation of the Creator, showing attributes of God also revealed in creation. In each edition the chapter ends with the caution that since God can be known more closely only "in the face of Jesus Christ," which can be known only with the eyes of faith, "what remains to be said of the knowledge of God is better deferred to the place where we will be speaking of faith's knowledge."[37] Then in chapter iv (or v) of these editions, De Fide, there occurs the same material, expanded, but in the same sequence leading up to the identical definition of faith that also continued unchanged into the edition of 1559. It was thus not only the final recasting of the *Institutio,* but the practice of Calvin through the years, to develop Scripture's authority for the revelation in creation as the background against which the Fall took place, then to develop saving knowledge of the "freely given promise in Christ" under the heading of faith. This procedure coincides exactly with the statement in the locus classicus of the duplex cognitio Domini:

> First in the fashioning of the universe and in the general teaching of Scripture the Lord shows himself to be the Creator. Then in the face of Christ he shows himself to be the Redeemer. From this arises a twofold knowledge of him, of which the former is now to be considered; the second will follow in its proper order.[38]

It is worth noting that Calvin's cross-reference at the end of chapter i (ed. 1539-1554)[39] was recast and moved in 1559 to I.vii.5 —

[37] Italics added. The Latin of 1539 is best observed in a modern edition in the French of 1540, ed. I. Pannier, *Institution de la Religion Chrestienne* (1936-39), Vol. 1, p. 79. Or *OS* III.87.36-40.

[38] I.ii.i, *OS* III.34.21-25.

[39] *Loc. cit., supra,* n. 37.

again, to alert the reader that the subject of knowledge was not yet complete. But this reference to developing the subject elsewhere, alibi, was not noticed either by the Strasbourg editors of the *Calvini Opera,* or by Barth and Niesel in the *Opera Selecta.*[40] It appears, however, in J.-D. Benoit's critical edition of the French of 1560[41] and in the McNeill-Battles American translation.[42] Since the Calvin literature generally tends to assimilate faith to biblical authority (Wernle may be an exception), often without even a serious analysis of faith, one might conclude that this failed cross-reference had dire effects. Both Werner Krusche and François Wendel all but ignore *Institutio* III.ii, as if the prime locus of the knowledge of God problem were in *Institutio* I.vi-viii. On the contrary I wish to argue that faith is the threshold of all Calvin's thought, because of the revelatory or cognitive priority of the soteriological.

The doctrines of Scripture and faith are separated throughout Calvin's thought on the basis of the duplex cognitio Dei. Scripture is always used in support of knowledge of the Creator, and faith in support of knowledge of the Redeemer. It is characteristic that the attributes (virtutes) of God the Creator presented in this context are claimed to be agreeable with or the same as those revealed through creation. Although justice and mercy are here included, they are not related to forgiveness and justification, but to God's patience with the wicked in history.[43] A quite different vocabulary characterizes the cognitio Dei Redemptoris: here the virtutes, attributes, drop away and the characteristic expression is free grace, or gratuitous mercy, coupled with the promise of God in Christ.[44] This description carries through all history among those patriarchs and prophets, and generally the "ancient" people, who — although Christ had not yet come — were distinguished from the rest of the human race in that their faith was directed toward the gratuitous promise in Christ. The

[40] *OS* III.71.14-17; Pluribus nunc supersedeo, quoniam hac de re alibi tractandi locus iterum se offeret: tantum nunc sciamus veram demum esse fidem quam Spiritus Dei cordibus nostris obsignat.

[41] *Institution de la Religion Chrestienne* (1957), Vol. 1, p. 99, n. 3.

[42] Vol. I, p. 81, n. 18. Even here a printer's error refers to III.i.1 instead of III.ii.

[43] I.x.2, *OS* III.86.6–87.19.

[44] Cf. Dowey, *Knowledge of God,* p. 207, notes 272-276, which contain about thirty-five occurrences of this terminology, a list which could be extended indefinitely.

virtutes Dei that Professor Stauffer points out in the sermons are of this same order.[45] One rather expects that when his fascinating work on the sermons advances to the topic of saving faith, the same parallels will be observed there.

But how are these two — Scripture and the internal witness of the Spirit, on the one hand, and Christ and the illumination of the Spirit, on the other — to be related? Elsewhere I have described this dialectical relation rather awkwardly as a "double presupposition." Each element presupposes the other, but in a different way. (1) The redemptive knowledge must be seen to have come from God, the Creator of heaven and earth, the same God to whom Scripture points in the natural order and the moral law, whom Scripture describes as the Triune Creator and Sustainer of the world. This is a logical or conceptual presupposition. It is not a propaedeutic or a first lesson in redemption, for merely opposing a Christian interpretation of the Creator to a heathen one does not produce faith; we know the Creator only in the gratuitous promise of mercy in Christ which is the other presupposition: (2) The knowledge of God the Creator comes only to those illuminated by the Spirit in faith, although the knowledge of faith, properly speaking, is not God as seen in his general creative activity, but as seen in the special work of redemption in Christ. Thus, the knowledge of the Redeemer is an "epistemological" presupposition of the knowledge of the Creator.[46]

The criticism that this description, although valid, appears to result in an exaggerated disparity within Calvin's thought structure, has been well taken in *Calvin's Catholic Christology* (1966) of David Willis, who offers through his study of Christology a fuller trinitarian setting for the twofold knowledge,[47] as does Werner Krusche.[48] The danger, however, remains (especially in Krusche's presentation) that the proper dialectic may be lost. An accurate estimate of the

45 Stauffer, *op. cit.*, Ch. 3.

46 Dowey, *Knowledge of God*, Ch. 5. The later influence of Calvin's distinction is traced in Richard A. Miller, "'Duplex Cognitio Dei' in the Theology of Early Reformed Orthodoxy." *The 16th Century Journal* (1979), pp. 51-61.

47 Pp. 120ff. and 130ff.

48 *Das Wirken des heiligen Geistes nach Calvin* (1957), pp. 127ff.

matter would seem to be: "Thus one may correctly emphasize the proper unity with Willis or the proper distinction with Dewey. Both are found in Calvin."[49,50]

The intent of the present argument is not to reduce dialectical procedures in Calvin's theology to a single type. On the contrary there are several levels and types of dialectic functioning as a result of Calvin's juristic background, rhetorical strategies, characterological traits, formal biblicism, polemic situations, and probably more. Our purpose is to locate the prime, basic disjuncture in Calvin's theological thought — one that is not reducible to method, but represents Calvin's dominant response to revelation, and itself calls for an appropriate method. The proposal is that the soteriological center of Calvin's thought, expressed in the twofold knowledge of God, structures the basic dialectic of his thinking.

It remains now to offer a comment on two other analyses and solutions of what is a proper statement of the basic dialectic of Calvin's theological thought.

[49] Charles Partee, *op. cit., supra,* n. 11, p. 45.

[50] H. A. Oberman's learned and penetrating article, "The 'Extra' Dimension in the Theology of Calvin," *JEH* XXI (1970), 43-64 — originally published as "Die 'Extra-Dimension' in des Theologie Calvins," in *Geist und Geschichte der Reformation, supra,* n. 30, pp. 323-356 — has been widely cited with approval. The "extra" dimension is offered as a device for expressing the structure of Calvin's theology in terms of the "mutuality" and "discontinuity" (English translation, p. 48) of soteriological and created elements of human life in the presence of God. Against the background of the history of Lutheran and Reformed polemic this generalized derivative of the so-called extra Calvinisticum is highly illuminating. But I would offer the following caveat: etiam extra carnem is an inappropriate and misleading terminology that is a foreign body in the exposition of Calvin's thought. Calvin did not use the expression at all (allegedly derived from *Institutio,* II.xviii.4 and IV.xvii.30) and the accompanying philosophical canard, finitum non capax infiniti, proposed as the root of Calvin's or Calvinism's error, is even less appropriate. Willis demonstated this fully in *Calvin's Catholic Christology,* and offered a trinitarian alternative. But not quite trusting his own success, he continues to refer to the "so-called" extra Calvinisticum. My suggestion would be that the full trinitarian setting as developed by Willis, entailing more adequate treatment of the Spirit and the Son in creation and providence, is adequate to give the quietus to the old "extra" formula, and that duplex, twofoldness, Calvin's own characteristic expression, better reflects the structure of his theology, in Christology and throughout.

Structure of "Bipolarity"?

One of the most serious and learned readings of Calvin's thought structure in recent decades, by Alexandre Ganoczy, locates the basic dialectic, not in the twofold knowledge, but in Calvin's perennial opening lines of the *Institutio*, on the knowledge of God and ourselves. This phrase points to an "antithetical" relation, an unrelieved "bipolarity," an "unstable balance" between God's transcendence and the human race enclosed in bodily existence. This bipolarity runs throughout Calvin's thought, and most seriously interferes with the unity of his Christology as well as the believer's unity with Christ.[51] Even with increasingly sympathetic modification as described by Hans Scholl,[52] partly in response to the careful critique of David Willis,[53] Ganoczy still locates here the rupture that runs throughout Calvin's theology.

It may be significant that Ganoczy takes very little notice of accommodation, and speaks pejoratively of the ubiquitous instrumentality in Calvin's thought through which accommodation (also within Christology!) functions. We have maintained above, and have published elsewhere, that what Ganoczy calls bipolarity shows even more strongly the quality of correlation. This is not humanity against God, but coram Dei.[54] Further, this accommodation-correlation characteristic applies to all knowledge of God, even apart from the fall. It is the rupture caused by sin, issuing in the twofold knowledge, not the cognitio Dei et homini that requires dialectical procedures to understand what was going on.

Ganoczy, of course, does not overlook the condition of sin in this foregoing connection. He writes, "the second dialectical relationship

51 *Ecclesia Ministrans* (1968), part A, Die Grundzüge der Theologie Calvins, *passim*, and see summary, p. 104.

52 *Calvinus Catholicus. Die Katholische Calvinforschung im* 20. Jahrhundert (1974), pp. 135ff.

53 "Notes on Ganoczy's *Calvin, Théologien de l'Église et du Ministère,*" *BHR* XXX (1968), pp. 185-198; and "Rhetoric and Responsibility in Calvin's Theology," in *The Context of Contemporary Theology,* Essays in Honor of Paul Lehmann, ed. McKelway and Willis (1974), pp. 43-63.

54 Willis, "Rhetoric and Responsibility," p. 57; and Dowey, *Knowledge of God,* pp. 18-24.

in Calvin's theocentric anthropology issues from original sin."[55] It may seem a fine point, but it is not, to insist that the rupture of sin is fundamental because it is sin that occasions a quite different divine approach to humanity than that of the just, omnipotent, merciful Creator. Here we meet the gracious promise of God the Redeemer in Christ, which is as different from the former as the grace of the gospel is from the curse of the law.

"Antithetical" Structure?

Another recent, impressive approach to the problem of structure in Calvin's theology appears in F. L. Battles: "Calculus Fidei."[56] Battles finds that an "anti-thetical structure" offers the "single principle that can sum up the theology of Calvin." This means that "every fundamental notion of his thought is defined in a field of tension — a true middle between false extremes." This is brought about by such actual historical errors and heresies as atheism (defect) and idolatry (excess), or a "spiritualist" (defect) as against a Roman (excess) understanding of the sacraments or the church. In a larger essay, not yet published,[57] Battles presents in meticulous detail, with 44 pages of diagrams, a "speculum" of the entire *Institutio* of 1559 analyzed according to this principle. This "field of tension" is, for Battles, rightly set within a strongly soteriological, history-of-salvation context, and hence is a practical, not theoretical or formal, exigency of Calvin's thought.

I wish to suggest that even if Battles' detailed observations and diagrams of the polemic elements of Calvin's theology are precisely correct, they do not demonstrate that his theological thought is

55 *Ecclesia Ministrans,* p. 42.

56 *Calvinus Ecclesiae Doctor,* ed. W. Neuser (1978), pp. 85-110.

57 Battles' published article is a reduced form of *Calculus Fidei. Some Ruminations on the Structure of the Theology of John Calvin* (1978), 136 pp., privately circulated, deposited in the library of Calvin Theological Seminary, Grand Rapids, Michigan, USA. The surprising title comes from Professor Battles' speculation that Calvin's application of a "true/false principle" along a spectrum of excess and defect (Aristotle) is similar to the theory of limits in Newton's calculus, "on which modern mathematics, and as a corollary, all modern science and technology depend, is actually a secularized form of the Scriptural view of reality." The validity of the Calvin analysis is our concern here, not the broader theory.

fundamentally structured by his polemic turned into an "antithetical" principle. Calvin's message is meant to be in the first place a timely interpretation and preaching of the gospel, whether in the form of commentary, treatises, or sermons, for the upbuilding of the church. As cast in the *Institutio,* this fundamental characteristic is reflected both in the overall creedal structure and in his announced and repeated indications concerning the knowledge of God. This appears in the knowledge "of God and ourselves" acting in relation to the twofold "species" of the revelation of the Creator and the revelation of the Redeemer "founded on the truth of the freely given promise in Christ, both revealed to our minds and sealed on our hearts through the Holy Spirit."[58] As sin and the work of the devil is always an "adventitious" or "accidental" quality in human history, not attributable to God or his creation as such, so the mediatorial work of Christ (*Institutio,* Book II) and the work of the Spirit in faith, regeneration, justification, and so on (*Institutio,* Book III) is controlled by the divine initiative toward the human race, not by alien strategies of the devil's minions among which Calvin finds a middle way. Theological truth for Calvin does not arise from a calculus or calculation based on an analysis of historical or theoretical error, but from the Word revealed. Granted that polemic strategies are ubiquitous, it appears wise of E. Saxer to conclude, "We do not wish this field of tension of true and false piety to be expounded as the principle of Calvin's thought."[59]

[58] III.ii.7, *CO* IV.16.31-35.

[59] Ernst Saxer's volume *Aberglaube, Heuchelei und Frömmigkeit* (1970) bears remarkable similarities to Battles' work. Saxer sees Superstition (excess) and Hypocrisy (defect) as the negative polarities between which Calvin's thought moves. Like Battles he sees Calvin's personal life, especially his conversion, and his views of salvation history as the existential setting of his thought. His caution, as quoted, however, is greater, p. 279.

APPENDIX I
A NOTE ON ANTHROPOMORPHISM[1]

IN CONDESCENDING to man's sinful state God "stammers (*balbultit*) to us in a rough and popular style." Com. Jn. 3:12 (CO XLVII.61c). He "accommodates (*accommodet*) himself to the ordinary way of speaking on account of our ignorance, and sometimes, if I may be allowed the expression, stammers." *Ibid.*, 21:24 (p. 485c). "When God descends to us, he in a certain sense abases (*extenuat*) himself, and stammers (*babultit*) with us. . . . And this is to be truly wise, when we embrace God in the manner in which he accommodates (*accommodat*) himself to our capacity. . . . Since God, in the gospel, takes upon himself the character of a tutor, let us learn to subject our minds to him: only let us remember that he descends to us in order to raise us up to himself." Com. Gen. 35:7, (CO XXIII.469b).

Calvin unfailingly points out the metaphoric quality of numerous Biblical anthropomorphisms, but with respect to their degrees of refinement. The coarser physical references to God's "mouth, ears, eyes," etc., are in effect baby talk, God lisping as a nurse to an infant, I.xiii.1 (OS III.109.13–15), cf. IV.xvii.23. The representations of moods or mental activities, God's "wrath" or his "repenting" of a decision, are of a higher order, but are still treated with extreme caution. "The word wrath, ἀνθρωποπαθῶς, according to the usage of Scripture, means the vengeance of God; for God in punishing, has (according to our notion) the appearance of one in wrath. It signifies therefore, no such emotion in God, but only has a reference to the perception and feeling of the sinner who is punished." Com. Rm. 1:18 (CO XLIX.23a). The same is true of God's "grief" or "repentance," Com. Gen. 6:6 (CO XXIII.118a–c). More positive terms, such as God's love and fatherhood, although still treated at times with a view to their analogical character, are generally regarded as much more adequate to the meaning they are meant to carry, thus are frequently used without warnings about their metaphorical quality.

Elsewhere Calvin takes God's representation of his residence to be "in heaven" as a symbol of transcendence. "Wherefore this is the same as if he had been said to be possessed of an infinite magnitude or sub-

[1] See above, pp. 9 ff.

limity, incomprehensible essence, immense power, and unlimited immortality. . . . that we may not fancy concerning him anything either terrestrial or carnal, that we may not measure him by our proportions or judge his will by our affections." III.xx.40 (OS IV.350.5–12) the same interpretation of "in heaven" is given in Com. Eph. 4:10 (CO LI.195).

APPENDIX II
CONSCIENCE AND THE SENSUS NATURAE [1]

BOHATEC puts beside conscience, "and not to be confused with it," the *sensus naturae* or *communis sensus*. "This is, like the conscience, innate, and performs a similar service. . . . The *sensus naturae* is usually excited when it is a matter of the maintenance or disturbance of order, when man inwardly rebels against an offense to public respectability which submerges justice and forgets human values. It is, briefly put, the *Rechtsgefühl* in which the sense of justice and the sense of order, therefore, the sense of moral and esthetic value are bound together, and out of which then an appropriate moral judgement issues, which we can call consciousness of justice (*Rechtsgewissen*)." *Calvin und das Recht*, pp. 8 f., cf. pp. 13–20. This is a masterfully brief exposition of the term where Bohatec finds it. But it is deceiving to separate it thus from conscience. Gloede, for whom Bohatec's work was evidently not available at the time of writing, citing the same passages, includes the *communis sensus* in his analysis of conscience as an "ethical guiding principle," but without sensing its esthetic aspect. *Theologia Naturalis bei Calvin*, pp. 110–113. This common (uni-ersal) or natural sense, it seems to me, can best be regarded as a synonym for conscience. It is a synonym having as its particular connotation a "sense of right." These phrases and similar ones are used most frequently where the sense is affected by an almost physical revulsion, such as illustrated by Calvin's examples of violations of the fifth, sixth, and seventh Commandments and their supplements in Com. Pent. as follows: Com. Ex. 21:15 (CO XXIV.607b), striking a parent; Com. Deut. 24:16 (CO XXIII.631b), death of children for crimes of their father; Com. Ex. 20:13 (CO XXIV.611a), murder; Com. Lev. 20:18 (CO XXIV.659a), cohabitation with a menstrous woman; Com. Lev. 18:1 (CO XXIV.661b), incest. The term disappears, except for one instance, Com. Ex. 23:24 (CO XXIV.695b), when Calvin describes the somewhat less revolting sins connected with the eighth Command. The same occurs in Com. Rom. 1:28, where physical perversions are called a violation of *communis sensus* (CO

[1] See above, pp. 68 ff.

XLIX.29a), and "not rendering to each his due" is *iniustiam, ibid.* (29b). Cf. Com. Mt. 10:37 (CO XLV.294a).

Some more uses showing the difficulty of fixing the concept exactly are the following: In Com. Isa. 58:7 it is ranked with *ius* and *humanitas* (CO XXXVII.329d-330a). In Com. Gen. 1:28, it is the *communis sensus* which declares the *lex naturae* to be inviolable (CO XXIII.29a); and in 1:16, it refers to naïve observation of the heavens as opposed to learned astronomy (CO XXIII.22c). In Com. Gen. 1:6 (CO XXIII.18c), *communis sensus* is used as the equivalent of the English "common sense" with no moral coloring at all: "For it is contrary to common sense and quite incredible that there should be water above the heaven." Again, "Nothing being more remote from common sense than that from the fault of one all should be deemed guilty, and thus sin be made general." II.i.5 (OS III.233.9). Cf. I.vii.1 (OS III.65.10).

APPENDIX III

THE BARTH-BRUNNER CONTROVERSY ON CALVIN[1]

THE HEATED THEOLOGICAL CONTROVERSY of fifteen years ago, in which Emil Brunner wrote *Nature and Grace* and received Karl Barth's *No!* in reply, was in part a controversy over the interpretation of Calvin. I offer the following comments solely on the Calvin issue as raised in the discussion and to relate our Chapter III to it at salient points.

1) Neither side used Calvin's own basic distinction, the *duplex cognitio Domini,* properly. The problem was formulated in terms of the revelation "from creation and in Christ," which is Barth's reading of the Calvin phrase,[2] and which Brunner uses, although without attributing it to Calvin.[3] This statement embraces two problems: that of the means of obtaining the knowledge of God (which according to Calvin are creation and Scripture) and that of the "species" of knowledge with regard to content (the knowledge of the Creator, and the knowledge of Christ the Redeemer).[4] The result of this formulation was that the specific problem of relating I.i–v (Calvin's natural theology over which he cast Paul's Biblical verdict, "inexcusable") to I.x–xviii (the Bible's teaching about the Creator) was confused with the problem of relating I.x–xviii (the Bible's teaching about the Creator) to Books II–IV (the Bible's teaching about the Redeemer). Hence developed Barth's suspicion that Brunner was trying to make of I.i–v an unrefracted piece of natural theology,[5] when Brunner was simply defending the Biblical doctrine of the revelation of the Creator (I.x ff.) in so far as the Bible itself, according to Calvin, points to creation as God's revelation. Barth's attack is centered largely on I.v, although Brunner cites from it only twice in *Nature and Grace,* even in the second edition.

Probably it is because these separable issues were not methodically distinguished by either theologian that Peter Barth (who cites the *duplex cognitio Domini* correctly, *Das Problem,* pp. 10 f., but makes no use of it), in supporting his brother against Brunner, wrote a piece

[1] See above, pp. 132 ff.
[2] *No!,* p. 105.
[3] *Nature and Grace,* p. 26.
[4] *Supra,* pp. 43, 144.
[5] *Supra,* p. 138.

which for all its heat is in its main outlines not inimical to what Brunner had written. In fact, both agree that for Calvin only the Christian can see the true God in creation, and then only by the aid of the "spectacles" of Scripture, not as if his "sight" had been perfectly restored.[6]

2) Brunner attributed to Calvin a "Christian *theologia naturalis.*"[7] By this term he meant a natural theology in an objective sense (the revelation in creation), but not in the Roman Catholic subjective sense (the ability to receive the revelation in creation unaided by Scripture). Peter Barth, denying the legitimacy of Brunner's term, proceeded to criticize him on the basis of what the term natural theology has meant in other times, without regard to the transforming adjective "Christian." Thus, he was criticizing an alleged independent natural theology, when Brunner himself was defending only the value of the revelation in creation to the Bible-instructed Christian. Gloede, Brunner's pupil, adopted the title *Theologia naturalis bei Calvin.* His first words were to explain that by the term he meant that part of Calvin's theology based on a Biblical view of creation.[8] He does, in spite of his intention, sometimes indulge in statements reminiscent of the old, not the "Christian" sense of the term.[9] These were seized upon in the attack by Wilhelm Niesel, which pays no attention to Gloede's avowed intention, to which, for the most part, he kept.[10]

In Chapter III I have used the name natural theology to refer only to that area of Calvin's theology where he speaks of the non-Christian's relation to God represented by either naïve or philosophical reflections outside the Biblical tradition and Calvin's effort (confined to I.v) on non-Biblical grounds (in the sense of non-authoritarian, but following Paul's example in Acts 17:16 ff.) to disprove certain philosophical misconceptions.

3) Peter Barth seized upon and condemned Brunner's term *Ergänzung* (complement) as expressing a complementary relationship between what is known directly from creation and what is known in Christ. In fact, Brunner never used the term in that sense. But within

[6] *Supra,* pp. 143 f.

[7] A term he has ceased to use; see *Man in Revolt,* p. 527, *Offenbarung und Vernunft,* pp. 60–63, 80.

[8] *Theologia Naturalis bei Calvin,* pp. 10 ff.

[9] *Ibid.,* pp. 67, 306.

[10] Niesel's review of Gloede, *Theologische Literaturbeilage der Reform. Kirchenztg.* October, 1936, pp. 15 f.

the concept as Brunner used it, it is possible to see two meanings, both of which are true to Calvin, but which, in the light of the *duplex cognitio Domini,* can be differentiated. One refers to the relation for the believer of the revelation in creation to the revelation in Scripture, and the other, to the relation of the knowledge of the Creator to the knowledge of the Redeemer. An example of the first is the following: "By *Ergänzung* I have never meant anything like a complementary relation (*Ergänzungsverhältnis*) of the reasoned and revealed knowledge of God of Thomism, but only this, that God when he commands us to take seriously the revelation in his works (*theatrum, speculum*) clearly wants to give us something that we, even as Bible believing Christians, would not have. Peter Barth himself recognizes—at least as Calvin's view—that astronomy, when carried on by a believer, is 'a useful means,' for seeing into the interrelations of the works of Creation." [11]

The second use is the following: "This *experientia*-knowledge of God is not made superfluous by faith in the Word of God, but on the contrary remains an important complement of the knowledge of God derived from Scripture. The knowledge of God to be gained from nature is only partial. To put it metaphorically: from nature we know the hands and feet, but not the heart of God . . . his wisdom and omnipotence, also his justice and even his goodness, but not his forgiving mercy." Then, "through Scripture the revelation in nature is both clarified and complemented. Scripture serves as a lens . . . the voice of God amplified. . . . And secondly, Scripture shows us that heart of God, which is not revealed in the natural revelation." [12]

Above, pp. 144–146, we have used the word "complement" to refer to additional knowledge of the Creator given by Scripture over and above what is revealed in creation.

[11] *Natur und Gnade,* 2d ed., p. 52.
[12] *Nature and Grace,* p. 38.

Appendix IV

KÖSTLIN'S CRITICISM OF CALVIN'S PREDESTINATION[1]

A strong interpretation, in some ways harmonious with, but for the most part opposed to, the one we have given is that of Köstlin. He comments that it is often said that when we consider the immediate religious-moral consciousness which is the ground on which Calvin looks back to the eternal decrees, we are driven to such a doctrine of predestination as he formulated. However, does not this consciousness also include in itself other elements which demand another solution—and is it not true that this other solution is not demanded for or possible for Calvin, because the peculiarity of his own basic point of view gave less weight to this element than did other theologians, and less, indeed, than the evangelical principle itself allows? "Does not there belong to it such a view of moral personality and at the same time of the opposition of God against evil, that at least excludes his view of the original fall of man? And has not a feeling for this held back Calvin himself from declaring himself more clearly over this [i.e., by treating of the decrees in Book I], and from beginning his theology with the decree of God? But he goes here only so far as we have seen him, because he supposes he must think the creature dependent and weak over against the absolute God. . . . It is, further, not merely the freedom of the divine love that this evangelical principle teaches, but it is above all love itself as the basic character of God. The question arises, if from here on the conclusion which one might wish to draw from this freedom is not, however, forbidden. According to Calvin this occurs in such a way that over against this love in God stands something else, ununited and with a certain preponderance." This is not merely God's punishing justice, but "we mean rather that all-dominating consciousness of the absolute divine sovereignty, freedom of will, and power as such; this it is that stands over the power of love and the condemning justice in such a way that purely by free choice it gives grace to some and condemns some, and in the equal performance of these various works it glorifies itself, and which finally by virtue of its nature prohibits and condemns all opposing questions in the moral-religious consciousness of men as infringement of its deserved reverence."

[1] See above, pp. 219 ff.

"It remains characteristic of Calvin to strive after strict consistency and the unity of his system. Certainly not less characteristic, however, is it for him that since he does not feel himself called upon to draw the final consequences and has not succeeded to a really inner synthesis of the various sides, motives, and interests of the evangelical principle —he bows himself in simple resignation before the divine Majesty on the limits which he here finds set and makes a similar resignation the duty of all," Köstlin, "Calvins Institutio nach Form und Inhalt," pp. 474–475, *passim*. We have said, on the contrary, that while God's freedom is such that no man can judge it, it is always the freedom or gratuitousness of mercy and remains in harmony with God's love. It does not develop in opposition to it as if the two had to be united in a system, but rather, for purposes of systematic thought, the two motives are analyzed out and therefore may seem conceptually separated from one another, while for Calvin they are not.

Appendix V
A REVIEW OF WILLIAM J. BOUWSMA'S *John Calvin* *A Sixteenth-Century Portrait*

William J. Bouwsma's task as a historian for many years has been to understand the multi-leveled transformation of Western culture that took place in early modern Europe. His chief mode of access has been the literature of the Renaissance. He now studies the Genevan church reformer John Calvin as he formerly studied Guillaume Postel, "as witnesses to the age that produced them." But in Calvin's case he does not write a biography in the usual sense. He sets out rather to paint a "portrait" in depth, taking for granted, except for a brief sketch, the external events of Calvin's career. This sketch takes strong positions on some contested issues, ignores others, and handles Servetus in just two mild sentences. Bouwsma's approach is through Calvin's lifelong humanism, and more especially through humanist rhetoric which has become prominent in Calvin studies of the last thirty years.

The author's procedure is to range through nearly the whole Calvin corpus, pulling together in often surprising clusters, and under carefully constructed topics, thousands of quotations and citations in the hope that he can, as Kant suggested for Plato, "understand him better than he understood himself." This is a bold and sophisticated move because Bouwsma programmatically pays little attention to the sequence, circumstance, or exegetical subject matter of Calvin's writings, and relatively minor attention to the categories in which Calvin himself understood himself as well as God, the world, and biblical revelation. Bouwsma's grounds for this are that in things that truly disclose the "historical Calvin" there was little growth or change throughout his life, and that Calvin reveals *himself* more in style and by implication than directly in subject matter and formally stated opinion. Bouwsma is seeking the human being behind the towering figure divested of the hagiography and demonology of Calvinism and anti-Calvinism. He arrives somewhat anticlimactically at a person "more heroic than most of us, if not necessarily more successful, in his struggle to come to terms with the tensions in himself" (231).

Bouwsma's Calvin is a complex, anxiety-ridden, divided, and often self-contradictory thinker, suspended between The Labyrinth of the traditional intricately ordered Christian cosmos (chs. 4-6) and The Abyss of uncertainty and freedom opened up by humanism among the "paradoxes and mystery at the heart of existence" (chs. 8-11). The philosophical-orthodox Calvin resists with dour rigidity as the humanist rhetor maneuvers the unknown with virtuosity and even delight: the one terrified by claustrophobic constriction and the other dizzied on the brink of the open void.

There are "two Calvins" both temperamentally and intellectually. The former is the less important since Bouwsma disclaims psychological analysis, despite some indulgence in father-dependence theory and some fairly confident mind-reading on miscellaneous matters usually thought to be best understood with professional psychological equipment. It is Calvin's twofold existential intellectual anxiety that is the main point of the whole study, for Bouwsma sees in Calvin a prominent example of the deeply divided mind of the sixteenth century, indeed of Everyman in the Christian West through the centuries. The chief yield of the volume in Bouwsma's own evaluation is to throw light on the anxiety at the core of the emerging new age. In an earlier article, "Anxiety and the Formation of Early Modern Culture," he displayed his preoccupation with this general theme, drawing on examples from Petrarch to Pascal and a wide spectrum of political, social, and economic literature.

Calvin was not paralyzed by anxiety, but driven by it to bring viable order to A World Out of Joint (ch. 3) through a reform of society, civil polity, and the church, here labeled "A Program for the

Times" (chs. 12-14). The "composite and political quality of Calvin's thought" which issues in "a triumph in principle of rhetoric over philosophy," of action over speculation, is much admired by Bouwsma. Thus in Calvin he finds the roots of both the structured dogmatic Calvinism which opposed modernity, and the skepticism, relativism, and pragmatism that characterize it.

With the above cultural-historical theme prescribing his goal and method (or as Dorothy Emett puts it, what is "important" to the historian in the selecting, arranging, and weighting of material), Bouwsma's project was bound to take a form different from the work of those who come to Calvin as a figure in church history, or a still relevant theologian, a landmark of fanaticism, or even an erudite student of the classics. One is thus more or less prepared to see Calvin's thought in a frame of reference in which Erasmus, Rabelais, Machiavelli, and Lefévre altogether outweigh the usual Augustine, Bernard, and Chrysostom in the attention they receive and the importance they are assigned. That "the genial Erasmus" is no help at all with the theme of anxiety does not discourage Bouwsma from mentioning him on every possible occasion, sometimes as a synonym for humanism. The "major respects" in which Calvin was not Erasmian (11) are never developed but reduced to a matter of temperament. Budé is all but ignored.

The overall structure of Bouwsma's presentation is a tour de force of Calvin study directed by the project and methods described. On every page there are insights and interconnections that enlighten the more theologically oriented reader of Calvin (I speak for myself) and send one back to the sources to see if 'tis like a camel indeed, or very like a whale. Various doctrines or teachings of the Christian faith that constituted both the substance and the vocabulary of Calvin's theological lifework do not appear at all. Other major themes are ingeniously reconstructed and reinterpreted. And it remains something of a salt bath to find that decorum gets more space than predestination, boundaries and mixture than regeneration and justification, Quintillian and Cicero than Jesus and Paul. Although this book "is not directly concerned with Calvin's theology" (3), Bouwsma has in effect constructed an alternative *summa* of Calvin's thought under the rubric of anxiety, "illuminating the momentous cultural crisis (of) his century" (4, 234). In the process, Calvin's own struggle for a quarter of a century as a Christian humanist thinker to revise, enlarge, and rearrange his *loci* into an *institutio* gets no attention at all. There may be some penalty in this, as follows:

It is an error to say that Calvin treated predestination as a part of providence in earlier editions of the *Institutes* (173). He did not. He always led into providence from predestination, and into predestination from faith. Always — even in 1559 where the new arrangement seems on the surface to be different. Is this important? It at least excludes Bouwsma's option of presenting providence apart from election and faith in a *locus* of his own invention, titled Power (ch. 10). Here Calvin's world tends to become sheer frightening power and a source of terror as he shakes in his boots during thunderstorms and fears the heaped-up Ptolemaic sea will inundate the earth. But for the Calvin I read, these dangers threaten only "if Fortune rules" and only if one does not know and trust God who falls with the sparrow, wills each drop of rain, and to whom Jesus called out forsaken on the cross (Calvin on Psalm 22). In this setting Calvin's rhetorical pyrotechnics about nature and human nature are foils or negative hyperbole for praising the trustworthiness of God. Bouwsma, too, takes brief account of this (171), but as a minor tint in a portrait of anxiety. Under his program anxiety becomes the dominating reality of Calvin's life and thought, around which all else (including this volume) is organized, and from which his lifework flows.

Is it of no consequence in seeking the "historical Calvin" that for Calvin himself anxiety was a persistent, threatening concomitant of faith, like Luther's *Anfechtungen,* but not the major fact of Christian existence? It seems to me that Calvin's writings reflect the priority of faith and election within the rhetor, coexisting with and dominating irrepressible anxiety. Through the christocentric mystery terror is commuted into religious awe *(timor religiosus)* more genuinely than appears in the antithetical Labyrinth/Abyss scheme.

Bouwsma's book, taken as a whole, seems to this reviewer to be a historical drama, beautifully constructed and highly informative, but lacking in certain central purposes and convictions of the main character.

One would certainly not want to reintroduce Calvin the sure-footed systematizer and flawless church father of "tulip" Calvinism, against whom much of Bouwsma's critique and correction are seemingly aimed. But this caricature has not really held sway in Calvin studies since Hermann Bauke designated Calvin's thought a *complexio oppositorum* in 1922. It may be that now the word will get out among general historians that Calvin is not an "iron logician" (Huizenga) — for Bouwsma's brilliant and imaginative work is bound to be their favorite and dominant book on Calvin for a long time to come. One hopes, however, that this paradoxical, troubled, sublime thinker will yet find an interpretation in which Bouwsma's contribution is incorporated into a more unified understanding of Calvin's theology and conscious intentions.

Oxford University Press is to be congratulated for producing this book very well, but not for omitting chapter titles and page references from the fifty-eight pages of endnotes, without which they are a Labyrinth indeed.

BIBLIOGRAPHY

This bibliography represents books actually used by the writer. It is not meant to be exhaustive.

Sources

Ioannis Calvini opera quae supersunt omnia; ed. by G. Baum, E. Cunitz, E. Reuss. 59 vols. (Corpus Reformatorum, vols. xxix sqq.) Brunsvigae, Schwetschke, 1863–1900.

Calvini opera selecta; ed. by P. Barth, G. Niesel. Monachii, Kaiser, 1926–1936. Vols. I, III, IV, V.

Jean Calvin, Institution de la religion chrestienne (Geneva, 1541); ed. by Jacques Pannier. Paris, Société les belles lettres, 1936.

Translations

The Commentaries of John Calvin. Various translators. 46 vols. Edinburgh, The Calvin Translation Society, 1843–1855.

Institutes of the Christian Religion. Trans. by Henry Beveridge. 3 vols. Edinburgh, The Calvin Translation Society, 1845.

Institutions of the Christian Religion. Trans. by John Allen. 7th ed., revised. 2 vols. Philadelphia, Board of Christian Education, 1936.

Tracts of Calvin; with his life by Theodore Beza. Trans. by Henry Beveridge. 3 vols. Edinburgh, The Calvin Translation Society, 1844.

Literature

Armstrong, W. P., ed. Calvin and the Reformation; four studies by Emile Doumergue, August Lang, Herman Bavinck, and Benjamin B. Warfield, New York, Revell, 1909.

Barth, Karl. Die kirchliche Dogmatik. Zollikon-Zürich, Evangelischer Verlag A.G., 1946. Vol. II, parts 1, and 2, and Vol. III, part 2.

—— No! Answer to Emil Brunner. Trans. by Peter Fraenkel, in *Natural Theology*. London, The Centenary Press, 1946.

Barth, Peter. "Calvin," in Die Religion in Geschichte und Gegenwart. 2d ed. Vol. I, part 2, 1425–1437. Tübingen, Mohr (Paul Siebeck), 1927.

—— "Fünfundzwanzig Jahre Calvinforschung," 1909–1934, *Theologische Rundschau,* Neue folge, 6. Jahrg. (1934), pp. 162–175, 246–267.

Barth, Peter. "Die fünf Einleitungskapitel von Calvins Institutio," *Kirchenblatt für die reformierte Schweiz,* 40. Jahrg., Nr. 11–13 (March 12, 19, and 26, 1925), pp. 41–42, 45–47, 49–50.

—— Das Problem der naturlichen Theologie bei Calvin, theologische Existenz Heute, Heft 18. Munich, Kaiser Verlag, 1935.

Bauke, Hermann. Die Probleme der Theologie Calvins. Leipzig, J. C. Hinrichs'schen Buchhandlung, 1922.

Beth, Karl. "Johann Calvin als reformatorischer Systematiker," *Zeitschrift der Theologie und Kirche,* XIX (1909), pp. 329–346.

Beyerhaus, Gisbert. Studien zur Staatsanschauung Calvins; mit besonderer Berücksichtigung seiner Souveränitatsbegriffs. Berlin, Trowitzsch, 1910.

Blanke, Fritz. Der verborgene Gott bei Luther. Berlin, Furche-Verlag, 1928.

Bodin, John. Method for the Easy Comprehension of History. Trans. by Beatrice Reynolds. New York, Columbia University Press, 1945.

Bohatec, Josef. Calvin und das Recht. Feudigen in Westphalen, Buchdruckerei G.m.b.H., 1934.

Breen, Quirinus. John Calvin: a Study in French Humanism. Grand Rapids, W. B. Eerdmans Publishing Company, 1931.

Brunner, Emil. Dogmatik. Zürich, Zwingli-Verlag, 1946. Vol. I, Die christliche Lehre von Gott.

—— Man in Revolt. Trans. by O. Wyon; from *Der Mensch in Widerspruch,* 1937. Philadelphia, The Westminster Press, no date.

—— Nature and Grace. Trans. by Peter Fraenkel, in *Natural Theology.* London, The Centenary Press, 1946.

—— Natur und Gnade, 2d ed. Tübingen, 1935.

—— Offenbarung und Vernunft. Zürich, Zwingli-Verlag, 1941.

Brunner, Peter. "Allgemeine und besondere Offenbarung in Calvins Institutio," *Evangelische Theologie,* 1. Jahrg. 1934, Heft 5, pp. 189–215.

—— Vom Glauben bei Calvin. Tübingen, Mohr (Paul Siebeck), 1925.

Camfield, F. R., ed. Reformation Old and New. London, Lutterworth Press, 1947.

Chenevière, M.-E. La Pensée Politique de Calvin. Paris, Imprimerie Labor, 1937.

Choisy, Eugène. Calvin et la science. Geneva, 1931. Recueil Faculté de théologie protestant.

Clavier, Henri. Etudes sur la Calvinisme. Paris, Librairie Fischbacher, 1936.

Dilthey, W. Gesammelte Schriften. Vol. II. Leipzig and Berlin, Teubner, 1914.

Dorner, I. A. Geschichte der protestantischen Theologie. Munich, Gotta'schen Buchhandlung, 1867.

Doumergue, E. Jean Calvin, les hommes et les choses de son temps. Paris, Librairie Fischbacher, Vol. IV, 1910; Vol. V, 1917.

Engelland, H. Gott und Mensch bei Calvin. Munich, Kaiser Verlag, 1934.

Frank, Erich. Philosophical Understanding and Religious Truth. New York, Oxford University Press, 1945.

Fuhrmann, Paul T. God-Centered Religion. Grand Rapids, Zondervan, 1942.

Gilson, Étienne. Christianity and Philosophy. New York: Sheed and Ward, 1939.

—— The Spirit of Medieval Philosophy. Trans. by A. H. C. Downes. New York, Scribner's Sons, 1940.

Gloede, Gunter. Theologia Naturalis bei Calvin. Stuttgart, Kohlhammer, 1935.

Heim, Karl. Das Gewissheitsproblem in der systematischen Theologie bis zu Schleiermacher. Leipzig, Hinrichs'schen Buchhandlung, 1911.

Heppe, H. Dogmatik der Evangelischen-reformierten Kirche. Elberfeld, Friederichs, 1861.

Hunter, A. M. The Teaching of Calvin. Glasgow, Maclehose, Jackson, 1920.

Jacobs, Paul. Prädestination und Verantwortlichkeit bei Calvin. Kassel, Oncken, 1937.

Kampschulte, J. W. Johann Calvin; seine Kirche und sein Staat in Genf. 2 vols. Vol. I, Leipzig: Duncker und Humblot, 1869; Vol. II, ed. after the author's death by W. Goetz, Leipzig, Duncker und Humblot, 1899.

Köstlin, J. "Calvins Institutio nach Form und Inhalt, in ihrer geschichtlichen Entwicklung." *Theologische Studien und Kritiken,* 1868, pp. 6–62, 410–486.

Kuyper, Abraham. Calvinism. New York, Revell, 1899.

Lang, August. "Die Reformation und das Naturrecht," *Beiträge zur Förderung christlicher Theologie,* 13. Jahrg., Heft 4 (1912), pp. 283–334.

Lecerf, A. An Introduction to Reformed Dogmatics. Trans. by S.L.-H. London, Lutterworth Press, 1949.

Lehmann, Paul. "The Reformers' Use of the Bible," *Theology Today,* III (October, 1946), 328–344.

Lelièvre, Charles. La Maîtrise de l'Esprit; essai critique sur le principe fondamental de la théologie de Calvin. Paris, Imprimerie A. Coueslant, 1901.

Lobstein, P. Die Ethik Calvins. Strassbourg, Schmidt, 1877.

—— "La Connaissance religieuse d'apres Calvin," *Revue de théologie et de philosophie* (Lausanne), XLII (1909), 53–110.

Mackinnon, James. Calvin and the Reformation. New York, Longmans, Green, and Co., 1936.

Mackintosh, H. R. Types of Modern Theology. London, Nisbet, 1937.

McNeill, John T. "Natural Law in the Theology of the Reformers," *Journal of Religion,* XXVI (July, 1946), 168–182.

Minear, Paul S. The Eyes of Faith. Philadelphia, The Westminster Press, 1946.

Mülhaupt, Erwin. Die Predigt Calvins. Berlin, de Gruyter, 1931.

Niebuhr, Reinhold. The Nature and Destiny of Man. 2 vols. New York, Scribners' Sons, 1943.

Niesel, Wilhelm. Die Theologie Calvins. Munich, Kaiser, 1938.

—— Review in *Literaturbeilage der reformierten Kirchenzeitung,* October, 1936, pp. 15 f.

Nygren, Anders. Agape and Eros. Part I trans. by A. G. Hebert, 1932; Part II (2 vols.) trans. by Philip S. Watson, 1938. London, Society for the Promotion of Christian Knowledge.

Otto, Rudolph. The Idea of the Holy. Trans. by J. W. Harvey. London, Oxford University Press, 1923.

Pannier, Jacques. Le Témoignage du Saint-Esprit. Paris, Librairie Fischbacher, 1893.

Parker, T. H. L. The Oracles of God; an introduction to the preaching of John Calvin. London, Lutterworth Press, 1947.

Reuss, E. Die Geschichte der Heiligen Schriften; Neuen Testaments. 5th ed. Part II. Braunschweig, Schwetschke, 1874.

Ritschl, Albrecht. Die christliche Lehre von der Rechtfertigung und Versöhnung. Vol. III. Bonn, Adolph Marcus, 1874.

Ritschl, Otto. Dogmengeschichte des Protestantismus. Vol. III. Göttingen, Vandenhoeck und Ruprecht, 1926.

Schweizer, A. Die protestantischen Centraldogmen in ihrer Entwicklung innerhalb der reformierten Kirche. Part II. Zürich, Orell, Fessli and Comp., 1854.

Seeberg, Reinhold. Lehrbuch der Dogmengeschichte. 2d ed. Vol. IV (part 2). Erlangen, A. Deicherische Verlagsbuchhandlung Werner Scholl, 1920.

Tillich, Paul. "Existential Philosophy," *Journal of the History of Ideas.* V (January, 1944), 44–70.

Warfield, Banjamin B. Calvin and Calvinism. New York, Oxford University Press, 1931. Contains "Calvin's Doctrine of the Knowledge of God," pp. 29–130, and "Calvin's Doctrine of God," et cetera.

Wernle, Paul. Der evangelische Glaube nach den Hauptschriften der Reformatoren. Tübingen, Mohr (Paul Siebeck), 1919. Vol. III, Calvin.

SUPPLEMENTARY BIBLIOGRAPHY

The following are selected from among recent works on themes treated in this volume. For more detailed lists with analyses, see surveys of Calvin literature by the author in *Church History,* XXIV (1955), 360–367, and XXIX (1960), 187–204.

Forstman, H. J. Word and Spirit; Calvin's Doctrine of Biblical Authority. Stanford, Stanford University Press, 1962.

Gerrish, B. A. "Biblical Authority in the Continental Reformation," *Scottish Journal of Theology,* X (1957), 337–360.

Haroutunian, Joseph. General Introduction to Calvin: Commentaries. Philadelphia, Westminster Press, 1958.

Johnson, R. C. Authority in Protestant Theology. Philadelphia, Westminster Press, 1959.

Kantzer, K. S., in J. S. Walvoord, ed., Inspiration and Interpretation. Grand Rapids, W. B. Eerdmans Publishing Company, 1957.

Kreck, W. "Wort und Geist bei Calvin," in *Festschrift für Günther Dehn,* ed. W. Schneemelcher. Neukirchen, Buchhandlung des Erziehungsvereins, 1957.

Krusche, Werner. Das Wirken des heiligen Geistes nach Calvin. Göttingen, Vandenhoeck and Ruprecht, 1957.

McNeill, J. T. "The Significance of the Word of God for Calvin," *Church History,* XXVIII (1959), 131–146.

Parker, T. H. L. The Doctrine of the Knowledge of God: a Study in the Theology of John Calvin. Edinburgh, Oliver and Boyd, 1952; Grand Rapids, W. B. Eerdmans Publishing Company, 1959.

Reid, J. K. S. The Authority of Scripture: a Study of Reformation and Post-Reformation Understanding of the Bible. New York, Harper and Brothers, 1957.

Stuermann, W. E. A Critical Study of Calvin's Concept of Faith. Tulsa, 1952 (privately published).

Willis, E. D. The Function of the So-Called Extra Calvinisticum in Calvin's Theology. Ph.D. dissertation, Harvard University, 1962.

Wallace, R. S. Calvin's Doctrine of the Word and Sacrament. Edinburgh, Oliver and Boyd. 1953.

INDEX